ECCLESIASTES;

OR,

THE PREACHER.

T0381811

ECCLESIASTES;

OR,

THE PREACHER,

WITH NOTES AND INTRODUCTION

BY

E. H. PLUMPTRE, D.D.

PROFESSOR OF NEW TESTAMENT EXEGESIS, KING'S COLLEGE,
LONDON; PREBENDARY OF ST PAUL'S; EXAMINING CHAPLAIN TO
THE ARCHBISHOP OF CANTERBURY.

EDITED FOR THE SYNDICS OF THE UNIVERSITY PRESS.

Cambridge:
AT THE UNIVERSITY PRESS.

London: CAMBRIDGE WAREHOUSE, 17, PATERNOSTER ROW.
Cambridge: DEIGHTON, BELL, AND CO.

1881

CAMBRIDGE UNIVERSITY PRESS
Cambridge, New York, Melbourne, Madrid, Cape Town,
Singapore, São Paulo, Delhi, Mexico City

Cambridge University Press
The Edinburgh Building, Cambridge CB2 8RU, UK

Published in the United States of America by Cambridge University Press, New York

www.cambridge.org
Information on this title: www.cambridge.org/9781107623972

First published 1881
First paperback edition 2013

A catalogue record for this publication is available from the British Library

ISBN 978-1-107-62397-2 Paperback

PREFACE.

AMONG the many enigmas of the Old Testament the book of Ecclesiastes is pre-eminently enigmatic. It comes before us as the sphinx of Hebrew literature, with its unsolved riddles of history and life. It has become almost a proverb that every interpreter of this book thinks that all previous interpreters have been wrong. Its very title has received some dozen discordant interpretations. The dates assigned to its authorship by competent experts range over very nearly a thousand years, from B.C. 990 to B.C. 10. Not less has been the divergence of opinion as to its structure and its aims. It has been regarded as a formal treatise, or as a collection of unconnected thoughts and maxims, like the *Meditations* of Marcus Aurelius, or Pascal's *Pensées*, or Hare's *Guesses at Truth;* or as a dialogue, though without the names of the interlocutors, after the manner of Plato; or like the discussions between the *Dotto* and the *Ignorante*, that form a prominent feature in the teaching of the Italian Jesuits, and in which the writer holds free debate with his opponents[1]. Those who take the latter view are, unfortunately, divided among themselves as to which interlocutor in the dialogue represents the views of the writer, and

---

[1] See Ginsburg's exhaustive survey of the literature of Ecclesiastes in the *Introduction* to his Commentary. Herder may be named as the author of the Dialogue theory, but he has been followed by many others.

which those that he is seeking to refute[1]. As to the drift
of the book, we meet with every conceivable variety of
hypothesis more or less skilfully maintained. Men have
seen in it the confessions of the penitent and converted
Solomon[2], or a bitter cynical pasquinade on the career
of Herod the Great[3], or a Chesterfield manual of policy
and *politesse* for those who seek their fortune in the palaces
of kings[4]. It has been made to teach a cloistral asceticism[5], or a healthy life of natural enjoyment[6], or a license
like that of a St Simonian "rehabilitation of the flesh[7]."
Those who looked on one side of the shield have found in
it a direct and earnest *apologia* for the doctrine of the
immortality of the soul[8]; those who approached it from
the other were not less sure that it was a polemic protest
against that doctrine as it was taught by Pharisees or
Essenes[9]. The writer aimed at leading men to seek the
things eternal, or sought to draw them away from the cloudland of the unknown that men call eternity. Dogmatism
and scepticism have alike claimed the author as their
champion. It has been made to teach the mysteries of the
Trinity and the Atonement[10], or to rebuke the presumption
that speculates on those mysteries.. It has been identified

---

[1] One school, *e.g.*, maintains that the seemingly Epicurean sentiments, another that the gloomier views of life, are stated only to be
rejected (Ginsburg, *ut supra*).

[2] This is, I need hardly say, the current traditional interpretation of
Jewish and Patristic and early Protestant writers (Ginsburg, *ut supra*).

[3] Grätz, *Comm. on Koheleth*, p. 13.

[4] Jacobi, quoted by Ginsburg, p. 186.

[5] The view was that of Jerome, Augustine, and the whole crowd of
Patristic and mediæval interpreters.

[6] Luther, *Comm. on Eccles.*   [7] Grätz, *Commentary*, p. 26.

[8] So most Patristic and early Protestant scholars; and Hengstenberg
and Delitzsch among those of our own time.

[9] So emphatically Grätz, p. 28.

[10] See the Commentaries of Jerome, Augustine, and others of the same
school, as collected by Pineda.

alike with the Creed of Athanasius and with that of the Agnostic.

Think, too, for a moment of the varying aspects which it presents to us when we come in contact with it, not as handled by professed interpreters, but as cropping up here and there in the pages of history, or the lives of individual men. We think of Gelimer, the Vandal king[1], led in chains in the triumph of Belisarius, and, as he walked on without a tear and without a sigh, finding a secret consolation in the oft-echoed burden of " *Vanitas vanitatum! omnia vanitas!*" or of Jerome reading the book with his disciple Blæsilla, that he might persuade her to renounce those vanities for the life of the convent at Bethlehem[2]; or of Thomas à Kempis taking its watchword as the text of the *De Imitatione Christi;* or of Laud writing to Strafford when the policy of "Thorough" had broken down, and counselling him to turn for consolation to its pages[3]. We remember how Luther found in it a healthy *Politica* or *Œconomica,* the very mirror of magistracy and active life, as contrasted with that of the monks and friars who opposed him[4]; how Voltaire dedicated his paraphrase of it to Frederick II., as that of a book which was the king's favourite study[5]. It has, in the history of our own literature, been versified by poets as widely contrasted as Quarles and Prior. It has furnished a name to the "Vanity Fair" of Bunyan and of Thackeray; and the latter in a characteristic poem[6] has moralized his song on the theme of its *Mataiotes Mataiotētōn*. Pascal found in it the echo of the restless scepticism which drove him to take refuge

---

[1] Gibbon, c. XLI.
[2] Hieron. *Præf. in Eccles.*
[3] Mozley, *Essays,* I. p. 60.
[4] Luther, *Præf. in Eccles.*
[5] Voltaire, *Œuvres,* Vol. X. p. 258 (ed. 1819).
[6] Thackeray, *Ballads and Tales,* 1869, p. 233.

from the uncertainty that tormented him apart from God, in the belief that God had revealed Himself, and that the Church of Rome was the witness and depository of that revelation[1]. Renan, lastly, looks on it as the only charming work—"*le seul livre aimable*"—that has ever been written by a Jew, and with his characteristic insight into the subtle variations of human nature, strives to represent to himself St Paul in his declining years—if only he had been of another race and of another temperament, *i.e.* if he had been quite another Paul than we have known—as at last discovering, *désillusionné* of the "sweet Galilean vision," that he had wasted his life on a dream, and turning from all the Prophets to a book which till then he had scarcely read, even the book Ecclesiastes[2].

It will be seen from the *Introduction* to this volume that I am not satisfied to rest altogether in any of these conclusions. I can honestly say that I have worked through the arguments by which the writers have supported them and have not found them satisfy the laws of evidence or the conditions of historical probability. It lies in the nature of the case that, as I have studied the book, month after month, I have felt its strangely fascinating and, so to speak, zymotic power, that side-lights have fallen on it now from this quarter and now from that, that suggestive coincidences have shewed themselves between its teaching and that of other writings in Hebrew, or Greek, or later literature, that while much remained that, like parts of St Paul's Epistles, was "hard to be understood" (2 Pet. iii. 16), much also seemed to become clear. The "maze" was not altogether "without a plan," and there was, at least, a partial clue to the intricate windings of the labyrinth. It

---

[1] Pascal, *Pensées*, Vol. I. p. 159, ed. Molines.
[2] Renan, *L'Antéchrist*, p. 101.

will be seen, in the course of the *Introduction* and the Notes that follow, that I have consulted most of the commentaries that were best worth consulting. It is not, I think, necessary to give a complete list of these or of other books which I have, in the course of my labours, laid under contribution, but I cannot withhold a special tribute of grateful admiration to the two works which have most helped me—the Commentary of Dr Ginsburg, the result of many years of labour, and characterized, as might be expected, by an exhaustive completeness; and that by Mr Tyler, which, though briefer, is singularly thoughtful and suggestive, and to which I am indeed indebted for the first impressions as to the date and character of the book, which have now ripened into convictions.

Those convictions I now submit alike to students and to experts. They will clash, it may be, in some points with inherited and traditional opinions. I can but hope, however, that those who are drawn to the study of the book may find in what I have written that which will help them to understand it better than they have done. They will find in it, if I mistake not, that it meets, and, we may believe, has been providentially designed to meet, the special tendencies of modern philosophical thought, and that the problems of life which it discusses are those with which our own daily experience brings us into contact. They will learn that the questions of our own time are those which vexed the minds of seekers and debaters in an age not unlike our own in its forms of culture, and while they recognize the binding force of its final solution of the problems, "Fear God and keep His commandments," on those who have not seen, or have not accepted the light of a fuller revelation, they will rejoice in the brightness of that higher revelation of the mind of God of which the Christian Church is the inheritor and the witness. If they feel, as they will do, that there is hardly any book of the Old Testament which presents so marked a contrast in its teaching to that of the Gospels or Epistles of the New Testament, they will yet acknowledge that it is not without a place in the Divine Economy of Revelation, and may become to those who use it rightly a παιδαγωγὸς εἰς Χρίστον—a "schoolmaster leading them to Christ."

BICKLEY VICARAGE,
Oct. 23rd, 1880.

CONTENTS.

PAGES

I. INTRODUCTION.

Chapter I. The Title .... 15—19

Chapter II. Authorship and Date .... 19—34

Chapter III. An Ideal Biography .... 35—55

Chapter IV. Ecclesiastes and Ecclesiasticus ...... 56—66

Chapter V. Ecclesiastes and the Wisdom of Solomon .... 67—75

Chapter VI. Jewish interpreters of Ecclesiastes... 75—87

Chapter VII. Ecclesiastes and its Patristic interpreters.............................. 88—97

Chapter VIII. Analysis of Ecclesiastes .... 97—101

II. TEXT AND NOTES... 103—230

III. APPENDIX.

   1. Koheleth and Shakespeare .... 231—249

   2. Koheleth and Tennyson .... 250—261

   3. A Persian Koheleth of the twelfth century ... 262—268

IV. INDEX .... 269—271

** The Text adopted in this Edition is that of Dr Scrivener's *Cambridge Paragraph Bible.* A few variations from the ordinary Text, chiefly in the spelling of certain words, and in the use of italics, will be noticed. For the principles adopted by Dr Scrivener as regards the printing of the Text see his Introduction to the *Paragraph Bible,* published by the Cambridge University Press.

INTRODUCTION.

CHAPTER I.

THE TITLE.

1. THE name *Ecclesiastes*, by which the book before us is commonly known, comes to us from the Greek version of the Old Testament, known as the Septuagint (the version of the *Seventy* who were believed to have been the translators), as the nearest equivalent they could find to the Hebrew title *Koheleth*. Jerome, the translator to whom we owe the Latin version known as the Vulgate, thought that he could not do better than retain the word, instead of attempting to translate it, and it has been adopted (in the title though not in the text) in the English and many other modern versions[1].

We are thrown back therefore upon the Hebrew word and we have, in the first instance, to ask what it meant, and why it was chosen by the author. In this enquiry we are met (1) by the fact that the word occurs nowhere else in the whole range of Old Testament literature, and the natural inference is that it was coined because the writer wanted a word more significant and adapted to his aim than any with which his native speech supplied him; possibly, indeed, because he wanted a word corresponding to one in a foreign language that was thus significant.

---

[1] Luther gives *Der Prediger Salomo,* which the English version reproduces in its alternative title.

Looking accordingly to the etymology of the Hebrew word we find that it is in form the feminine participle of an unused conjugation of a verb *Kâhal* and as such would have a meaning connected with the root-idea of the verb, that of "gathering" or "collecting." The verb is always used in its other conjugations of gathering persons and not things (Exod. xxxv. 1; Num. i. 18, viii. 9, xvi. 19, *et al.*), and from it is formed the noun which in our English version appears as "congregation" (Lev. iv. 14; Num. x. 7; Deut. xxiii. 1 *et al.*), "assembly" (Num. xiv. 5; Deut. v. 22; Judges xx. 2 *et al.*) or "company" (Jer. xxxi. 8; Ezek. xvi. 40, xvii. 17 *et al.*), while in the LXX it appears almost uniformly as *Ecclesia.* It is accordingly an all but certain inference that the meaning of the new-coined word was either "one who calls an assembly" or, looking to the usual force of the unused conjugation from which it is formed[1], "one who is a member of an assembly." The choice of the feminine form may be connected with the thought that the writer wished to identify himself with Wisdom (a noun which was feminine in Hebrew as in other languages), who appears as teaching in the bold impersonation of Prov. i. 20, viii. 1—4. On the other hand the noun is always treated throughout the book (with, possibly, the solitary exception of chap. vii. 27, but see note there) as masculine, partly, perhaps, because the writer identified himself with the man Solomon as well as with the abstract wisdom, partly, it may be also, because usage had, as in the case of Sophereth (Neh. vii. 57), Pochereth (Ezra ii. 57), Alemeth and Azmaveth (1 Chron. viii. 36) sanctioned the employment of such feminine forms as the names of men.

It follows from this that the LXX translators were at least not far wrong when they chose *Ecclesiastes* as the nearest equivalent for the Hebrew title of the book, *Koheleth.* Our word "Preacher," however, which has been adopted from Luther, is altogether misleading. Taken in connexion with the associa-

---

[1] The participle *Koheleth* is formed as if from the *Kal* conjugation, which commonly denotes intransitive state or action. No example of the verb *Kâhal* is found in this form. The two forms most in use are the transitive, "to gather," and the passive "to be gathered."

tions which the very sound of *Ecclesia* in any of its compounds calls up, it suggests the idea of a teacher delivering a set discourse to a congregation of worshippers. That is, to say the least, an idea which it is hard to reconcile with the structure and contents of Koheleth. It may be added that it is just as foreign to the meaning of the Hebrew and Greek words. The verb *Kâhal* is never used in connexion with the idea of vocal utterance of any kind. The *Ecclesiastes* was not one who called the *Ecclesia* or assembly together, or addressed it in a tone of didactic authority, but much rather one who was an ordinary member of such an assembly (the political unit of every Greek State) and took part in its discussions. He is, as Aristotle says, not an *archon* or a ruler (*Pol.* III. 11), but a part of the great whole (*Ibid.*). So the *Ecclesiazusai* of Aristophanes are women who meet in an assembly to debate, and the word is used in the same sense by Plato (*Gorg.* p. 452, E). In the LXX, the word does not occur outside the book to which it serves as a title, and we have therefore no reason for thinking that they used it in any other than its ordinary sense. It follows from this that the more natural equivalent for it in English would be *Debater* rather than *Preacher*, and looking to the fact that the Hebrew writer apparently coined the word, it would be a natural inference that he did so, because he wanted a substantive which exactly expressed the idea of one who desired to present himself in that character and not as a teacher. He claimed only to be a member, one of many, of the great *Ecclesia* of those who think. If we could assume that he had any knowledge of Greek, it would be a legitimate inference that he formed the new word as an equivalent to the Ecclesiastes which had that significance. It is obvious that this is a meaning which fits in far more aptly with the nature of the book, its presentment of many views, more or less contrasted with each other, its apparent oscillation between the extremes of a desponding pessimism and a tranquil Epicureanism. To use the title of a modern book with which most readers are familiar, the writer speaks as one who takes his part in a meeting of *Friends in Council*.

The true meaning of the title having thus been established, both on philological grounds and as being in harmony with the character of the work itself, it will be sufficient to note briefly the other meanings which have been assigned to it by different scholars. (*a*) It cannot mean, as Grotius thought, one who was a συναθροιστής (*synathroistes*) a *collector sententiarum* or "compiler," one who does not maintain a theory or opinion of his own but brings together those of other thinkers; for this, though it agrees fairly with the nature of the contents of the book, is incompatible with the fact that the Hebrew verb is used, without exception, in the sense of collecting, or calling together, persons and not things. (*b*) More, perhaps, is to be said for Ginsburg's view (*Koheleth, Introd.* p. 2) that the title expresses the act of bringing together those that have been scattered, assembling men, as the historical Solomon assembled them, to meet as in the Divine presence (1 Kings viii. 1—5), calling back those that have wandered in the bye-ways of doubt, "a gatherer of those far off to God." The word thus taken expresses the thought which was uttered in the words of the true Son of David: "How often would I have gathered thy children together" (Matt. xxiii. 34; Luke xiii. 34). It is, however, against this view, that the writer forms the word *Koheleth* as has been said above, from a conjugation not in use (*Kal*), which would naturally express being in a given state or position, and passes over the conjugation which was in use (*Hiphil*) and expressed the transitive act of bringing into such a position or state. To that latter form belongs, in this case, the meaning of "gathering together" into an assembly. It can scarcely be questioned that the writer's motive in not using it, when it was ready to his hand, was that he deliberately sought to avoid the sense of "gathering an assembly," and coined a word, which, as the LXX translators rightly felt, conveyed the sense of being a member of such an assembly and taking part in its proceedings. (*c*) Jerome's view, followed as we have seen by Luther, that the word describes a *concionator* or "preacher" is that also of the *Midrash Rabba* (a Jewish commentary of uncertain date, but not earlier than the sixth, nor later than the twelfth century,

Steinschneider, *Jewish Literature*, p. 53) which explains the name as given by Solomon, "because his discourses were delivered before the congregation" (Ginsburg, p. 3, Wünsche, *Midr. Koh.* p. 2), but this also, as shewn above, is both wrong etymologically and at variance with the character of the book. (*d*) The word cannot mean, as a few commentators have thought, "one who has been gathered," as describing the state of the repentant and converted Solomon, for this would involve a grammatical solecism in the opposite direction to that already examined, and would assign a passive meaning to a form essentially active, though not factitive, in its force. (*e*) Other more far-fetched interpretations, resting on hazardous Arabic etymologies, as that the word meant "penitent" or "the old man," or "the voice that cries," may be dismissed, as not calling for any serious discussion.

CHAPTER II.

AUTHORSHIP AND DATE.

1. It lies on the surface that the writer of the book, who, though he does not introduce the name of Solomon, identifies himself (ch. i. 12—16) with the historical son of David, was either actually the king of Israel whose name was famous for "wisdom and largeness of heart" or that, for some reason or other, he adopted the dramatic personation of his character as a form of authorship. On the former hypothesis, the question of date is settled together with that of authorship, and the book takes its place almost among the earliest treasures of Hebrew literature, side by side with the Psalms that actually came from David's pen and with the inner kernel of the Book of Proverbs. On the latter a wide region of conjecture lies opens to us, from any date subsequent to that of Solomon to the time when we first get distinct traces of the existence of the book, and the problem, in the absence of external evidence, will have to be decided on

*

the ground of internal notes of time and place as seen in the language, thought, and structure of the book. A preliminary question meets us, however, which turns, not upon evidence either external or internal, but upon an *à priori* assumption. It has been urged that when a writer adopts a personated authorship he is guilty of a fraudulent imposture, that such an imposture is incompatible with any idea of inspiration, however loosely that inspiration may be defined, and that to assume a personated authorship is therefore to assert that the book has no right to the place it occupies in the Canon of the Old Testament[1]. On this view Ecclesiastes, if not written by Solomon, takes its place on the same level as Ireland's *Vortigern*, or Chatterton's *Rowley*, or Macpherson's *Ossian*. It may fairly be said, however, of this view that it ignores the fact that a dramatic personation of character has, at all times, been looked upon as a legitimate form of authorship, not necessarily involving any *animus decipiendi*. With some writers of the highest genius, as *e.g.*, with Robert Browning and Tennyson, a monologue or soliloquy of this character has been a favourite form of composition. The speeches in Herodotus and Thucydides, the *Apologies* written in the name of Socrates by Xenophon and Plato, the Dialogues of Plato throughout, are instances in which no one would dream of imputing fraud to the writers, though in all these cases we have, with scarcely the shadow of a doubt, the thoughts and words of the writers and not of the men whom they represent as speaking. The most decisive, and in that sense, crucial instance of such authorship is found, however, in the book which presents so striking a parallel to Ecclesiastes, the Apocryphal Wisdom of Solomon. There also, both in the title and the body of the book (Wisd. vii. 5, 7, ix. 7, 8) the writer identifies himself with the Son of David. It was quoted by early Greek and Latin fathers as by Solomon (Clem. Alex. *Strom.* VI. 11, 14, 15; Tertull. *Adv. Valent.* c. 2 ; *De Præscr. Hæret.* c. 7). From

---

[1] The argument may be found in most English Commentaries, but see especially an elaborate treatise on *The Authorship of Ecclesiastes*, pp. 1—12 (Macmillan and Co., 1880).

the time of the Muratorian Fragment[1], it has been commonly
ascribed to Philo or some other writer of the Alexandrian
school of Jewish thought[2]. No one now dreams of ascribing
it to Solomon. No one has ever ventured to stigmatize it as
a fraudulent imposture. It has been quoted reverentially even
by Protestant writers, cited as Scripture by many of the Fathers,
placed by the Church of Rome in the Canon of Scripture (*Conc.
Trident. Sep.* IV. *de Can. Script.*), and recognized by Church of
England critics as entitled to a high place of honour among the
books which they receive as deutero-canonical (Art. VI.). In
the face of these facts it can scarcely be said with any probability that we are debarred from a free enquiry into the
evidence of the authorship of Ecclesiastes, other than the statement of ch. i. 12, or that we ought to resist or suppress the
conclusion to which the evidence may point, should it tend to a
belief that Solomon was not the author. If dramatic personation be, in all times and countries, a legitimate method of instruction, there is no *à priori* ground against the employment of
that method by the manifold and "very varied wisdom" (the
πολυποίκιλος σοφία of Eph. iii. 10) of the Eternal Spirit. It may
be added that this is, at least, a natural interpretation of the
structure of the Book of Job. It can hardly be supposed that
that work is the report of an actual dialogue.

Returning to the enquiry accordingly, we may begin by admitting freely that the Solomonic authorship has in its favour
the authority of both Jewish and Christian tradition. The
Midrash Koheleth (= Commentary on Ecclesiastes, probably, as
has been said above, between the sixth and twelfth centuries)
represents the opinions of a large number of Rabbis, all of whom

---

[1] The words of the Fragment as they stand are "*Et sapientia ab
amicis in honorem ipsius scripta*," but it has been conjectured that this
was a blundering translation of the Greek ὑπὸ Φίλωνος ("by Philo"),
which the writer mistook for ὑπὸ φίλων ("by friends"), Tregelles,
Canon Murator. p. 53.

[2] So Jerome (*Præf. in lib. Salom.*); Luther (*Pref. to Wisd. Sol.*)
and many others (Grimm's *Weisheit, Einleit.* p. 22). The present
writer has shewn what appear to him strong reasons for ascribing it to
Apollos (*Expositor*, vol. I. "The Writings of Apollos").

base their interpretations on the assumption that Solomon was the writer. The *Targum* or Paraphrase of the book (assigned by Ginsburg (*Koheleth*, p. 36) to the sixth century after Christ) follows in the same track. A line of Jewish Commentators from Rashi (Rabbi Solomon Yitzchaki) in the eleventh century to Moses Mendelssohn in the eighteenth, and some yet later authors (Ginsburg, *Introduction*, pp. 38—80) wrote on the same assumption. The testimony of Patristic literature is as uniform as that of Rabbinic. The book was paraphrased by Gregory Thaumaturgus (d. A.D. 270), commented on by Gregory of Nyssa (d. A.D. 396), referred to and in part explained by Augustine (d. A.D. 430), and accepted by their mediæval successors, Hugo of St Victor (d. A.D. 1140), Richard of St Victor (d. A.D. 1173), Bonaventura (d. A.D. 1274), and Nicholas de Lyra (d. A.D. 1340), whose testimony, as having been born a Jew, comes with a two-fold weight, as the work of the historic Solomon.

Uniform, however, as this *consensus* is, amounting almost to the "*semper, ubique, et ab omnibus*" which Vincent of Lerins made the test of Catholicity, it can scarcely be regarded as decisive. The faculty of historical criticism, one might almost say, of intellectual discernment of the meaning and drift of a book or of individual passages in it, is, with rare exceptions, such as were Origen, Eusebius, Jerome, Dionysius of Alexandria, and Theodore of Mopsuestia, wanting in the long succession of the Christian Fathers, and no one can read the Targum or the Midrash on Koheleth, or the comments of not a few of their successors, without feeling that he is in the company of those who have eyes and see not, and who read between the lines, as patristic interpreters also do, meanings which could, by no conceivable possibility, have been present to the thoughts of the writer. It is true alike of all of them that they lived at too remote a date from that of the book of which they write for their opinion to have any weight as evidence, and that they had no materials for forming that opinion other than those which are in our hands at the present day.

The first voice that was heard to utter a conclusion adverse to this general *consensus* was, as in the case of so many other traditional beliefs, that of Luther. The same bold insight which led him to the conjecture, now accepted by many scholars as approximating to a certainty, that the Epistle to the Hebrews was the work not of St Paul but of Apollos (Alford, *Commentary on N. T., Int. to Ep. to Hebrews*) shewed itself also in regard to Ecclesiastes. In his short Commentary on that book, indeed, written in A. D. 1532 (*Opp.* IV. p. 230, ed. 1582), he treats it throughout as by Solomon, but in his *Table Talk* (*Tischreden*, LIX. 6, ed. Leipzig, 1846) he speaks more freely. " Solomon did not write the book, ' the Preacher,' himself, but it was composed by Sirach in the time of the Maccabees... It is, as it were, a Talmud put together out of many books, probably from the Library of Ptolemy Euergetes, king of Egypt." He goes on to point to the Book of Proverbs as having been composed in the same way, the maxims which came from the king's lips having been taken down and edited by others. It is probable, though we have no evidence of the fact, that Luther may have derived this opinion from some of the " *Humanists,*" the more advanced scholars, of his time, or, possibly, from the Jewish students with whom his work as a translator of the Bible brought him into contact.

The line of free enquiry was followed up by Grotius (A. D. 1644) who, in his *Commentary on the Old Testament*, after discussing the meaning of the title (see above, p. 18) and the aim and plan of the book, gives his judgment as to authorship : "With good reason was it " (in spite of apparent difficulties) "received into the Canon. And yet I, for my part, do not hold it to be the work of Solomon, but to have been written later under the name of that king as one who was moved with repentance. What is to me the ground of this conclusion is that there are many words in it which are not found elsewhere than in Daniel, Esdras (Ezra) and the Chaldæan paraphrasts " (*Opp.* I. p. 258, ed. 1679). Elsewhere he assigns the authorship to Zerubbabel or one of his contemporaries. Luther and Grotius were, however, before their time, and although the suggestion of the latter received a favourable mention in a note of Gibbon's (*Decline and Fall,* C. XLI.), Protestant and Roman Catholic commentators went on following the received tradition till Döderlein in 1784, Jahn in 1793, J. E. C. Schmidt in 1794, revived the objections urged by Grotius and gave them currency among European scholars. From that time onward the stream of objections to the Solomonic authorship has flowed with an ever-increasing volume. Among them we find not only those who are conspicuous for a bold and destructive criticism but men whose position in German theology is that of orthodox Conservatism. Hengstenberg, Keil, Delitzsch, Vaihinger, are on this point at one with Ewald and with Hitzig. In America Noyes and Stuart, in England Davidson and Ginsburg and Cox (*Quest of the Chief Good, Introd.*), have followed in the same track.

The chief ground of agreement among writers representing such very different schools is mainly that given by Grotius. Delitzsch gives a list of about a hundred words or forms or meanings either peculiar to Ecclesiastes or found only in the post-exilian books of the Old Testament, or even not appearing till the time of the later Aramaic of the Mishna literature. It would be out of place to give this list fully here; some of them will be noticed as they occur. Delitzsch's summing up of the results of the induction is that "If the Book of Koheleth be of old Solomonic origin, then there is no history of the Hebrew language" (Delitzsch, *Introd.* p. 190). Ginsburg (p. 253) asserts, with equal emphasis, that "we could as easily believe that Chaucer is the author of Rasselas as that Solomon wrote Koheleth." Ewald's judgment is hardly less decisive when he says that "this work varies more widely than any other in the Old Testament from the old Hebrew speech, so that one might easily be tempted to believe that it was the latest of all the books now included in the Canon" (*Poet. Büch.* IV. p. 178). Ewald himself does not adopt that conclusion, holding that in the gradual admixture of the older and the newer forms of speech, it might easily happen that an earlier writer might use more of the newer forms than a later one, but he places the date of the Book as certainly not before the last century of the Persian Monarchy. The same conclusion as to the date is maintained by Knobel, Davidson and other writers. It may be noted that if we accept that conclusion it forms, in part at least, an answer to the objection drawn from the idea that the personated authorship involves fraudulent imposture. A man who deliberately writes with the *animus decipiendi*, as in the cases of Chatterton and Ireland, aims at archaic forms, avoids modernisms, appears, as it were, in the full dress of a masquerade. The writer who simply adopts the personation as a means of attracting, suggesting, teaching, more powerful than writing in his own name, is content to use the style of his time. He practically says to his readers, as in this case and in the Wisdom of Solomon, and perhaps also (though here there are more traces of fraudulent intention) in the Orphic poems of Aristobulus and the Second Book of Esdras, " I am not what I seem."

It must, however, be admitted that the conclusion thus strongly stated is not even now universally accepted. It is urged that Solomon's foreign diplomacy or foreign marriages may have made him familiar with Aramaic forms and words which did not come into common use till later, that we know too little of colloquial Hebrew in the time of Solomon to form an estimate of the extent to which it varied from that of poetry like the Psalms, or formal maxims like the Proverbs, and that the number of Aramaisms has been exaggerated by prepossessions in favour of a foregone conclusion[1]. And this position also has been taken by men of very different schools of thought. From Bishop Wordsworth (*Commentary*) and Dr Pusey and Mr Bullock (*Speaker's Commentary, Introd. to Eccles.*) we might naturally look for a defence of the traditional belief. From the opposite extreme Renan (*Hist. des Langues Semitiques*, p. 131) declares his belief (mainly resting, however, on the absence of the sacerdotal element) that "Job, the Song of Songs, and Kohe-

[1] A more elaborate discussion of this linguistic problem, in which the writer seeks to minimise the number and force of Delitzsch's list, is found in the anonymous treatise on *The Authorship of Ecclesiastes* already referred to (pp. 26—39). See note p. 20.

leth are all productions of the period of Solomon," though he thinks it possible that they have been edited and partly re-written at a later date. In his treatise *Le Livre de Job*, however (p. xxviii.), he modifies his opinion and speaks of the Book of Proverbs as compiled under the kings and of Ecclesiastes as still later. Dean Milman (*Hist. of Jews*, I. p. 325) writes that he is "well aware that the general voice of German criticism assigns a later date (than that of Solomon) to this book. But," he adds, "I am not convinced by any arguments from internal evidence which I have read." By Herzfeld's objections, the force of which he admits, he is "shaken but not convinced."

To the argument on purely linguistic grounds others have been added, of which it can scarcely be denied that while each of them taken by itself might admit of a more or less satisfactory answer, they have, taken together, a considerable cumulative force. Thus it has been urged (1) that the words "I the Preacher was king over Israel" (ch. i. 12) could not have been written by Solomon, who never ceased to be king; (2) that a book coming from the son of David was hardly likely to be characterised, as this is, by the omission of the name of Jehovah which is so prominent in the Psalms and Proverbs, or of all reference to the history of Israel, or to the work which Solomon had done in the erection of the Temple as well as of his palaces and gardens; (3) that, if written, as the traditional belief, for the most part, assumes, in the penitence of Solomon's old age, we might have looked not merely for the sigh of disappointment uttered in the "vanity of vanities," but for the confession of his own sins of apostasy and idolatry; (4) that the historical Solomon, the second king of his dynasty, the first who had begun his reign in the Holy City, was hardly likely to speak of "all that had been before him in Jerusalem" (ch. i. 16); (5) that the language, as of an observer from without in which the writer speaks of the disorder and corrupt government that prevailed around him (ch. iv. 1, v. 8, viii. 9, x. 5), is not such as we should have expected from one who, if such evils existed, was himself responsible for them; (6) that the book presents many striking parallelisms with that of Malachi[1] which is confessedly later than the exile and written under the Persian monarchy, probably circ. B.C. 390; (7) that it also contains, as will be shewn further on, allusive references to events in the history of Persia, or, as some have thought, to events in the history of Egypt under the Ptolemies[2]; (8) that, to anticipate what will be hereafter shewn in detail, it presents at least the germs of the three tendencies which were developed in the later days of Judaism in the forms of Pharisaism, Sadducaism and the asceticism of the Essenes[3]; (9) that there are not a few passages which indicate the writer's acquaintance with the philosophy and literature of Greece[4].

More decisive, perhaps, in its bearing upon the question now before us is the manner in which the book was treated by the Jewish leaders of the Rabbinic schools in the century before the Christian era. Absolutely the first external evidence which we have of its existence is found in a Talmudic report of a discussion between the two schools of Hillel and of Shammai as to its admission into the Canon of the sacred books. It was debated under the singular form of the question whether the Song of Songs and Koheleth polluted the hands, *i.e.* whether they were so sacred that it was a sacrilege for common or unclean hands to touch them. Some took one side, some another. As usual, the school of Shammai "loosed," *i.e.* pronounced against the authority of the book, and that of Hillel "bound" by deciding in its favour. Different Rabbis held different opinions (Mishna, *Yadayim*, v. 3, Gemara, *Megila* 7, *a*), quoted in full by Ginsburg, p. 14). So again another Talmudic tract (*Shabbath*, quoted *ut supra*) reports that the "wise men wanted to declare Koheleth apocryphal, because its statements contradicted each other," and in the *Midrash Koheleth*, that they did so, because "they found in it sentiments that tended to infidelity" (Ginsburg, *ut supra*). They were at last led to

---

[1] See Notes on ch. v. 1—6.
[2] See Notes on chs. iv. 13, v. 8, ix. 14, x. 7, 16, 17, 20.
[3] See Notes on chs. iii. 19—21, vii. 1—6, 16.
[4] See Notes on chs. i. 3—11, ii. 24, iii. 20, v. 18, vi. 6, xii. 11, 12.

acquiesce in its admission by the fact that at least it began and ended with words that were in harmony with the Law (Mishna, *Yadayim*, v. 3, quoted by Ginsburg, p. 14). The memory of the discussion lingered on till the time of Jerome who reports (*Comment. on Eccles.* XII. 13) that "the Hebrews say that among the works of Solomon which have been rejected (*antiquata*) and have not remained in the memory of men, this book also ought to be cancelled or treated as of no value (*obliterandus*) because it maintained that all the creatures of God are vain." Without discussing now the view as to the teaching of Ecclesiastes thus expressed, it is scarcely conceivable that a book that had come down from a remote 'antiquity with the prestige of Solomonic authorship, and had all along been held in honour as the representative of his divinely inspired wisdom, could have been so spoken of. Such a discussion, in such a case, would have been an example of a bold criticism which has no parallel in the history of that period of Jewish thought. It is not without significance as bearing upon a question to be discussed hereafter, that it was the narrow exclusive school of Shammai that raised the objection, that held, *i.e.*, that Koheleth was not canonical, and therefore did not pollute the hands, while that of Hillel with its wider culture, and sympathy with Greek thought, was ready to admit its claim, and finally turned the balance of opinion in its favour (Gemara, *Megila* 7, *a*, *Shabbath* 30, *b*, quoted by Ginsburg, p. 15).

An inference of a like kind may be drawn, if I mistake not, from the existence of the Apocryphal Book known as the Wisdom of Solomon, written, beyond the shadow of a doubt, by an Alexandrian and probably not long before, or possibly after, the Christian era. If the book Ecclesiastes were, at the time when that author wrote, generally recognized as having the authority which attached to the name of Solomon, there would have been something like a bold irreverence in the act of writing a book which at least seemed to put itself in something like a position of rivalry, and in some places, to be a kind of corrective complement to its teaching. (Comp. Wisd. ii. iii. with Eccles. ii. 18—26, iii. 18—22, and other passages in ch. v.) If, however, it were known to be a comparatively recent work, and that the schools of Jerusalem had been divided in opinion as to its reception into the Canon, it is quite intelligible than an earnest and devout Jew, such as the writer of the *Wisdom of Solomon* manifestly was, should have thought himself justified in following the example that had been set of a personated authorship, and have endeavoured to make his ideal Solomon a truer representative of a wisdom which was in harmony with the faith and hope of Israel. How far he succeeded in this aim is a question which will meet us in a later stage of our enquiry. (See ch. v.)

On the whole, then, weighing both the facts themselves, and the authority of the names which are arranged on either side as to the conclusions to be drawn from them, the balance seems to incline somewhat decisively to another than Solomonic authorship. Assuming this conclusion as established, we have to ask to what later period in Jewish history it is to be referred, and here the opinions of scholars divide themselves into three chief groups.

I. There are those who, like Ewald, Ginsburg, and Hengstenberg, fix its date during the period in which the Jews were subject to the rule of the Persian kings. They rest their belief on the fact that the book contains words that belong to that period, such as those for "orchards" (see Note on ch. ii. 5) and "province" (see Note on ch. ii. 8). In the use of the word "angel" apparently for "priest" (see Note on ch. v. 6), they find an indication that the writer was not far from being a contemporary of the prophet Malachi, who uses that word in the same sense (Mal. ii. 7). The tone of the book, in its questionings and perplexities, indicates, they think, a general spiritual condition of the people, like that which Malachi reproves. The "robbery" in "tithes and offerings" (Mal. iii. 8) agrees with the "vowing and not paying" of ch. v. 5. The political situation described in chs. iv. 1, vii. 7, viii. 2—4, the hierarchy of officials, the tyranny, corruption and extortion of the governors of provinces (see Note on ch. v. 8), the supreme authority of the great King practically issuing in the despotism of a queen, a minister, or a slave, the revelry and luxury of the court (see Note on ch. x.

16), are all painted with a vividness which implies experience of misgovernment such as that which meets us in Neh. v. 15, ix. 36, 37; Esth. i. 7, 8, iii. 9 (see Notes on ch. x. 4, 7, 16). More specific references have also been found to events in Persian history, to the influence of the eunuch Bagoas (see Note on ch. x. 5) under Artaxerxes Ochus, to the treatment of that king's corpse in ch. vi. 3, to Artaxerxes Mnemon as one whose likeness we may recognize in the "old and foolish king" of ch. iv. 13. The facts thus stated cannot be regarded as otherwise than interesting and suggestive, but it is obvious that they are compatible with a later date, which presented the same political and social conditions, and at which the historical facts, assuming the reference to them to be sufficiently definite, would still be in the memories of men.

II. And there is, it is believed, overwhelming evidence in favour of that later date. Mr Tyler, in the Introduction to his singularly interesting and able treatise on *Ecclesiastes* (1874), finds in the book traces not to be mistaken of the influence of the teaching both of Stoic and Epicurean philosophy. In the view of life as presenting a recurrence of the same phenomena, the thing which is being as that which hath been (see Notes on chs. i. 5—7, 11, iii. 14, 15), he finds the Stoic teaching of the cycles of events presented by history, such as that which we find in its later form in the *Meditations* of Marcus Aurelius (XI. 1). The thought of the nothingness of man's life and strivings, his ambitions and his pleasures (chs. i. 2, 3, 17, ii. 21—26, vi. 3, and *passim*), has its parallel in the apathy and contempt of the world which characterised the teaching of the Stoics when they taught that they were transient "as the flight of a swift-winged bird;" and that all human things (τὰ ἀνθρώπινα) were "as a vapour, and as nothingness" (Marc. Aur. *Meditt.* VI. 15, X. 31). The Stoic destiny (εἱμαρμένη), and the consequent calm acceptance of the inevitable, on which the Stoic prided himself, is echoed in the teaching of Koheleth as to the events that come to man by a power which his will cannot control, the "time and chance" that happeneth alike to all (chs. viii. 8, ix. 11). The stress laid on the common weaknesses of mankind as being of the nature of insanity, as in the frequently recurring combination of "madness and folly" (see Notes on chs. i. 17, ii. 12, vii. 25, x. 13), is altogether in harmony with the language of the Stoics (Diog. Laert. VII. 124). Nor are the traces of the teaching of Epicurus less distinctly visible. We know that teaching indeed mainly through later writers, and the "many books" of the great Master himself have perished altogether, but for that very reason we know perhaps better than if we had the latter only, what were the points of his system which most impressed themselves on the minds of his followers. Lucretius and Horace are for us the representatives of Epicurean thought as Epictetus and Marcus Aurelius are of Stoic, and the parallelisms of language and idea which these writers present to the book now before us, may legitimately suggest the conclusion that they drank from a common source. We note accordingly that the Debater is acquainted with the physical science of Epicurus as represented by Lucretius. They speak in almost identical terms of the phenomena of the daily rising and setting of the sun, of the rivers flowing into the sea, and returning to their source (see Note on i. 5, 6). Their language as to the dispersion at death of the compound elements of man's nature (see Notes on chs. iii. 19, 20, xii. 7) ; as to our ignorance of all that comes after death (see Note on ch. iii. 21); as to the progress of man in the arts of civilized life (see Note on ch. vii. 29); as to the nature of man standing, as far as we know, on the same level as that of beasts (see Note on ch. iii. 18, 19), presents an identity of tone, almost even of phrase. Still more in accord with popular Epicureanism as represented by Horace is the teaching of Koheleth as to the secret of enjoyment, consisting in the ἀταραξία (tranquillity) of a well regulated life (chs. ii. 24, iii. 22, v. 18, ix. 7), in the avoidance of passionate emotions and vain ambitions, and anxious cares, in learning to be content with a little, but to accept and use that little with a deliberate cheerfulness (chs. v. 11, 12, 19, vii. 14). Even the pessimism of the Epicurean, from which he vainly seeks to find a refuge in this *pococurante* life, is echoed by the Debater. The lamentations over the frailty and shortness of man's life (ch. vi. 4, 5, 12), over the disorders which prevail in nature and in society (chs. v. 8, vii. 7, viii. 9, 14, ix. 16, x. 16—18), the ever-recurring burden of the "vanity of vanities" (chs. i. 2, 17, ii. 26, iv. 16, viii. 10, ix. 9, xi. 10, xii. 8), are all characteristic of the profounder tendencies of the same school, which culminated in the "*tantâ stat prædita culpâ*" of Lucretius (II. 181).

But it is not only in its affinity with the later philosophical systems of Greece that we find a proof of the later date of Ecclesiastes. It is throughout absolutely saturated with Greek thought and language. In the characteristic phrase of "under the sun" to express the totality of human things (see Notes on chs. i. 14, iv. 15, vi. 1, ix. 3), of "seeing the sun" for living (see Notes on chs. vi. 5, xi. 7), in the reference to the current maxims of Greek thought, the Μηδὲν ἄγαν ("Nothing in excess") in ch. vii. 16, in the stress on opportuneness (καιρός) in ch. iii. 1—8, in the "many books" of ch. xii. 12, recalling the 300 volumes of the writings of Epicurus, and the 400 of his disciple Apollodorus, and the 200,000 of the library at Alexandria, in the characteristic, "Who knows?" of the rising school of Scepticism in ch. iii. 21, in the cynical disparagement of women which made Euripides known as the misogynist, and cast its dark shadow over Greek social life (see Note on ch. vii. 28), in the allusive reference to a Greek proverb in the "bird in the air" that reports secrets (see Note on ch. x. 20), in the goads as representing the stimulating effect of all true teaching (see Note on ch. xii. 11), perhaps also in the knowledge shewn (see Note on ch. xii. 5) of the Greek pharmacopœia,—in all this evidence, in its cumulative force, we find what compels us to admit that the book could not well have been written before the schools of the Garden and the Porch had obtained a prominent position, *i.e.* not earlier than B.C 250. With less confidence I bring before the reader the substance of Mr Tyler's argument as to the probable limits of the period within which Ecclesiastes may have been written (*Ecclesiastes, Introd.* § 5). The earlier of these limits he fixes as above, at about B.C. 250. The later he finds in the coincidence between it and the book known as the Wisdom of the Son of Sirach, the Ecclesiasticus of the English Apocrypha.

I present these, as he gives them, and leave the reader to judge of their evidential force[1].

Eccles. vii. 13—15	and	Ecclus. xxxiii. 13—15.
Eccles. viii. 1	......	Ecclus. xiii. 25, 26.
Eccles. x. 11	......	Ecclus. xii. 13.
Eccles. vii. 20—22	......	Ecclus. xix. 16.
Eccles. x. 2, 3, 12—14	......	Ecclus. xx. 7, xxi. 25, 26.
Eccles. x. 8	......	Ecclus. xxvii. 26.
Eccles. vii. 27	......	Ecclus. xxxiii. 15.
Eccles. i. 7	......	Ecclus. xl. 11.

Assuming these resemblances to imply derivation and that Ecclesiasticus was the later book of the two, and identifying the Euergetes of his grandson's Preface with Ptolemy Physcon, Mr Tyler concludes that the book now before us could not well have been written before B.C. 180 and is inclined to name B.C. 200 as the most probable date. From this point of view the name given to the latter book in the earliest Latin Version, from which it passed into the Vulgate, is not altogether without significance. The term *Ecclesiasticus* presupposes that the book was looked on as following in the wake of *Ecclesiastes*, belonging to the same class of didactic literature. It is, of course, true that another account of the name was given by patristic writers (Rufinus, *Comm. in Symb.* c. 38) and has been adopted by many modern scholars (Westcott in *Smith's Dict. of Bible*, Art. *Ecclesiasticus*), as though it meant that the book was an "Ecclesiastical" one in the later sense of the word as contrasted with "canonical," fit to be read in the *Ecclesia* though not of authority as a rule of faith. Looking, however, to the fact that there was a book already current in which the word Ecclesiastes was distinctly used in its pre-Christian sense, it is a more natural conclusion to infer that the old meaning was kept in view and that the book was therefore named with the significance now suggested. This is at all events in harmony with the use which the writer himself makes of the word *Ecclesia*, —in ch. xxxviii. 33, when he says of the unlearned workers of the world that they "shall not sit high in the congregation," *i.e.*

[1] The subject is more fully discussed in ch. iv.

in the *ecclesia*, or academy of sages, and falls in with Mr Tyler's theory that his work was more or less influenced by Ecclesiastes. Another commentator (Hitzig) is led to the same conclusion on different grounds. In the picture of the political evils of which the writer complains in ch. iv. 13, vii. 10, 26, or of a young and profligate one in ch. x. 16, he finds definite allusions to the history of Egypt under Ptolemy Philopator and Ptolemy Epiphanes respectively, and, although it may be admitted that the references are not sufficiently definite to establish the point, if taken by themselves, yet, as supervening on other evidence, it will be felt, I think, that they have a considerable corroborating force.

As the result to which these lines of inference converge we have accordingly to think of Ecclesiastes as written somewhere between B.C. 240, the date of the death of Zeno, and B.C. 181, that of the death of Ptolemy Epiphanes.

III. A recent critic (Grätz) has gone a step further, assigning the book to the reign of Herod the Great, and treats it as practically in part a protest against the mal-administration of his government, and in part a polemic against the rising asceticism of the Essenes. I cannot say, however, that the arguments which he advances in support of this hypothesis seem to me sufficiently weighty to call in this place for examination in detail (some of them will find mention in the notes), and they are, to say the least, far outweighed by the evidence that has led Tyler and Hitzig, travelling on distinct lines of investigation, to their conclusion.

It remains, with this date, thus fairly established, to enquire into the plan and purpose of the book, its relation to the environment of the time, to earlier and to later teaching in the same region of thought. The peculiar character of the book, its manifest reproduction, even under the dramatic personation of its form, of a real personal experience, has led me to think that I can do this more effectively in the form of an ideal biography of the writer, based upon such *data* as the book itself presents, than by treating the subject in the more systematic way which would be natural in such a treatise as the present. To that biography I accordingly now invite the attention of the reader.

CHAPTER III.

AN IDEAL BIOGRAPHY.

It would be a comparatively easy task, of course, to write the life of the traditional author of Ecclesiastes. The reign of Solomon "in all his glory" and with all his wisdom has often furnished a subject both for the historian and the poet. There would be a special interest, if we could treat the book before us as leading us into the region that lies below the surface of history, and find in it an autobiographical fragment in which the royal writer laid before us his own experience of life and the conclusions to which he had been led through it. The Confessions of Solomon would have on that assumption a fascination not less powerful than those of Augustine or Rousseau. For the reasons which have been given in the preceding chapter, I cannot adopt that conclusion, and am compelled to rest in the belief that Ecclesiastes was the work of an unknown writer about two hundred years before the Christian era. To write his life under such conditions may seem a somewhat adventurous enterprise. One is open to the charge of evolving a biography out of one's inner consciousness, of summoning a spectral form out of the cloudland of imagination. I have felt, however, looking to the special character of the book, that this would be a more satisfactory way of stating the view that I have been led to hold as to the occasion, plan, and purpose of the book than the more systematic dissertation with which the student is familiar in Commentaries and Introductions. The book has so little of a formal plan, and is so much, in spite of the personated authorship, of the nature of an autobiographical confession, partly, it is clear, deliberate, partly, perhaps, to an extent of which the writer was scarcely conscious, betraying its true nature beneath the veil of the character he had assumed, that the task of portraying the lineaments that lie beneath the veil is comparatively easy. As with the *Pensées* of Pascal or of

3 — 2

Joubert, or the *Sonnets* of Shakespeare, we feel that the very life of the man stands before us, as *votivâ...veluti descripta tabellâ*, in all its main characteristics. We divine the incidents of that life from the impress they have left upon his character, and from chance words in which more is meant than meets the ear.

Koheleth (I shall use the name by anticipation, as better than the constant repetition of "the writer," or "the subject of our memoir") was born, according to the view stated above, somewhere about B.C. 230. He was an only son, "one alone and not a second," without a brother (ch. iv. 8). His father lived in Judæa[1], but not in Jerusalem, and to find "the way to the city," the way which none but the proverbial "fool" among grown-up men could miss, came before the child's mind at an early age as the test of sagacity and courage (ch. x. 18). The boy's education, however, was carried on in the synagogue school of the country town near which he lived, and was rudimentary enough in its character, stimulating a desire for knowledge which it could not satisfy. He learnt, as all children of Jewish parents learnt, the *Shemà* or Creed of Israel, "Hear, O Israel, the Lord thy God is one Lord" (Deut. vi. 4), and the sentences that were written on the Phylacteries which boys, when they reached the age of thirteen and became Children of the Law, wore on their forehead and their arms. He was taught many of the Proverbs which proclaimed that "the fear of the Lord is the beginning of knowledge" (Prov. i. 7), and learnt to reverence Solomon as the ideal pattern of the wisdom and largeness of heart that grow out of a wide experience (1 Kings iv. 29). But it was a time of comparative deadness in the life of Israel. The last of the prophets had spoken some two centuries before, and there were few who studied his writings or those of his predecessors. The great masters of Israel and teachers of the Law had not yet raised the fabric of tradition which was afterwards embodied in the Talmud. The expectations of the Anointed King were for the time dormant, and few were looking for "redemption in Jeru-

---

[1] So Ewald, *Introd. to Ecclesiastes.*

salem" or for "the consolation of Israel." Pharisees and
Sadducees and Essenes, though the germs of their respective
systems might be found in the thoughts of men, were not as yet
stimulating the religious activity of the people by their rivalry
as teachers. The heroic struggle of the Maccabees against the
idolatry of Syria was as yet in the future, and the early history
of the nation, the memories of Abraham and Isaac and Jacob,
did not kindle the patriotic enthusiasm which they came to
kindle afterwards. There was a growing tendency to fall into
the modes of thought and speech and life of the Greeks and
Syrians with whom the sons of Abraham were brought into
contact. Even the sacred name of Jahveh or Jehovah, so
precious to their fathers, had dropped into the background, and
men habitually spoke of "God," or "the Creator," after the
manner of the Greeks (ch. xii. 1). It was a time, such as all
nations and Churches have known, of conventionality and
routine. The religion of the people, such as the boy saw it,
was not such as to call out any very deep enthusiasm. The
wealth of his parents had attracted a knot of so-called devout
persons round them, and his mother had come under their
influence, and in proportion as she did so, failed to gain any
hold on her son's heart, and left no memory of a true pattern of
womanhood for him to reverence and love. Even she formed
no exception in after years to the sweeping censure in which he
declared that among all the women he had met he had never
known one who satisfied his ideal of what a true woman
should be (ch. vii. 28). The religionists who directed her conscience called each other by the name of "Friend," "Brother,"
or "Companion," and claimed to be of those of whom Malachi
had spoken, "who feared the Lord and spake often one to
another" (Mal. iii. 16). Koheleth saw through their hypocrisy,
watched them going to the house of God, *i.e.*, to temple or
synagogue (Ps. lxxiv. 8), and heard their long and wordy and
windy prayers—the very sacrifice of fools (ch. v. 1, 2). He saw
how they made vows in time of sickness or danger, and then,
when the peril had passed away, came before the priest, on
whom they looked as the messenger or angel of the Lord, with

frivolous excuses for its non-fulfilment (ch. v. 4—6); how they told their dreams as though they were an apocalypse from heaven (ch. v. 7). It was necessary to find a phrase to distinguish the true worshippers from these pretenders, and just as men, under the influence of the maxim that language was given to conceal our thoughts, came to speak of *la vérité vraie* as different from the ordinary *vérité*, so Koheleth could only express his scorn of the hypocrites by contrasting them, as with the emphasis of iteration, with "those who fear God, who indeed fear before him" (ch. viii. 12).

As Koheleth grew to years of manhood, he was called to take his part in the labours of the cornfield and the vineyard. The wealth of his father did not lead him to bring up his son to a soft-handed leisure, for men had not then ceased to recognize the blessedness of toil, and it had become a proverb that a father who does not teach his sons to labour with their hands teaches them to be thieves. The teachers of Israel remembered that the "king himself was served by the field" (ch. v. 9) and "despise not husbandry" was one of the maxims of the wise. In after years, when pleasure had brought satiety and weariness, and dainties palled on the palate, Koheleth looked back regretfully on that "sweet sleep" of the labour of earlier days, which followed on the frugal, or even scanty, meal (ch. v. 12).

As he grew up to manhood, however, there came a change. Like the younger son in the parable (Luke xv. 12) he desired to see the world that lay beyond the hills, beyond the waters, and asked for his portion of goods and went his way into a far country. Among the Jews, as among the Greeks, and partly, indeed, as a consequence of their intercourse with them, this had come to be regarded as one of the paths to wisdom and largeness of heart. So the Son of Sirach wrote a little later: "A man that hath travelled knoweth many things." "He shall serve among great men, and appear before princes; he will travel through strange countries; for he hath tried the good and evil among men" (Ecclus. xxxiv. 9, xxxix. 4. Comp. Homer, *Od.* I. 3). And if a Jew travelled anywhere at that period, it was almost a matter of course that he should direct his steps to Alexandria. Intercourse between the two nations of Egypt and Judah was, indeed, no new thing. Psammetichus, in the days of Manasseh, had invited Jews to settle in his kingdom[1]. There had been Israelites "beyond the rivers of Ethiopia" in the days of Josiah (Zeph. iii. 10). Alexander, in founding the new city which was to immortalize his name, had followed in the footsteps of Psammetichus. The first of the Ptolemies had brought over many thousands, and they occupied a distinct quarter of the city[2]. Philadelphus had, as the story ran, invited seventy-two of the elders of Israel to his palace that they might translate their Law as an addition to the treasures of his library, had received them with all honour, and invited them to discuss ethical questions day by day with the philosophers about his court[3]. A wealthy Jew coming to such a city, not without introductions, was sure to be well received, and Koheleth sought and found admission to that life of courts, which the Son of Sirach pointed out as one of the paths of wisdom (Ecclus. xxxix. 4). It was a position not without its dangers. It tempted the Jew to efface his nationality and his creed, and his hopes in the far-off future. It tempted him also to exchange the purity to which he was pledged by the outward symbol of the covenant and by the teaching of his home life, for the license of the Greek. Koheleth for a time bowed his neck to the yoke of a despotic monarch, and learnt the suppleness of the slaves who dare not ask a king, What doest thou? (ch. viii. 4). He watched the way the court winds blew, and learnt to note the rise and fall of favourites and ministers (ch. x. 67). He saw or heard how under Ptolemy Philopator the reins of power had fallen into the hands of his mistress, Agathoclea, and her brother; how the long minority of his son Epiphanes had been marked by the oppression of the poor and "violent perverting of judgment and justice" in the provinces (ch. v. 8), by all the evils which come on a land when its "king is a child" and its "princes revel in the morning" (ch. x. 16, 17)[4]. He had seen the pervading power of a system

[1] Letter of Pseudo-Aristeas.
[3] Letter of Pseudo-Aristeas.
[2] Joseph. *Ant.* XII. 1.
[4] Justin, XXX. 1.

of police espionage, which carried what had been spoken in whispers to the ears of the ruler (ch. x. 20). A training such as this could scarcely fail to make the man who was subject to it something less of an Israelite—to turn his thoughts from contemplating the picture which the prophets had drawn of a true and righteous King, to the task of noting the humours of kings who were neither true nor righteous, and flattering them with an obsequious homage, in the belief that "yielding" in such a case "pacifieth great offences" (ch. x. 4) [1].

Temptations of another kind helped to complete the evil work. The wealth of Koheleth enabled him to surround himself with a certain magnificence, and he kept before himself the ideal of a glory like that of Solomon's: the wine sparkled at his banquets, and singing men and singing women were hired to sing songs of revelry and love, and the Greek *hetæræ*, the "delights of the sons of men," the *demi-monde* of Alexandria, surrounded him with their fascinations (ch. ii. 3—8). His life became one of reckless sensuality. Like the Son in the parable, to whom I have before compared him, he wasted his substance in riotous living, and devoured his wealth with harlots (Luke xv. 13, 30). The tendency of such a life is, as all experience shews, to the bitterness of a cynical satiety. Poets have painted the Nemesis which dogs the footsteps of the man who lives for pleasure. In the Jaques [2], perhaps to some extent even in the Hamlet, of Shakespeare, in the mental history, representing probably Shakespeare's own experience, of his Sonnets, yet more in the Childe Harold of Byron, in the "Palace of Art" and the "Vision of Sin," of Tennyson, we have types of the temper of meditative scorn and unsatisfied desire that uttered itself in the cry, "All is vanity and feeding upon wind" (ch. i. 14).

But what is true more or less of all men except those who live—

"Like a brute with lower pleasures, like a brute with lower pains,"

---

[1] So Bunsen, *God in History*, I. p. 159.
[2]   " For thou thyself hast been a libertine,
              As sensual as the brutish sting itself."
                                        As You Like It, II. 7.

was true then, as it has been since, in its highest measure, of the Jew who abandons the faith of his fathers and drifts upon the shoreless sea of a life of license. *Corruptio optimi pessima.* He has inherited higher hopes and nobler memories than the men of most other nations, and when he falls he sinks even to a lower level than they sink. The "little grain of conscience" that yet remains "makes him sour," and the features are stamped with the sneer of the mocker, and he hates life, and yet, with the strange inconsistency of pessimists, shrinks from death. He denies, or at least questions, the possibility of knowing that there is a life beyond the limits of this life (ch. iii. 18—21), and yet draws back from the journey to the undiscovered country, and clings passionately (ch. xi. 7) to the life which he declares to be intolerable (ch. ii. 17, vi. 3, vii. 1). The literature of our own time presents two vivid pictures of the character and words of one who, being a Jew, has passed through this experience. In the life of the Raphael of Kingsley's *Hypatia*, yet more in that of Heinrich Heine at Paris[1], we have the counterpart of the life of Koheleth at Alexandria.

Under the thinly veiled disguise of the person of the historic Solomon he afterwards retraced his own experience and the issue to which it had brought him. He had flattered himself that he was not making himself the slave of pleasure, but even in his wildest hours was gaining wider thoughts and enlarging his knowledge of good and evil, that even then his "wisdom remained with him" (ch. ii. 3, 9). Like Goethe, he was philosophic, or, to speak more truly, artistic, in the midst of his sensuality, and watched the "madness and folly" of men, and yet more of women, with the eye of a connoisseur (ch. ii. 12). It was well for him, though it seemed evil, that he could not rest in the calmly balanced tranquillity of the supreme artist, which Goethe, and apparently Shakespeare, attained after the "*Sturm und Drang*" period of their life was over. The utter weariness and satiety, the mood of a *blasé* pessimism, into which he fell was as the first stepping-stone to higher things.

The course of his life at Alexandria had been marked by two

---

[1] Comp. Stigand's *Life of Heine*, II. chap. I.

strong affections, one of which ended in the bitterness of despair, while the other, both at the time and in its memory afterwards, was as a hand stretched forth to snatch him as "a brand from the burning." He had found a friend, one of his own faith, a true Israelite, who had kept himself even in Alexandria pure from evil, and gave him kindly sympathy and faithful counsel, who realised all that he had read in the history of his own country of the friendship of David and Jonathan, or in that of Greece of Theseus and Peirithous, or Orestes and Pylades (chs. iv. 9, 10, vii. 28). He was to him what Pudens, the disciple of St Paul, was to Martial, touching the fibres of reverence and admiration where the very nerve of pudicity seemed dead and the conscience seared[1]. The memory of that friendship, perhaps the actual presence of the friend, saved Koheleth from the despair into which the other passion plunged him. For he had loved, in one instance at least, with a love strong as death, with a passion fiery and fond as that of Catullus for Lesbia; had idealized the object of his love, and had awakened, as from a dream, to find that she was false beyond the average falsehood of her class—that she was "more bitter than death," her heart "as snares and nets," her hands as "bands." He shuddered at the thought of that passion, and gave thanks that he had escaped as a bird out of the snare of the fowler; yet more, that the friend of whom he thought as one that "pleased God," had not yielded to her temptation[2] (ch. vii. 26). We

---

[1]　　"O quam pæne tibi Stygias ego raptus ad undas,
　　　　Elysiæ vidi nubila fusca plagæ !
　　Quamvis lassa, tuos quærebant lumina vultus,
　　　　Atque erat in gelido plurimus ore Pudens."

　　"Yea, all but snatched where flows the gloomy stream,
　　　　I saw the clouds that wrap the Elysian plain.
　　Still for thy face I yearned in wearied dream,
　　　　And cold lips, Pudens, Pudens! cried in vain."
　　　　　　　　　　　　　　　　　MART. *Epigr.* VI. 58.

[2] Here, too, identity of experience produces almost identity of phrase:—
　　　　"Non jam illud quæro, contra ut me diligat illa
　　　　　Aut quod non potis est, esse pudica velit;
　　　　Ipse valere opto, et tetrum hunc deponere morbum,
　　　　　O Di! reddite mî hoc pro pietate meâ."

are reminded, as we look first on this picture and then on that, of the marvellous and mysterious sonnet (cxliv.) in which Shakespeare writes—

> "Two loves I have of comfort and despair
> Which, like two spirits, do suggest me still.
> The better angel is a man right fair,
> The worser spirit a woman coloured ill.
> To win me soon to hell, my female evil
> Tempteth my better angel from my side,
> And would corrupt my saint to be a devil,
> Wooing his purity with her foul pride."

The life of Heine, to which I have already referred as strikingly resembling that of Koheleth, presents hardly less striking a parallel. He, too, had known one friend—"the only man in whose society I never felt *ennui;* on whose sweet, noble features I could see clearly the aspect of my own soul[1]." He, too, in what seems to have been the one real passion of his life, had found himself deceived and disappointed—

> "She broke her faith; she broke her troth;
> For this I feel forgiving;
> Or else she had, as wedded wife,
> Embittered love and living[2]."

The heart-wound thus inflicted was not easily healed. Art, culture, pleasure failed to soothe him. There fell on him the "blank misgivings" of which Wordsworth speaks, the profound sense of nothingness which John Stuart Mill describes so vividly in his Autobiography, what the Germans call the *Weltschmerz,* the burden of the universe, or, in Koheleth's own phrase, the "world set in the heart" (ch. iii. 11); the sense of

> "I ask not this, that she may love me still,
>   Or, task beyond her power, be chaste and true;
> I seek for health, to free myself from ill;
>   For this, ye gods, I turn in prayer to you."
>   CATULL. *Carm.* LXXVI.

[1] Stigand, *Life of Heine*, I. p. 88.   [2] *Ibid.* I. p. 47.

an infinity and an eternity which man strives in vain to measure or apprehend.

It was in this frame of mind that Koheleth turned to the literature and philosophy of Greece. The library founded by the first Ptolemy, enlarged by Philadelphus, arranged and catalogued by Demetrius Phalereus, and thrown open as a free library to all students, claimed, we may well believe, not less than that of Thebes, which had the title graved upon its portals, to be the Ἰατρεῖον ψυχῆς, the "Hospital for the diseases of the Soul[1]." He had by this time gained sufficient knowledge of Greek to read at least the writings of the three previous centuries. They opened a new world of thought and language to him. He had grown weary of psalms and prophecies and chants, as men of our own time have grown weary of their Bible and Prayer-Book and Christian Year, and had not turned to them for comfort and counsel. His new reading brought him, at any rate, distraction. The lyric and dramatic poets he read indeed chiefly in the extracts which were quoted by lecturers, or the anthologies that were placed in the hands of young students; but in these he found words that relieved and even interpreted his own feelings. He learnt from Sophocles and Theognis to look on "not being" as better than any form of life (ch. iv. 2, 3); with the misogynist Euripides, who echoed his own wailing scorn, to utter bitter sneers at women's falsehood and frailty; with the pessimist Glycon to say of life that it was

πάντα γέλως, καὶ πάντα κόνις καὶ πάντα τὸ μηδέν.

"All is a jest, and all is dust, and all is nothingness."

From the earlier sages he learnt the maxims that had become the ornaments of school-boys' themes, and yet were new to him —the doctrine of the Μηδὲν ἄγαν, "nothing in excess" (the "*Surtout, point de zèle*" of Talleyrand); the not being "overmuch righteous or overmuch wicked" (ch. vii. 16). From Chilon he learnt to talk of the time, or καιρός, that was fixed for all things, of opportuneness, as almost the one ethical criterion

[1] Diodorus, I. 49.

of human action (ch. iii. 1—11). He caught up the phrase "under the sun" as expressing the totality of human life (ch. i. 9, and thirty other passages).

It was, however, to the philosophy of Greece, as represented by the leading sects of Stoics and Epicureans, that he turned with most eagerness. The former had in its teaching much that attracted him. That doctrine of recurring cycles of phenomena, not in the world of outward nature only, but of human life, history repeating itself, so that there is nothing new under the sun (ch. i. 9, 10), gave to him, as it did afterwards to Aurelius, a sense of order in the midst of seemingly endless changes and perturbations, and led him to look with the serene tranquillity of a *Nil admirari* at the things that excited men's ambition or roused them to indignation. If oppression and corruption had always been the accompaniments of kingly rule, such as the world had then known it, why should he wonder at the "violent perverting of justice and judgment in a province" under an Artaxerxes or a Ptolemy? (ch. v. 8). From the followers of Zeno he learnt also to look on virtue and vice in their intellectual aspects. The common weaknesses and follies of mankind were to him, as to them, only so many different forms and degrees of absolute insanity (chs. i. 17, ii. 12, vii. 25, ix. 3). He studied "madness and folly" in that mental hospital as he would have studied the phenomena of fever or paralysis. The perfect ideal calm of the Stoic seemed a grand thing to aim at : as much above the common life of men as light is above darkness (ch. ii. 13). The passion, or the fashion, of Stoicism, however, soon passed away. That iteration of events, the sun rising every day, the winds ever blowing, the rivers ever flowing, the endless repetition of the follies and vices of mankind (ch. i. 5—8), became to him, as the current of the Thames did to the jaded pleasure-seeking duke who looked on it from his Richmond villa[1], unspeakably wearisome. It seemed to mock him with the thought of monotony where he had hoped to find the pleasure of variety. It mocked him also with the thought of the permanence of nature, or even of the mass of human existence

---

[1] Cox's *Quest of the Chief Good*, p. 81.

considered as part of nature, and the fleeting nothingness of the
individual life. The voice of the rivulet--

> "Men may come and men may go,
> But I go on for ever"

brought no pleasant music to his ear. And, to say the truth,
the lives of the Stoics of Alexandria did not altogether commend
their system to him. They talked much of the dignity of virtue,
and drew fine pictures of it; but when he came to know them,
they were as vain, irritable, egotistic, sometimes even as sordid
and sensual, as the men whom they despised. Each man was,
in his own eyes, and those of his little coterie, as a supreme
sage and king, almost as a God. There was something in them
like the mutual apotheosis of which Heine complained in the
pantheistic followers of Fichte and of Schelling[1]. Against that
system, which ended in making every man his own deity, there
rose in the heart of the Israelite, who had not altogether
forgotten the lessons of his earlier life, a protest which clothed
itself in the words, "Fear thou God" (ch. viii. 12, 13). And so
Koheleth turned from the Porch to the Garden. It was at least
less pretentious, and did not mock him with its lofty ideal of an
unattained and unattainable perfection. Even the physics and
physiology of the school of Epicurus were not without their
attractions for a mind eager in the pursuit of knowledge of all
kinds. Their theory of the circulation of the elemental forces,
the rivers flowing into the sea yet never filling it, but returning
as through arteries and veins, filtered in their progress from the
sea's saltness, to the wells and fountains from which they had
first sprung to light (ch. i. 5—7); their study of the growth of
the human embryo, illustrated as it was by dissections in the
Museum of Alexandria[2], shewing how the "bones grow in the
womb of her that is with child" (ch. xi. 5); their discoveries, not
quite anticipating Harvey, yet on the same track, as to the
action of the heart and the lungs, the lamp of life suspended by

---

[1] Stigand's *Life of Heine*, II. p. 162.
[2] Dissection, and even vivisection, were first practised in the medical
schools of Alexandria.—*Quarterly Review*, LXVI. p. 162.

its silver chain, the pitcher drawing every moment fresh draughts from the fountain of the water of life (ch. xii. 6)[1]; all this came to him as a new interest, a new pleasure. It was as fascinating, that wonderland of science, as a new poem or a new *mythos*, or, in modern phrase, as a new novel or romance. And then its theory of life and death, did not that seem to point out to him the secret of a calm repose? The life of man was as the life of brutes (ch. iii. 19). His soul was compound, and so discerptible. All things had been formed out of the eternal atoms, and into the eternal atoms all things were evermore resolved. Admitting even, for the sake of hypothesis, that there was something more than the forms of matter which are palpable and visible in man's nature, some vital force or ethereal spark, yet what had been brought together at birth was, at any rate, certain to be dissolved at death. Dust to dust, the ether which acted in man's brain to the ether of the infinite azure, was the inevitable end (ch. iii. 21, but *not* xii. 7). Such a view of life served at least to strip death of the terror with which the δεισιδαιμονία, the superstition, the *Aberglaube*, of men had clothed it. It did not leave him to dread the passage into the dim darkness of Sheol, the land of the shadow of death, as Hezekiah (Isa. xxxviii. 11, 18) and the Psalmist (Psa. vi. 5, xxx. 9, lxxxviii. 11) had dreaded it (ch. ix. 10). It freed him from the terrors of the Gehenna of which his countrymen were beginning to talk, from the Tartarus and Phlegethon and Cocytus, the burning and the wailing rivers, in which the Greeks who were outside the philosophic schools still continued to believe. It left him free to make the most and the best of life. And then that "best of life" was at once a pleasant and an attainable ideal. It confirmed the lessons of his own experience as to the vanity and hollowness of much in which most men seek the satisfaction of their desires. Violent emotions were followed by a reaction, the night's revel by the morning headache; ambition and the favour of princes ended in disappointment. What the wise man should strive after was just the maximum of enjoyment, not over-

---

[1] I purposely refrain from including the other anatomical references which men have found in Eccles. xii. 4, 5.

balanced by the *amari aliquid* that rises even *medio de fonte leporum*—a life like that of the founder of the school—moderate and even abstemious, not disdaining the pleasures of any sense, yet carrying none to an excess. He had led a life of calm serene tranquillity, almost one of total abstinence and vegetarianism, and so the ἀταραξία which had become identified with his name, had been protracted to extreme old age[1]. The history of men's lives had surely "nothing better" to show than this. This, at any rate, was good (ch. iii. 12, 14, 22, v. 18, viii. 15). In such a life there was nothing that the conscience condemned as evil. It admitted even of acts of kindness and benevolence, as bringing with them a moral satisfaction (chs. vii. 1, 2, xi. 1, 2), and therefore a new source of enjoyment. Even the sages of Israel would have approved of such a life (Prov. v. 15—19, xxx. 7), though it might not satisfy the heroic aspirations and high-soaring dreams of its prophets. Enjoyment itself might be received as a gift from God (ch. ii. 26, v. 19).

Into this new form of life accordingly Koheleth threw himself, and did not find it altogether a delusion. Inwardly it made him feel that life was, after all, worth living (ch. xi. 7). He began to find the pleasure of doing good, and visiting the fatherless and widow in their affliction. He learnt that it was better to go to the house of mourning than to the house of feasting. The heart of the wise was in that house and not in the house of mirth (ch. vii. 2—4). Even the reputation of doing good was not to be despised, and the fragrance of a good name was better than the odorous spikenard or rose-essence of the king's luxurious banquets (ch. vii. 1). And he gained, as men always do gain by any acts of kindness which are not altogether part of the ostentatious or self-calculating egotism of the Pharisee, something more than enjoyment.

> "Sunt lachrymae rerum, et mentem mortalia tangunt."

> "We needs must weep for woe, and, being men,
> Man's sorrows touch our hearts."
>
> VIRG. *Æn.* I. 462.

[1] Diog. Laert. X. I. p. 6.

The flood-gates of sympathy were opened. His self-love was expanding almost unconsciously into benevolence. He began to feel that altruism and not egotism was the true law of humanity. He was in this point, partly, perhaps, because here too the oracle in his inmost heart once more spoke out the secret of the wisdom of Israel, "Fear thou God," wiser than his teachers (ch. v. 7).

A wealthy Jew with this turn for philosophizing was not likely to be overlooked by the lecturers and *littérateurs* of Alexandria. From the Library of that city Koheleth passed to the Museum[1], and was elected, or appointed by royal favour, a member of the august body who dined in its large hall at the public expense, and held their philosophical discussions afterwards. It was a high honour for a foreigner, almost as much so as for an Englishman to be elected to the Institute of France, or a Frenchman to a Fellowship of the Royal Society. He became first a listener and then a sharer in those discussions, an *Ecclesiastes*, a *debater*, and *not* a preacher, as we count preaching, in that *Ecclesia*. Epicureans and Stoics, Platonists and Aristotelians met as in a Metaphysical Society, and discussed the nature of happiness and of the supreme good, of the constitution of life and of the soul's immortality, of free will and destiny. The result of such a whirl of words and conflict of opinions was somewhat bewildering. He was almost driven back upon the formula of the scepticism of Pyrrho, "Who knows?" (ch. iii. 21). It was to him what a superficial study of Hobbes and Shaftesbury, of Voltaire and Rousseau, of Kant and Schelling, of Bentham and Mill, of Comte and Herbert Spencer, have been to English students of successive generations. One thing, at least, was clear. He saw that here also "the race was not to the swift, nor bread to the wise, nor riches to men of understanding" (ch. ix. 11). The charlatan too often took precedence of the true man: silent and thoughtful wisdom was out-talked by an eloquent

---

[1] For the fullest account of the Alexandrian Museum accessible in English, see the article on Alexandria in Vol. LXVI. of the *Quarterly Review*. It is, I believe, no secret, that it was written by the late Rev. William Sewell.

declaimer (ch. ix. 15, 16). Here also, as in his life of revelry, there was much that could only be described as vanity and much "feeding upon wind."

So for a short time life passed on, looking brighter and more cheerful than it had done. There came before him the prospect, destined not to be realized, of the life of a happy home with wife and children round him (ch. ix. 7—9). But soon the evil day came in which there was no more any pleasure to be found (ch. xii. 1). The life of revelry and pleasure had sapped his strength, and the strain of study and the excitement of debate had made demands upon his vital powers which they could not meet, and there crept over him the slow decay of a premature old age, of the paralysis which, while it leaves consciousness clear and the brain free to think and muse over many things, attacks first one organ of sense or action and then another. The stars were darkened and the clouds of dark thoughts "returned after the rain" of idle tears, and "the keepers of the house trembled and the strong men bowed themselves." Sight failed, and he no longer saw the goodly face of nature or the comeliness of man or woman, could no longer listen with delight to the voice of the "daughters of music" (ch. xii. 2—4). Even the palate lost its wonted sense of flavour, and the choicest dainties became distasteful. His voice passed into the feeble tones of age (ch. xii. 4). Sleep was more and more a stranger to his eyes, and his nights were passed, as it were, under the branches of the almond tree, the "early waking tree" that was the symbol of *insomnia* (ch. xii. 5; Jer. i. 11, 12). Remedies were applied by the king's physicians, but even the "caper-berry," the "sovereign'st thing on earth," or in the Alexandrian pharmacopœia, against that form of paralysis, was powerless to revive his exhausted energies. The remainder of his life—and it lasted for some six or seven years; enough time to make him feel that "the days of darkness" were indeed "many" (ch. xii. 8)—was one long struggle with disease. In the language of the Greek writers with whom he had become familiar, it was but a long νοσοτροφία, a βίος ἀβίωτος ("a chronic illness," a "life unliveable"). His state, to continue the parallel already more than once suggested, was like that which made the last eight years of Heine's life a time of ceaseless suffering[1]. It added to the pain and trouble which disease brought with it that he had no son to minister to his wants or to inherit his estate. House and garden and lands, books and art-treasures, all that he had stored up, as for a palace of art and a lordly pleasure-house, would pass into the hands of a stranger (ch. iv. 8). It was a sore travail, harder than any pain of body, to think of that as the outcome of all his labours. It was in itself "vanity and an evil disease" (ch. vi. 2). And beyond this there lay a further trouble, growing out of the survival, or revival, of his old feelings as an Israelite, which neither Stoic apathy nor Epicurean serenity, though they would have smiled at it as a superstition, helped him to overcome. How was he to be buried? (ch. vi. 3). It was, of course, out of the question that his corpse should be carried back to the land of his fathers and laid in their tomb in the valley of Jehoshaphat. The patriotic zeal which had been roused by the struggle of the Maccabees against Antiochus Epiphanes would not have allowed the body of one who was suspected of apostasy to desecrate the holy city. And even in Alexandria itself the more rigorous Jews had been alienated by his Hellenizing tendencies. He could not expect that their mourners would attend at his funeral, crying, after their manner, Ah, brother! or Ah, sister! Ah, Lord! and Ah, his glory! (Jer. xxii. 18). He had before him the prospect of being buried as with the burial of a dog.

And yet the days were not altogether evil. The friend whom he had found faithful, the "one among a thousand," did not desert him, and came and ministered to his weakness, to raise up, as far as he had the power, the brother who had fallen (ch. iv. 10). He could no longer fill his belly with the husks that

[1] Heine's description of his own state, in its piteous frankness, can scarcely fail to remind us of the contrast between the pictures drawn by Koheleth in ch. ii. and ch. xii. "I am no longer a Hellene of jovial life and somewhat portly person, who laughed cheerily down upon dismal Nazarenes. I am now only a poor death-sick Jew, an emaciated image of trouble, an unhappy man." Stigand's *Life of Heine*, II. p. 386.

the swine did eat. Sensual pleasures and the fragments of a
sensuous philosophy, the lower and the higher forms of popular
Epicureanism, were alike unsatisfying, and the voice within
once more spoke in clearer notes than ever, Fear thou God.
With him, as with Heine (to refer once more to the Koheleth
of our time), there was a religious reaction, a belief in a personal
God, as that to which men must come when they are "sick to
death," a belief not unreal even though the habitual cynicism
seemed to mock it in the very act of utterance[1]. It was not,
indeed, like the cry of the prodigal, "I will arise and go to my
father;" for that thought of the Divine Fatherhood was as yet
but dimly revealed to him; but the old familiar thought that
God was his Creator, the Giver of life and breath and all things
(ch. v. 19, xii. 1), returned in its fulness and power, and in his
own experience he was finding out that his pleasant vices had
been made whips to scourge him, and so he learnt that, though
he could not fathom the mystery of His judgments, the Creator
was also the Judge (ch. xi. 9). It was in this stage of mental
and spiritual growth, of strength growing out of weakness, that
he was led to become a writer, and to put on record the results
of his experience. He still thought in the language of his
fatherland, and therefore in that language he wrote.

A book written under such conditions was not likely to

---

[1] It may be well once more to give Heine's own words. He de-
clines, in his will, the services of any minister of religion, and adds,
"This desire springs from no fit of a freethinker. For four years I
have renounced all philosophic pride, and have returned back to religious ideas and feelings. I die in the belief of one only God, the
Eternal Creator, whose pity I implore for my immortal soul" (Stigand's
Life of Heine, II. p. 398). Still more striking is the following extract
from a letter to his friend Dr Kolb which is quoted in the *Globe* of
Oct. 11, 1880, from a German newspaper: "My sufferings, my physical
pains are terrible, and moral ones are not wanting. When I think
upon my own condition, a genuine horror falls over me and I am
compelled to fold my hands in submission to God's will (*Gott-ergeben*)
because nothing else is left for me." In somewhat of the same tone he
says somewhere (I have forgotten where), "God will pardon me; *c'est
son métier*." Elsewhere he writes, in spite of his sufferings, with the
lingering love of life which we note in Koheleth (ch. ix. 4—9, xi. 7),
"O God, how ugly bitter it is to die! O God, how sweetly and snugly one
can live in this snug, sweet nest of earth" (Stigand's *Life*, II. p. 421).

present the characteristics of a systematic treatise. It was, in part, like Pascal's *Pensées*, in part, like Heine's latest poems—the record of a conflict not yet over, though it was drawing near its close. The "Two Voices" of our own poet were there; or rather, the *three* voices of the pessimism of the satiated sensualist, and the wisdom, such as it was, of the Epicurean thinker, and the growing faith in God, were heard in strange alternation; now one, now another uttering itself, as in an inharmonious discord, to the very close of the book. Now his intellect questioned, now his faith affirmed, as Heine did, the continued existence of the spirit of man after death (chs. iii. 19, xii. 7). As conscious of that conflict, and feeling the vanity of fame, as Keats did, when he desired that his only epitaph might be, "Here lies one whose name was writ in water," he shrank from writing in his own person, and chose as the title of his book that which at once expressed its character and embodied the distinction which at one time he had prized so highly. As men have written under the names of Philalethes or Phileleutheros, as a great thinker of the last century, Edward Tucker, wrote his *Light of Nature Pursued*, under the pseudonym of Abraham Search, so he came before his readers as Koheleth, Ecclesiastes, the Debater. He was free in that character to utter varying and conflicting views. It is true he went a step further, and also came before them, as though the book recorded the experience of one greater than himself as the seeker after, and possessor of, wisdom. The son of David, king over Israel in Jerusalem, was speaking as through his lips (ch. i. 1, 12, 16). It was a trick, or rather a fashion, of authorship, such as was afterwards adopted in the *Wisdom of Solomon* by a man of purer life and higher aim, though less real inspiration, but not a fraud, and the fashion was a dominant one and deceived no one. The students of philosophy habitually conveyed their views in the shape of treatises by Aristotle, or letters or dialogues by Plato. There was scarcely a medical writer of eminence at Alexandria who had not published his views as to the treatment of disease under the name of Hippocrates[1]. Plato

[1] Sprengel, *Hist. de Médecine*, I. p. 430.

and Xenophon had each written an *Apologia* which was represented as coming from the lips of Socrates. The latter had
also composed an ideal biography of Cyrus. And in this case
Koheleth might well think that the analogy between his own
experience and that of the sage of Israel was more than enough
to justify the personation as a form of quasi-dramatic art.
Both had gone through a like quest after the chief good, seeking first wisdom and then pleasure, and then the magnificence
and the culture that comes from art, and then wisdom again.
Both had found that all this was, in the end, unsatisfying.
Might he not legitimately hold up the one experience embodied
in the form of the other, and put on for the nonce the robes of
Solomon, alike in his glorious apparel, and in the sackcloth and
ashes, in which, as the legend ran, he had ended his days as a
penitent? In his early youth Koheleth had gazed on the ideal
picture of Solomon as a pattern which he strove to reproduce.
The surroundings of his manhood, the palaces, and gardens,
and groves, and museums, and libraries of the Ptolemies
enabled him to picture what the monarch's kingly state had
been. In his picture of the close of the life, as was natural, the
subjective element predominated over the objective, and we
have before us Koheleth himself, and not the Solomon of
history.

The analysis of the book itself will, it is believed, confirm the
theory now suggested. It will be enough, for the present, to
note that from first to last it was, on the view now taken,
intensely personal, furnishing nearly all the materials for a
memoir; that its main drift and purpose, broken, indeed, by
many side eddies, now of cynical bitterness, now of worldly
wisdom, now of keen observation, was to warn those who were
yet in quest of the chief good against the shoals and rocks and
quicksands on which he had well-nigh made utter shipwreck of
his faith; that his desire was to deepen the fear of God in
which he had at last found the anchor of his soul; that that
fear had become more and more a reality as the shadows closed
around him; that it had deepened into the conviction that the
Creator was also the Judge, and that the Judge of all the earth,

sooner or later, would assuredly do right. The close of the book all but coincided with the close of life. He waited, if not with the full assurance of faith, yet with a calm trustfulness, for the hour when the few mourners should "go about the street," and he should go to his eternal home (ch. xii. 6); when "the dust should return to the earth as it was, and the spirit should return to God who gave it" (ch. xii. 7). "Return to God"—that was his last word on the great problem, and that was at once his dread and his consolation.

So the life and the book ended; and it will remain for a distinct enquiry to trace the after history of the latter. Not without reason was it brought by the grandson of Sirach, or some other seeker after truth, from Alexandria to Palestine, and translated by him into Greek[1]. Not without reason did he, or some later Rabbi, add the commendatory verses with which the book now closes, truly describing its effect as that of the goad that spurs on thought, of the nails that, once driven in, cannot easily be plucked out (ch. xii. 11). Not without reason did the wiser thinkers of the school of Hillel resist the narrow scruples of those of the school of Shammai when the question was debated whether the new unknown book should be admitted to a place side by side with all that was noblest and most precious in their literature[2], and, in spite of seeming contradictions, and Epicurean or heretical tendencies, recognize that in this record of the struggle, the fall, the recovery of a child of Israel, a child of God, there was the narrative of a Divine education told with a genius and power in which they were well content, as all true and reverential thinkers have been content since, to acknowledge a Divine inspiration.

[1] See next Chapter.
[2] See pp. 27, 28.

CHAPTER IV.

ECCLESIASTES AND ECCLESIASTICUS.

Some evidence tending to shew that the influence of the former of these books is traceable in the latter has already been laid before the reader in ch. ii. as fixing a date below which we cannot reasonably carry the date of its composition. The relation between the two books requires, however, a closer scrutiny and leads to results of considerable interest. It will be seen that, making allowance for the fact that the one writer is marked by an almost exceptional originality and that the other is avowedly a compiler, there is throughout a striking series of parallelisms, over and above those already noted, such as make the conclusion that the one had the work of the other in his hands all but absolutely certain. The evidence of this statement is necessarily inductive in its character, and the following instances are submitted as an adequate, though not an exhaustive, basis for the induction.

Ecclus. i. 13. Whoso feareth the Lord it shall go well with him.

Eccles. viii. 13. But it shall not be well with the wicked, neither shall he prolong his days, which are as a shadow; because he feareth not before God.

Ecclus. iv. 6, vii. 30, xxiv. 8, xxxix. 5. "He that made" or the "Creator," as a name for God.

Eccles. xii. 1. Remember now thy Creator in the days of thy youth, while the evil days come not, nor the years draw nigh, when thou shalt say, I have no pleasure in them.

Ecclus. iv. 20. Observe the opportunity (καιρός).

Eccles. iii. 1—8. To every thing there is a season, and a time to every purpose under the heaven: a time to be born, and a time to die; a time to plant, and a time to pluck up that which is planted; a time to kill, and a time to heal;

a time to break down, and a time to build up; a time to weep, and a time to laugh; a time to mourn, and a time to dance; a time to cast away stones, and a time to gather stones together; a time to embrace, and a time to refrain from embracing; a time to get, and a time to lose; a time to keep, and a time to cast away; a time to rend, and a time to sew; a time to keep silence, and a time to speak; a time to love, and a time to hate; a time of war, and a time of peace.

Ecclus. vi. 6. Have but one counseller of a thousand.

Eccles. vii. 28. Which yet my soul seeketh, but I find not: one man among a thousand have I found; but a woman among all those have I not found.

Ecclus. viii. 8. Of them thou shalt learn how to serve great men with ease.

Eccles. viii. 2–4, x. 20. I counsel thee to keep the king's commandment, and that in regard of the oath of God. Be not hasty to go out of his sight: stand not in an evil thing; for he doeth whatsoever pleaseth him....Where the word of a king is, there is power: and who may say unto him, What doest thou?...Curse not the king, no, not in thy thought; and curse not the rich in thy bed-chamber: for a bird of the air shall carry the voice, and that which hath wings shall tell the matter.

Ecclus. vi. 14. A faithful friend is a strong defence, and he that hath found such an one hath found a treasure.

Eccles. iv. 9. Two are better than one; because they have a good reward for their labour.

Ecclus. ix. 3. Meet not with a harlot, lest thou be taken with her snares.

Eccles. vii. 26. And I find more bitter than death the woman, whose heart is snares and nets, and her hands as bands: whoso pleaseth God shall escape from her; but the sinner shall be taken by her.

Ecclus. x. 3. An unwise (ἀ-παίδευτος) king destroyeth his people.

Eccles. iv. 13. Better is a poor and a wise child than an old and foolish king, who will no more be admonished.

Eccles. x. 16. Woe to thee. O land, when thy king is a child, and thy princes eat in the morning.

Ecclus. x. 9. Why is earth and ashes proud?

Eccles. xii. 7. Then shall the dust return to the earth as it was: and the spirit shall return unto God who gave it.

Ecclus. x. 23. It is not meet to despise the poor man that hath understanding.

Eccles. ix. 15. Now there was found in it a poor wise man, and he by his wisdom delivered the city; yet no man remembered that same poor man.

Eccles. x. 7. I have seen servants upon horses, and princes walking as servants upon the earth.

Ecclus. xi. 5. Many kings have sat down upon the ground; and one that was never thought of hath worn the crown.

Ecclus. xi. 17. The gift of the Lord remaineth with the godly, and his favour bringeth prosperity for ever.

Eccles. iii. 13. And also that every man should eat and drink, and enjoy the good of all his labour, it is the gift of God.

Ecclus. xi. 18, 19. There is that waxeth rich by his wariness and pinching, and this is the portion of his reward: whereas he saith, I have found rest, and now will eat continually of my goods; and yet he knoweth not what time shall come upon him, and that he

Eccles. ii. 18, 19, v. 13, vi. 2. Yea, I hated all my labour which I had taken under the sun: because I should leave it unto the man that shall be after me. And who knoweth whether he shall be a wise man or a fool? yet shall he have rule over all my labour

must leave those things to others, and die.

wherein I have laboured, and wherein I have shewed myself wise under the sun. This is also vanity....There is a sore evil which I have seen under the sun, namely, riches kept for the owners thereof to their hurt....A man to whom God hath given riches, wealth, and honour, so that he wanteth nothing for his soul of all that he desireth, yet God giveth him not power to eat thereof, but a stranger eateth it : this is vanity, and it is an evil disease.

Ecclus. xii. 13. Who will pity a charmer that is bitten with a serpent?

Eccles. x. 8, 11. Whoso breaketh an hedge, a serpent shall bite him....Surely the serpent will bite without enchantment ; and a babbler is no better.

Ecclus. xiii. 23. When a rich man speaketh, every man holdeth his tongue.

Eccles. ix. 11, 16. I returned, and saw under the sun, that the race is not to the swift, nor the battle to the strong, neither yet bread to the wise, nor yet riches to men of understanding, nor yet favour to men of skill; but time and chance happeneth to them all. ...Then said I, Wisdom is better than strength; nevertheless the poor man's wisdom is despised, and his words are not heard.

Ecclus. xiii. 26. The finding out of parables is a wearisome labour of the mind.

Eccles xii. 12. Of making many books there is no end; and much study is a weariness of the flesh.

Ecclus. xiv. 12. Remember that death will not be long in coming, and that the covenant of the grave (Hades) is not shewn to thee.

Eccles. viii. 8. There is no man that hath power over the spirit to retain the spirit; neither hath he power in the day of death : and there is no discharge in that

Ecclus. xv. 5. In the midst of the congregation (ἐκκλησία) shall wisdom open his mouth.

Ecclus. xvi. 4. By one that hath understanding shall the city be replenished.

Ecclus. xvii. 28. Thanksgiving perisheth from the dead as from one that is not.

Ecclus. xvii. 30. All things cannot be in men, because the son of man is not immortal.

Ecclus. xviii. 6. As for the wondrous works of the Lord, there may be nothing taken from them, neither may anything be put unto them, neither can the ground of them be found out.

Ecclus. xix. 16. Who is he that hath not offended with his tongue?

Ecclus. xx. 7. A wise man will hold his tongue till he see opportunity (καιρόν).

Ecclus. xxv. 7, xxvi. 5, xxvi. 28, There be nine things which I have

war; neither shall wickedness deliver those that are given to it.

Eccles. xii. 10. The Preacher sought to find out acceptable words: and that which was written was upright, even words of truth.

Eccles. ix. 15. Now there was found in it a poor wise man, and he by his wisdom delivered the city; yet no man remembered that same poor man.

Eccles. ix. 4. For to him that is joined to all the living there is hope: for a living dog is better than a dead lion.

Eccles. iii. 20, 21. All go unto one place; all are of the dust, and all turn to dust again....Who knoweth the spirit of man that goeth upward, and the spirit of the beast that goeth downward to the earth?

Eccles. vii. 13, xi. 5. Consider the work of God: for who can make that straight, which he hath made crooked?...As thou knowest not what is the way of the spirit, nor how the bones do grow in the womb of her that is with child, even so thou knowest not the works of God who maketh all.

Eccles. vii. 22. For oftentimes also thine own heart knoweth that thou thyself likewise hast cursed others.

Eccles. iii. 7. A time to rend, and a time to sew; a time to keep silence, and a time to speak.

Eccles. xi. 2. Give a portion to seven, and also to eight; for

judged in mine heart...and the tenth I will utter with my tongue. ...There be three things that mine heart feareth; and for the fourth I was sore afraid....There be two things that grieve my heart; and the third maketh me angry.

Ecclus. xxvi. 13. The grace of a wife delighteth her husband.

Ecclus. xxvi. 23. A wicked woman is given as a portion to a wicked man : but a godly woman is given to him that feareth the Lord.

Ecclus. xxvii. 25, 26. Whoso casteth a stone on high casteth it on his own head; and a deceitful stroke shall make wounds....Whoso diggeth a pit shall fall therein.

Ecclus. xxxiii. 15, xlii. 24. So look upon all the works of the most High; and there are two and two, one against another....All these things are double one against another.

thou knowest not what evil shall be upon the earth.

Eccles. ix. 9. Live joyfully with the wife whom thou lovest all the days of the life of thy vanity, which he hath given thee under the sun, all the days of thy vanity : for that is thy portion in this life, and in thy labour which thou takest under the sun.

Eccles. vii. 26. And I find more bitter than death the woman, whose heart is snares and nets, and her hands as bands : whoso pleaseth God shall escape from her; but the sinner shall be taken by her.

Eccles. x. 8, 9. He that diggeth a pit shall fall into it; and whoso breaketh an hedge, a serpent shall bite him....Whoso removeth stones shall be hurt therewith; and he that cleaveth wood shall be endangered thereby.

Eccles. vii. 27, iii. 1—8. Behold, this have I found, saith the Preacher, counting one by one, to find out the account....To every thing there is a season, and a time to every purpose under the heaven : a time to be born, and a time to die; a time to plant, and a time to pluck up that which is planted; a time to kill, and a time to heal; a time to break down, and a time to build up; a time to weep, and a time to laugh; a time to mourn, and a time to dance; a time to cast away stones, and a time to gather stones together; a time to embrace, and a time to refrain from embracing; a time to get, and a time to lose; a time to keep, and a time to cast away; a time to rend, and a time to sew; a time to keep silence, and a time to speak; a time to love, and a time to hate; a time of war, and a time of peace.

Ecclus. xxxiv. 7. Dreams have deceived many, and they have failed that put their trust in them.

Eccles. v. 7. For in the multitude of dreams and many words there are also divers vanities: but fear thou God.

Ecclus. xxxv. 4. Thou shalt not appear empty before the Lord.

Eccles. v. 5. Better is it that thou shouldest not vow, than that thou shouldest vow and not pay.

Ecclus. xxxiii. 13. As the clay is in the potter's hand, to fashion it at his pleasure, so man is in the hand of him that made him.

Eccles. vii. 13. Consider the work of God: for who can make that straight, which he hath made crooked?

Ecclus. xxxviii. 16. Cover his body according to the custom, and neglect not his burial.

Eccles. vi. 3. If a man beget an hundred children, and live many years, so that the days of his years be many, and his soul be not filled with good, and also that he have no burial; I say, that an untimely birth is better that he.

Ecclus. xl. 1. Great travail is created for every man, and an heavy yoke is upon the sons of Adam.

Eccles. i. 3, 5. What profit hath a man of all his labour which he taketh under the sun?...... All things are full of labour.

Ecclus. xl. 11. All things that are of the earth shall return to the

Eccles. i. 7, xii. 7. All the rivers run into the sea; yet the

earth again : and that which is of the waters doth return into the sea.

sea is not full; unto the place from whence the rivers come, thither they return again....Then shall the dust return to the earth as it was: and the spirit shall return unto God who gave it.

Ecclus. xli. 4. There is no inquisition in the grave, whether thou hast lived ten, or a hundred, or a thousand years.

Eccles. vi. 3—6, ix. 10. If a man beget an hundred children, and live many years, so that the days of his years be many, and his soul be not filled with good, and also that he have no burial; I say, that an untimely birth is better than he. For he cometh in with vanity, and departeth in darkness, and his name shall be covered with darkness. Moreover he hath not seen the sun, nor known any thing: this hath more rest than the other. Yea, though he live a thousand years twice told, yet hath he seen no good: do not all go to one place?...Whatsoever thy hand findeth to do, do it with thy might; for there is no work, nor device, nor knowledge, nor wisdom, in the grave, whither thou goest.

Making all due allowance, in considering this evidence, for the fact that some at least of the passages cited are of the nature of maxims that form the common stock of well-nigh all ethical teachers, there is enough, it is submitted, to leave little doubt on the mind that the later writer was acquainted with the earlier. Essentially a compiler, and not entering into the deeper genius of Ecclesiastes, the son of Sirach found in it many epigrammatic precepts, summing up a wide experience, and used it as he used the Proverbs of Solomon, and those of his grandfather Jesus, in the collection which he aimed at making as complete as possible.

Assuming this connexion between the two books to be proved we may find, perhaps, in the Prologue and Epilogue of the later work, something that throws light upon the history of the earlier. In the former the son of Sirach tells his readers that he was led to the task of translating and editing the maxims which his grandfather Jesus had written by a previous experimental work of a like nature. When he had come to Egypt at the age of thirty-eight[1], under Euergetes II. (B.C. 170—117) better known in history by his nickname of Physcon, or the Fat, he had found a MS. (ἀφόμοιον, used like the Latin "exemplum") of no small educational value (οὐ μικρᾶς παιδείας) and "thought it most necessary to give diligence and travail to interpret it." It is obvious that this must have been altogether distinct from the "Wisdom" of his grandfather Jesus with which he must naturally have become familiar in Palestine, and the question which meets us is, what was the book? and what became of the son of Sirach's translation of it? The answer which I venture to suggest is that the book was none other than the Ecclesiastes of the Old Testament Canon[2]. The character of the book was precisely such as would attract one who was travelling in search of wisdom, though, as we have seen, he was caught more by its outwardly gnomic character than by its treatment of the deeper underlying problems with which it deals, and which have exercised, as with a mysterious fascination, the ingenuity of later writers.

---

[1] This is held by most scholars (e.g. Westcott) to be the natural rendering of the sentence. By some, however, it has been taken as referring to the thirty-eighth year of the king's reign. Neither of the two Ptolemies, however, who bore the name of Euergetes, had so long a reign as this, unless we include in that of Euergetes II. the time in which he ruled conjointly with his brother Ptolemy Philometor. Another interpretation refers the words to the thirty-eighth year of the son of Sirach's stay in Egypt. On any supposition the words bring us to a later date than that to which we have assigned the composition of Ecclesiastes.

[2] It is perhaps worth mentioning that this view of the passage in its general meaning has been maintained by Arnold in his *Commentary on Ecclesiasticus*. He supposes, however, that the MS. in question was the Wisdom of Solomon. It will be seen in the next chapter that there are good grounds for assigning to that book a considerably later date.

The context seems to imply, though the words do not necessarily involve the idea of a fixed canon, that the book had come to take its place on nearly the same level with "the law and the prophets and the other books" which had been translated from Hebrew into Greek. On this assumption then we may have in this obscure passage the first trace of the reception of Ecclesiastes into the Hebrew Canon, a reception which we may in part, at least, attribute to the commendatory verses in ch. xii. 9, 10 which were clearly added by some one other than the writer and which, on this assumption, may well have been written by the son of Sirach himself. Is it not, we may add, a probable inference that it was this connexion that led to the title Ecclesiasticus by which the book, which in the Hebrew MSS. that Jerome had seen bore the title of "Proverbs" and in the LXX. that of the "Wisdom of Sirach" (a title singularly misleading, as that was the name neither of the author or the translator), was known in the Latin Version? Would it not be natural, if the Greek Version came from the pen of the son of Sirach, and if his own book presented manifest traces of its influence, that he should sooner or later come to be known as belonging to the same school, an *Ecclesiasticus* following in the track of an *Ecclesiastes?* The common traditional view, adopted without question, from Rufinus (*Comm. in Symb.* c. 38), that here the word has the distinctly Christian sense which is altogether absent from Ecclesiastes, and describes the character of the book as "Ecclesiastical," *i.e.* read in church or used in the public instruction of catechumens and young men, is surely a less probable explanation, to say nothing of the absence of any proof that it was so used[1], and of any sufficient reason why a name, which in this sense, must have been common to many books, should have been confined to this one.

---

[1] The nearest approach to such a proof is found in the statement of Athanasius (*Ep. Fest.* s. f.) that the book was "one of those framed by the fathers for the use of those who wished to be instructed in the way of godliness," (Westcott, Art. *Ecclesiasticus*, in Smith's *Dict. of Bible*). It is obvious however that this applied to a whole class of books, not to this in particular.

One more conjecture presents itself as throwing light on the prayer of the son of Sirach, in all probability the translator and not the original author of the book[1], which forms the last chapter of Ecclesiasticus. The occasion of that prayer was the deliverance of the writer from some extreme peril. He had been accused to the king and his life had been in danger. He does not name the king, probably because he had already done so in the Prologue, and had fixed the time when he had come under his power. He does not name the nature of the charge, but the *Apologia* that follows (Ecclus. li. 13—30) seems to imply that in what he had done he had been pursuing the main object of his life, had been seeking wisdom and instruction (παιδείαν). May not the charge have been connected with the Greek translation of Ecclesiastes which we have seen good reason to look on as his handiwork? Those pointed words as to the corrupt and oppressive government of the king's provinces (ch. v. 8), those vivid portraits of the old and foolish, or of the young and profligate, king (chs. iv. 13, x. 16), of princes revelling in luxury while the poor were starving (ch. x. 16), might well seem to the cruel and suspicious king to be offensive and dangerous, while the turn for literature which led him to become an author, would naturally also lead him to take cognizance of a new Greek book beginning to be circulated among his Jewish subjects. That the translator's *Apologia* was successful may partly have been due to the fact that he could point to passages which more than balanced what had given occasion of offence by apparently enjoining the most entire and absolute submission to the king's lightest words, and prohibiting even the mere utterance of discontent (ch. x. 4, 20).

---

[1] This, it may be mentioned, is the view taken by Grotius and Prideaux. They agree in assigning the incident of the peril to the reign of Ptolemy Physcon.

CHAPTER V.

ECCLESIASTES AND THE WISDOM OF SOLOMON.

The coincidences between the teaching of the unknown author of Ecclesiastes and that of the Son of Sirach are, it will be admitted, whatever estimate may be formed of the inferences drawn from them, interesting and suggestive. They at least shew that the one writer was more or less influenced by the other. Those that present themselves on a comparison of the former book with the Wisdom of Solomon are of a very different yet not less suggestive character. Before entering on an examination of them it will be well to sum up briefly all that is known as to the external history of the book to the study of which that comparison invites us. The facts are few and simple. It is not mentioned by name by any pre-Christian writer. The earliest record of its existence is found in the Muratorian Fragment (A.D. 170) where it is said to have been "ab amicis Solomonis in honorem ipsius scripta." An ingenious conjecture of Dr Tregelles suggests, as has been stated above (Note p. 15), that this was a mistaken rendering of a Greek text on which the Latin writer of the Fragment based his Canon, and that the original ascribed the authorship of the book to Philo of Alexandria. The statement that Philo was probably the writer of the book is repeated by Jerome. The book is found in all the great MSS. of the LXX. but these do not carry us further back than the 4th or 5th century of the Christian æra. We have, however, indirect evidence of its existence at an earlier period. Two passages are found in Clement of Rome which make it all but absolutely certain that he must have been acquainted with the book.

(1) Who will say to him, What didst thou? or who will resist the might of his strength? Clem. R. 1. 27.

(1) For who will say, What didst thou? or who will resist thy judgment? Wisd. xii. 12.

Who will resist the might of thine arm? Wisd. xi. 22.

(2) Unrighteous envy … by which also death entered into the world. Clem. R. I. 3.	(2) By envy of the devil death entered into the world. Wisd. ii. 24.

Among the earlier post-apostolic Fathers, and we need not go beyond these for our present purpose, Irenæus is said to have written a book "on various passages of the Wisdom of Solomon and the Epistle to the Hebrews" (Euseb. *Hist. Eccles.* V. 26). Clement of Alexandria quotes the teaching as "divine" (*Strom.* IV. 16, 17). Tertullian quotes it, sometimes without naming it (*Adv. Marc.* III. 22), sometimes as being the work of Solomon (*Adv. Valent.* c. 2). So far we have evidence of its being read and held in honour at the latter part of the first and throughout the second century, but not earlier.

A comparison of the Book of Wisdom with some of the writings of the New Testament leads, however, to the conclusion that it must have been more or less studied between A.D. 50 and A.D. 70. Dr Westcott has called attention (Smith's *Dict. of the Bible.* Art. *Wisdom of Solomon*) to some striking parallelisms with the Epistles of St Paul, and these it may be well to bring before the reader.

(1) Wisd. xv. 7. The potter, tempering soft earth, fashioneth every vessel with much labour for our service: yea, of the same clay he maketh both the vessels that serve for clean uses, and likewise all such as serve to the contrary.	(1) Rom. ix. 21. Hath not the potter power over the clay, of the same lump to make one vessel unto honour, and another unto dishonour?
(2) Wisd. xii. 20. If thou didst punish the enemies of thy people, and the condemned to death, with such deliberation, giving them time and place to repent of their malice…	(2) Rom. ix. 22. What if God, willing to shew his wrath, and to make his power known, endured with much longsuffering the vessels of wrath fitted to destruction.
(3) Wisd. v. 17—19. He shall put on righteousness as a breastplate, and true judgment instead of an helmet. He shall take holiness for an invincible shield.	(3) 1 Thess. v. 8, Eph. vi. 13—17. But let us, who are of the day, be sober, putting on the breastplate of faith and love; and for an helmet, the hope of sal-

His severe wrath shall he sharpen for a sword.

vation....Wherefore take unto you the whole armour of God, that ye may be able to withstand in the evil day, and having done all, to stand. Stand therefore, having your loins girt about with truth, and having on the breastplate of righteousness; and your feet shod with the preparation of the gospel of peace; above all, taking the shield of faith, wherewith ye shall be able to quench all the fiery darts of the wicked. And take the helmet of salvation, and the sword of the Spirit, which is the word of God.

The coincidences of the Wisdom of Solomon with the thoughts and language of the Epistle to the Hebrews are yet more numerous. They are enough, as I have elsewhere endeavoured to shew[1], to suggest the thought of identity of authorship. With that hypothesis, however, we are not now concerned, and I content myself with noting a few that are sufficient to establish the conclusion that the former book must have been known to the writer of the latter. Thus in the opening of the Epistle we have the two characteristic words πολυμερῶς ("in sundry parts," or "times") agreeing with the πολυμερές ("manifold") of Wisd. vii. 22, and ἀπαύγασμα ("brightness") with Wisd. vii. 26. In Wisd. xviii. 22 the "Almighty Word" is represented as bringing "the unfeigned commandment as a sharp sword" and in Heb. iv. 12 that Word is described as "sharper than any two-edged sword." In Wisd. i. 6, "God is witness of his reins and a true beholder of his heart," and in Heb. iv. 12 the divine Word is "a discerner of the thoughts and intents of the heart." The following characteristic words are common to both: the "place of repentance" (Wisd. xii. 10; Heb. xii. 17), Moses as the servant (θεράπων = "attendant") of God (Wisd. xvii. 21; Heb. iii. 5), Enoch translated, μετετέθη (Wisd. iv. 10; Heb. xi. 5),

---

[1] See *Expositor*, Vol. II. Two papers on "the Writings of Apollos."

ὑπόστασις (="substance" or "confidence" Wisd. xvi. 21; Heb. i. 3, iii. 14), τελειότης (="perfection" Wisd. vi. 15; Heb. vi. 1), βεβαίωσις (="confirmation" Wisd. vi. 18; Heb. vi. 6), ἀπολείπεται (="there remaineth" Wisd. xiv. 6; Heb. iv. 6), πρόδρομος (="fore-runner" Wisd. xii. 8; Heb. vi. 20). The above instances are but a few out of a long list, but they are sufficient for our present purpose. It may be added that both books present numerous parallelisms with the writings of Philo[1].

It follows from the facts thus brought together, as well as from an examination of the book itself, that the Wisdom of Solomon was known to Hellenistic Jews early in the Apostolic age, that it probably had its origin in the Jewish School of Alexandria, or that its writer was acquainted with the works of the greatest of the teachers of that school. Looking to the work itself we find that he had at least some knowledge of the ethical teaching of Greek philosophers, and enumerates the four great virtues, of "courage, temperance, justice, prudence" (ἀνδρεία, σωφροσυνή, δικαιοσυνή, φρόνησις), as they enumerated them (Wisd. viii. 7). With these data we may proceed to examine the relation in which he stands to the two books which have already been discussed in their relation to each other. The title of his book "Wisdom" indicates that he challenged comparison with the "Wisdom" of the son of Sirach. The form which he adopts for his teaching, his personation of the character of Solomon (Wisd. vii. 7—11, viii. 14, ix. 7, 8), shews that he did not shrink from challenging comparison with Ecclesiastes. A closer scrutiny shews, if I mistake not, that a main purpose of his book was to correct either the teaching of that book, or a current misinterpretation of it. Let us remember in what light it must have presented itself to him. It had not, if our conclusion as to its authorship be right, the claim which comes from the reverence due to the authority of a remote antiquity or an unquestioned acceptance. He must have known that it had not been received as canonical without a serious opposition, that the strictest school of Pharisees had been against its reception, that it had seemed to them tainted with the heresy of Epicureanism and Sadduceeism. If it was

---

[1] See the papers on "the Writings of Apollos" already referred to.

interpreted then as it has often been interpreted since, it may have seemed to him to sanction a lawless sensuality, to fall in with the thoughts of those who said "let us eat and drink, for to-morrow we die," to throw doubt, if not denial, on the soul's immortality. Was this, he seems to have asked himself, the true ideal of wisdom? Was it not his duty to bring before men another Solomon than that whose experience seemed to end in materialism and pessimism, in the scepticism of an endless doubt? And so he too adopts, without any hesitation, the form of personated authorship. He has indeed less dramatic power than his predecessor. His Solomon is more remote from the Solomon of history than that of Koheleth. The magnificence, the luxury, the voluptuousness, which the earlier writer portrays so vividly, not less than the idolatry which is so prominent in the historical Solomon, are passed over here. The Son of David, as painted by him, is simply an ideal sage, a kind of Numa Pompilius, consecrating his life from beginning to end to the pursuit of wisdom, blameless and undefiled (Wisd. vii. viii.). Looked at from this point of view the opening of his book is in its very form sufficiently significant. He will not call himself an *Ecclesiastes* or *Debater*. It seems to him that the work of a teacher is to teach and not merely to discuss. The wisdom which inspires him is authoritative and queen-like. He is, what Koheleth is not, a "preacher" in the modern sense of the word, and calls on men to listen with attention (Wisd. i. 1). Had his predecessor counselled submission to the tyranny of kings, and accepted the perversion of judgment and justice as inevitable (Eccles. v. 8, x. 4, 20), he, for his part, will call on the judges of the earth and kings, and rebuke them for their oppressions (Wisd. i. 1, vi. 1—10). Had Koheleth spoken of seeking wisdom in wine and revelry, and the "delights" of the sons of men (Eccles. ii. 1—8), he will proclaim that "wisdom will not dwell in the body that is subject unto sin" (Wisd. i. 4) and that "the true beginning of her is the desire of discipline" (Wisd. vii. 17). Had the earlier writer spoken bitter things of men and yet more of women (ch. vii. 28), he will remind his hearers that wisdom is a "loving," a "philanthropic," spirit (φιλάνθρωπον πνεῦμα, Wisd. i. 6). To the ever-recurring complaint that all things are "vanity and feeding upon wind" (Eccles. i. 14, 17, ii. 26, *et al.*) he opposes the teaching that "murmuring is unprofitable" (Wisd. i. 11). The thought that death was better than life, to be desired as an everlasting sleep (Eccles. vi. 4, 5), he meets with the warning "seek not death in the error of your life" (Wisd. i. 12), ventures even on the assertion that "God made not death," that it was an Enemy that had done this, that life and not death was contemplated in the Divine Purpose as the end of man (Wisd. i. 13). It was only the ungodly who counted death their friend (Wisd. i. 16). In the second chapter of the book, there is a still more marked antagonism. He puts into the mouth of the "ungodly" what appears in Ecclesiastes as coming from the writer himself. It is they who say "our life is short and miserable" (Wisd. ii. 6; Eccles. viii. 6), that "we shall be hereafter as though we had never been" (Wisd. ii. 2; Eccles. ix. 5, 6), that death and life are both determined by a random chance, "at all adventure" (Wisd. ii. 2; Eccles. ix. 11), that "our body shall be turned into ashes, and our spirit vanish in the soft air" (Wisd. ii. 3; Eccles. iii. 19, xii. 7)[1], that after death the doom of oblivion soon overtakes man and all his actions (Wisd. ii. 4; Eccles. i 11). They take up almost the very words of Koheleth when they say "Let us enjoy the good things that are present...Let us fill ourselves with costly wine and ointments" (Wisd. ii. 7; Eccles. ix. 7—9). Had the despondent pessimist mourned over the fact that the "wise man dieth as the fool," that there is one event to the righteous and the wicked" (Eccles. vii. 15, ix. 2), the answer is ready—that it was only "in the sight of the unwise they seemed to die," and that their hope is full of immortality (Wisd. iii. 2). Had he declared that he had not found one righteous woman after all his searching (Eccles. vii. 26), he is met with the half-personal answer that that was but natural, that it was true of all who despised wisdom and nurture that "their wives are foolish and their children wicked" (Wisd. iii. 12). Had he taught, or been thought to

---

[1] I hold this to be a misinterpretation of the meaning of Eccles. xii. 7, but it was not the less a natural interpretation at the time, and has often been accepted since.

teach, a life which was emancipated from all restraints and welcomed on almost equal terms children born in and out of wedlock (see Notes on Eccles. ix. 9, xi. 1, 2), entering as it were, a protest against the asceticism which afterwards developed itself into the rule of the more rigid Essenes, the voice of the writer of Wisdom declares that "blessed is the barren who is undefiled" and "the eunuch, which with his hands hath wrought no iniquity" (Wisd. iii. 14), that it is better "to have no children and to have virtue" (Wisd. iv. 1), that "the multiplying brood of the ungodly shall not thrive." Had the sceptical thinker spoken in terms which suggested the thought that he looked on the hope of immortality and the enthusiasm of virtue as no less a form of insanity than the passionate vices of mankind (Eccles. i. 17, ii. 12, vii. 25), the author of the Wisdom of Solomon puts into the mouth of the scoffers the confession "we fools counted his life madness" (Wisd. iv. 4).

And the corrective antagonism of the later writer to the earlier is seen not less clearly in the fact that he gives prominence to what had been before omitted than in these direct protests. It seemed to him a strange defect that a book professing to teach wisdom should contain from first to last no devotional element, and therefore he puts into the mouth of his ideal Solomon a prayer of singular power and beauty for the gift of wisdom (Wisd. ix.). He, an Israelite, proud of the history of his fathers, could not understand a man writing almost as if he had ceased to be an Israelite, one to whom the names of Abraham and Isaac and Jacob were unknown, and therefore he enters on a survey of that history to shew that it had all along been a process manifesting the law at once of a Divine retribution, and of a Divine education (Wisd. x. xi.). He could as little understand how a son of Abraham, writing in Egypt with all the monuments of its old idolatries and later developments of the same tendency to anthropomorphic and theriomorphic worship around him, could have let slip the opportunity of declaring that God is a spirit (Wisd. xii. 1) and must be worshipped in spirit and in truth; that the worship of "fire or wind, or the swift air or the circle of the stars, or the violent water or the lights of heaven" (Wisd.

xiii. 1—4) was relatively noble, "less to be blamed" as compared with the gross idolatry which stirred his spirit within him —as that of Athens stirred the spirit of St Paul—as he walked through the streets of Alexandria. The one idea of God presented in Ecclesiastes seemed to him to be that of Power, hardly of Law, predestinating times and seasons (Eccles. iii. 1—10) and the chances and changes of men's lives (Eccles. ix. 11), working out a partial retribution for man's misdeeds within the limits of earthly experience (Eccles. xi. 9, xii. 14), but leaving many wrongs and anomalies unredressed (Eccles. v. 8, viii. 11). He seeks therefore to bring before men that thought of the Fatherhood of God, which was beginning to dawn upon men's minds, some echoes of which (if our conclusion as to the date of the book be right) had perhaps floated to him from the lips that proclaimed that Fatherhood in its fulness. He had heard, it may be, that One had appeared in Galilee and Jerusalem who "professed to have the knowledge of God, and called himself the 'child' or 'servant' (παῖδα) of the Lord and made his boast that God was his Father" (Wisd. ii. 13—16), that He had been slandered, conspired against, mocked, and put to death, that Sadducean priests had stood by his cross deriding Him, "if the righteous man be the son of God, He will help him and deliver him from the hands of his enemies. Let us examine him with despitefulness and torture and condemn him with a shameful death" (Wisd. ii. 18—20) and that marvellous history had stirred him into a glow of admiration for Him whom as yet he knew not. He could not subside after that into the tone of mind which looks on "life as a pastime and our time here as a market for gain" (Wisd. xv. 12).

It will be seen in the Commentary that follows that I look on the estimate which the author of the Wisdom of Solomon formed of Ecclesiastes as a wrong one, that he was wanting in the insight that sees the real drift which is the resultant of cross currents and conflicting lines of thought. The mystical ascetic who had been trained in the school of Philo, who was, it may be, to develope afterwards, under a higher teaching, into the writer of the Epistle to the Hebrews, lived and moved in a region of thought and feeling altogether different from that of the man who had passed through a multiform experience of wine and wisdom, of love and madness, of passion and "feeding upon wind." But it is not the less instructive to note how such a writer treated the earlier book which also professed to embody the Wisdom of Solomon, of which he could not possibly have been ignorant, and which seemed to him to tend to the popular easy-going Epicureanism that was destructive of all lofty aims and nobleness of character.

CHAPTER VI.

JEWISH INTERPRETERS OF ECCLESIASTES.

It is, perhaps, natural in dealing with a book which presents so many difficulties both in particular passages and in its general drift, to turn to the interpreters who belonged to the same race and spoke the same language as the writer. How did they understand this. or that expression? What did they gather from the book as its chief substantial lesson? And of these we look naturally, in the first instance, with most interest and expectation to the book which gives us the expression, not of an individual opinion, but of the collective wisdom of Israel. We have heard, it may be, high things of the beauty of the Haggadistic mode of interpretation that prevailed in the schools out of which the Mishna, the Gemara, the Targum, and the Midrashim sprang[1]. We open the Midrash, or Commentary,

[1] The terms may be briefly explained for the reader to whom they are wholly or comparatively new. The Targums (= Interpretation) are the Chaldee or Aramaic Paraphrases of the Books of the Old Testament. The Mishna (=repetition or study) is a collection of Treatises on various points, chiefly ceremonial or juristic, in the Mosaic Law. The Gemara (=completeness) is a commentary on, or development of, the Mishna, the contents of which have been classified as coming under two categories, (1) the Halachah (=Rule), which includes the enactments of the Mishna in their application to life, and answers accordingly to the casuistic systems of Scholastic Theology, and (2) the Haggadah (= Legend, or *Saga*) which comprises a wide range of legendary, allegorical, and mystical interpretation. The Midrashim (=studies,

on Koheleth in the hope that we shall see our way through passages that have before been dark, that some light will be thrown on the meaning of words and phrases that have perplexed us. What we actually find answers to the parable of the blind leading the blind and both falling into the ditch (Matt. xv. 14); rules of interpretation by which anything can be made to mean anything else; legends of inconceivable extravagance passing the utmost limits of credibility; an absolute incapacity for getting at the true meaning of a single paragraph or sentence,—this makes up the store of accumulated wisdom to which we had fondly looked forward. Instead of a "treasure" of "things new and old," the pearls and gems, the silver and the gold, of the wisdom of the past, we find ourselves in an old clothes' shop full of shreds and patches, of rags and tatters. We seem, as we read, to be listening to "old wives' fables" and old men's dreams. A suspicion floats across our mind that the interpretations are *delirantium somnia* in the most literal sense of the word. We involuntarily ask, Can these men have been in their right minds? Are we not listening to a debate of insane Commentators? Is not the Midrash as a *Critici Sacri* compiled and edited within the walls of Colney Hatch? Of other expositions it is true that they "to some faint meaning make pretence." Of this alone, or almost alone, it may be said that it "never deviates into sense."

Would the reader like to judge for himself and try his luck at *Sortes Midrashianæ?* I take a few samples at a venture.

(1) Eccles. i. 7, "All the rivers run into the sea, yet the sea is not full." Of this verse we have a wide variety of interpretations: (*a*) All wisdom is in the heart of man and the heart is not full. (*b*) The whole law goes into the heart and the heart is not satisfied. (*c*) All people will join themselves to Israel and yet the number of Israel will still grow. (*d*) All the dead pass into Hades and Hades is not full. (*e*) All Israelites go on their

or expositions) are commentaries, collecting the opinions of distinguished Rabbis on the Books of the Old Testament, and these also contain the Halachah and Haggadah as their chief elements. Deutsch. *Essays*, pp. 17—20, 41—51.

yearly pilgrimage to Jerusalem and yet the Temple is never crowded. (*f*) All riches flow into the kingdom of Edom (= Rome), but in the days of the Messiah they shall be brought back.

(2) Eccles. iv. 8, "There is one alone, and there is not a second; yea, he has neither child nor brother." (*a*) He who is alone is God, the ever-blessed One. (*b*) Or he is Abraham, who had no son or brother or wife when he was thrown into Nimrod's furnace, when he was told to leave his father's house, and when he was commanded to offer up his only son Isaac; or (*c*) He who is alone, is the tribe of Levi, who found "no end of all his labour" in erecting the Tabernacle; or (*d*) that which is alone is the evil lust which leads a man to sin and breaks the ties of kindred; or (*e*) the words describe Gebini ben Charson who was his mother's only son and was blind and could not see his wealth and had no end of trouble with it.

(3) Eccles. ix. 14—16. "There was a little city and few men within it, and there came a great king and besieged it, and built great bulwarks against it. Now there was found in it a poor wise man, and he by his wisdom delivered the city." Here again the expositions are manifold. (*a*) The city is the world, and the few men are those that lived at the time of the Flood and the king is Jehovah, and the wise man is Noah. (*b*) The city is Egypt and the king is Pharaoh, and the poor wise man is Joseph. (*c*) The city is Egypt and the few men are Joseph's brethren and the king is Joseph, and the wise man is Judah. (*d*) The city is Egypt and the men are the Israelites, and the king is the Pharaoh of the Exodus, and the wise man is Moses. (*e*) The city is Sinai, the men are the Israelites and the king is the King of kings, and the bulwarks are the 653 precepts of the Law, and the wise man is Moses. (*f*) The city is Sinai and the few men are the Israelites, and the king is the lust of the flesh, and the wise man is Moses. (*g*) The little city is the Synagogue, and the men are the assembly in it, and the king is the King of kings and the wise man is the elder of the Synagogue. (*h*) The city is the human body, and the men are its limbs, and the king is the lust of the flesh, and the

bulwarks are temptations and errors, and the wise man is Conscience.

A few more specimens will be enough to complete the induction. The "dead flies" of Eccles. x. 1 are (a) Korah and his company; or (b) Doeg and Ahithophel. The precept, "give a portion to seven and also to eight" of Eccles. xi. 3, is explained as referring (a) to the Laws of the Sabbath on the seventh day of the week and of Circumcision on the eighth day after birth; or (b) to Moses as in the seventh generation from Abraham and Joshua as representing the eighth; or (c) to the ceremonial precept of Lev. xii. 1—3; or (d) to the seven days of the Feast of Tabernacles and the closing festival of the eighth day. The maxim, "in the morning sow thy seed and in the evening withhold not thine hand" of Eccles. xi. 6, means Marry in thy youth and beget children, and if thy wife dies, marry again in thine age and beget more children. "Rejoice, O young man, in thy youth..." means "Rejoice in the study of the Law and let thy heart cheer thee with the doctrine of the Mishna and walk in the ways of thy heart, i.e. of the higher knowledge of the Talmud." The "evil days" of Eccles. xii. 1 are the days of the Messiah and of the great tribulation that accompanies them. The "mourners that go about the streets" are the worms that feed upon the carcase (Eccles. xii. 5). The "clouds that return after the rain" are the stern prophecies of Jeremiah that came after the destruction of the Temple. The "pitcher broken at the fountain" (Eccles. xii. 6) is the potter's vessel of Jer. xxxvi. 18. The "grasshopper" of Eccles. xii. 6 is the golden image of Nebuchadnezzar.

The student will probably think that he has had enough and more than enough of the insanities of the *Midrash Koheleth*.

If the Midrash fail us, shall we fare better with the Targum, or Paraphrase, of Ecclesiastes? Here at any rate we are not involved in a labyrinth of conflicting interpretations each more monstrous than the other. The mass of opinions has been sifted, and the judicious editor, compiling, as it were, a Commentary for use in families and schools, has selected that which seems to him most in accordance with the meaning of the original, explaining its hard passages so as to make them easy and edifying for the unlearned reader. Let us see what he will find in this instance and how the edification is obtained.

TEXT.	TARGUM.

TEXT.

Eccles. i. 3. What profit hath a man of all his labour which he taketh under the sun?

TARGUM.

What advantage is there to a man after his death, from all his labour which he laboured under the sun in this world, except he studied the word of God, in order to receive a good reward in the world to come?

Eccles. i. 11. Neither shall there be any remembrance of things that are to come with those that shall come after.

There will be no remembrance of them among the generations which will be in the days of the King Messiah.

Eccles. i. 17. I the Preacher was king over Israel in Jerusalem.

When king Solomon was sitting upon the throne of his kingdom, his heart became very proud of his riches, and he transgressed the word of God, and he gathered many horses, and chariots, and riders, and he amassed much gold, and silver, and he married from foreign nations; whereupon the anger of the Lord was kindled against him, and he sent to him Ashmodai the king of the demons, who drove him from the throne of his kingdom, and took away the ring from his hand, in order that he should wander about the world to reprove it, and he went about in the provincial towns and cities of the land of Israel, weeping and lamenting, and saying, I am Koheleth whose name was formerly called Solomon, who was king over Israel in Jerusalem.

TEXT.	TARGUM.
Eccles. ii. 4. I made me great works: I builded me houses; I planted me vineyards.	I multiplied good works in Jerusalem. I built houses, the Temple, to make atonement for Israel, and a royal palace, and a conclave, and the porch, and a house of judgment of hewn stones where the wise men sit, and the judges to give judgment. I made a throne of ivory for the sitting of royalty. I planted vineyards in Jabne, that I and the Rabbis of the Sanhedrin might drink wine, and also to make libations of wine new and old upon the altar.
Eccles. ii. 10. My wisdom remained with me.	Whatsoever the Rabbis of the Sanhedrin asked of me respecting pure and impure, innocent and guilty, I did not withhold from them any explanation of these things.
Eccles. ii. 18. Because I should leave it unto the man that shall be after me.	Because I must leave it to Rehoboam my son who comes after me, and Jeroboam his servant will come and take away out of his hands ten tribes, and will possess half of the kingdom.
Eccles. iii. 1. A time to be born, and a time to die.	There is a special time for begetting sons and daughters, and a special time for killing disobedient and perverse children, to kill them with stones according to the decree of the judges.
Eccles. iii. 11. He hath made everything beautiful in his time.	King Solomon said by the spirit of prophecy, God made everything beautiful in its time; for it was opportune that there should be the strife which was in the days of Jeroboam son of Nebat: for if it had

TEXT.

TARGUM.

been in the days of Sheba, son of Bichri, the Temple would not have been built because of the golden calves which the wicked Jeroboam made...He concealed from them also the great Name written and expressed on the foundation stone.

Eccles. iii. 19. That which befalleth the sons of men befalleth beasts.

For as to the destiny of the wicked and the destiny of the unclean beast, it is one destiny for both of them.

Eccles. iv. 13. Better is a poor and wise child than an old and foolish king.

Better Abraham, who is the poor youth and in whom is the spirit of prophecy from the Lord, and to whom the Lord was known when three years old, and who would not worship an idol, than the wicked Nimrod who was an old and foolish king. And because Abraham would not worship an idol he threw him into the burning furnace, and a miracle was performed for him of the Lord of the world, and He delivered him from it... For Abraham went out from the family of idolaters, and reigned over the land of Canaan; for even in the reign of Abraham Nimrod became poor in the world....[Then follows a long prediction like that in the paraphrase of chap. iii. 11 of the revolt of the ten tribes under Jeroboam.]

Eccles. v. 7. In the multitude of dreams and many words there are also divers vanities: but fear thou God.

In the multitude of the dreams of the false prophets, and in the vanities of sorcerers, and in the many words of the wicked, be-

TEXT.	TARGUM.
	lieve not, but serve the wise and just.
Eccles. v. 6. Neither say thou before the angel that it was an error.	In the day of the great judgment thou wilt not be able to say before the avenging angel who exercises dominion over thee, that it is an error.
Eccles. vi. 6. Do not all go to one place?	If he...had not studied the law ...in the day of his death he will go to Gehenna, to the place whither all sinners go.
Eccles. vi. 8. What hath the poor, that knoweth to walk before the living?	What is this poor man to do but to study the law of the Lord, that he may know how he will have to walk in the presence of the righteous in Paradise?
Eccles. vii. 4. The heart of the wise is in the house of mourning.	The heart of the wise mourns over the destruction of the Temple, and grieves over the captivity of the house of Israel.
Eccles. vii. 15. All things have I seen in the days of my vanity.	All this I saw in the days of my vanity, that from the Lord are decreed good and evil to be in the world according to the planets under which men are created.
Eccles. vii. 16. Be not righteous over much.	Be not over-righteous when the wicked is found guilty of death in the court of judgment: so as to have compassion on him, and not to kill him.
Eccles. vii. 24. That which is far off, and exceeding deep, who can find it out?	Who is he that will find out by his wisdom the secret of the day of death, and the secret of the day when the King Messiah will come?
Eccles. vii. 28. One man among a thousand have I found;	From the days of the first Adam till the righteous Abraham was

TEXT.	TARGUM.
but a woman among all those have I not found.	born, who was found faithful and just among the thousand kings that gathered together to build the tower of Babel? and a woman, as Sarah, among all the wives of those kings I have not found.
Eccles. viii. 14. There be just men to whom it happeneth according to the work of the wicked; again, there be wicked men to whom it happeneth according to the work of the righteous.	There are righteous to whom evil happens as if they had done like the deeds of the wicked; and there are wicked to whom it happens as if they had done like the deeds of the righteous; and I saw by the Holy Spirit that the evil which happens to the righteous in this world is not for their guilt, but to free them from a slight transgression, that their reward may be perfect in the world to come; and the good that comes to sinners in this world is not for their merits, but to render them a reward for the small merit they have acquired, so that they may get their reward in this world, and to destroy their portion in the world to come.
Eccles. ix. 2. All things come alike to all.	Everything depends upon the planets; whatever happens to any one is fixed in heaven.
Eccles. ix. 8. Let thy garments be always white; and let thy head lack no ointment.	At all times let thy garment be white from all pollution of sin, and acquire a good name, which is likened to anointing oil.
Eccles. ix. 14. There was a little city, and few men within it...	Also this I saw...the body of a man which is like a small city... and in it are a few mighty men just as the merits in the heart of man are few; and the evil spirit

TEXT.	TARGUM.
	who is like a great and powerful king, enters into the body to seduce it...to catch him in the great snares of Gehenna, in order to burn him seven times for his sin. And there is found in the body a good spirit, humble and wise, and he prevails over him and subdues him by his wisdom, and saves the body from the judgment of Gehenna.
Eccles. x. 7. I have seen servants upon horses, and princes walking as servants.	King Solomon said by the spirit of prophecy, I saw nations who were before subject to the people of the house of Israel, now prosperous and riding on horses like princes, whilst the people of the house of Israel and their princes walk on the ground like slaves.
Eccles. xi. 9. Whoso removeth stones shall be hurt therewith; and he that cleaveth wood shall be endangered thereby.	King Solomon the prophet said, It is revealed to me that Manasseh, the son of Hezekiah, will sin and worship idols of stone; wherefore he will be delivered into the hands of the king of Assyria, and he will fasten him with halters: because he made void the words of the law which are written on the tables of stone from the beginning, therefore he will suffer from it; and Rabshakeh his brother will worship an image of wood, and forsake the words of the law which are laid in the ark of shittim-wood; therefore he shall be burned in a fire by the angel of the Lord.
Eccles. x. 16, 17. Woe to thee,	Woe to thee, O land of Israel,

TEXT.	TARGUM.
O land, when thy king is a child, and thy princes eat in the morning. Blessed art thou, O land, when thy king is the son of nobles, and thy princes eat in due season.	when wicked Jeroboam shall reign over thee, and remove from thee the morning sacrifices, and thy princes shall eat bread before offering the daily morning sacrifice. Well to thee, O land of Israel, when Hezekiah son of Ahaz, from the family of the house of David, king of Israel, who is mighty in the land, shall reign over thee, and shall perform the obligations of the commandments, and thy nobles, after having brought thee the daily sacrifice, shall eat bread at the fourth hour.
Eccles. x. 20. Curse not the king, no not in thy thought; and curse not the rich in thy bed-chamber; for a bird of the air shall carry the voice, and that which hath wings shall tell the matter.	Even in thy mind, in the innermost recesses of thy heart, curse not the king, and in thy bed-chamber revile not a wise man, for the angel Raziel proclaims every day from heaven upon Mount Horeb, and the sound thereof goes into all the world; and Elijah the high-priest hovers in the air like an angel, the king of the winged tribe, and discloses the things that are done in secret to all the inhabitants of the earth.
Eccles. xii. 5. The mourners go about the streets.	The angels that seek thy judgment walk about like mourners, walking about the streets, to write the account of thy judgments.
Eccles. xii. 11. The words of the wise are as goads, and as nails fastened by the masters of assemblies, which are given from one shepherd.	The words of the wise are like goads that prick, and forks which incite those who are destitute of knowledge to learn wisdom as the goad teaches the ox; and so are the words of the rabbis of the

TEXT.	TARGUM.
	Sanhedrin, the masters of the Halachas and Midrashim which were given through Moses the prophet; who alone fed the people of the house of Israel in the wilderness with manna and delicacies.
Eccles. xii. 12. And further, by these, my son, be admonished; of making many books there is no end, and much study is a weariness of the flesh.	And more than these, my son, take care to make many books of wisdom without an end, to study much the words of the law and to consider the weariness of the flesh.

It will be felt from the extracts thus brought together[1] that the Targum is on the whole pleasanter reading than the Midrash. The traces of discordant interpretation are carefully effaced. All flows on smoothly as if there never had been and never could be any doubt as to what the writer of the original book had meant. Hard sayings are made easy. A spiritual, or at least an ethical, turn is given to words which seemed at first to suggest quite other than spiritual conclusions. The writer of the book, whose identity with Solomon is not questioned for a moment, is made to appear not only as a moral teacher but in the higher character of a prophet. The illustrations drawn from the history of Israel, the introduction of the name of Jehovah, the constant reference to the Shechinah and the Law, give the paraphrase a national and historical character not possessed by the original. The influence of the planets as determining men's characters and the events that fashion them is brought in as a theory of predestination easier to receive than that which ascribes all that happens to the direct and immediate action of the Divine Will. All is done, in one sense, to edification.

The misfortune is, however, that the edification is purchased at the cost of making the writer say just the opposite, in many cases, of what he actually did say. As Koheleth personates

---

[1] I have to acknowledge my obligations for these extracts to the translation of the Targum appended to Dr Ginsburg's *Koheleth*.

Solomon, so the paraphrast personates Koheleth, and the confessions of the Debater, with their strange oscillations and contrasts, become a fairly continuous homily. In all such interpretations, and the Targum of Koheleth is but a sample of a widespread class which includes other than Jewish commentators, there is at once an inherent absence of truthfulness and a want of reverence. The man will not face facts, but seeks to hide them or gloss them over. He assumes that he is wiser than the writer whom he interprets, practically, *i.e.* he claims for himself a higher inspiration. He prefers the traditions of the school in which he has been brought up to the freshness of the Divine word as it welled forth out of the experience of a human heart.

With the eleventh century we enter on a fresh line of Jewish interpreters of the book. The old rabbinical succession had more or less died out, and the Jewish school of Europe began to be conspicuous for a closer and more grammatical exegesis of the sacred text. An interesting survey of the literature which thus grew up, so far as it bears on the interpretation of Ecclesiastes, will be found in the Introduction to Dr Ginsburg's Commentary. It is marked, as might be expected, by more thoroughness and more individual study, a truer endeavour to get at the real meaning of the book. Each man takes his place in the great army of Commentators and works on his own responsibility. To go through their labour would be an almost interminable task. It was worth while to give some account of the Midrash and the Targum because they represented certain dominant methods and lines of thought, but it does not fall within the scope of this volume to examine the works of all Jewish interpreters simply because they are Jewish, any more than of those that are Christian.

CHAPTER VII.

ECCLESIASTES AND ITS PATRISTIC INTERPRETERS.

It does not fall, as has been just said, within the plan of the present book, to give a review of the Commentaries on Ecclesiastes that have preceded it, so far as they represent only the opinions of individual writers. The case is, however, as before, altered when they represent a school of thought or a stage in the history of interpretation, and where accordingly the outcome of their labours illustrates more or less completely the worth of the method they adopted, the authority which may rightly be given to the *dicta* of the School.

It has been said (Ginsburg, p. 99), that Ecclesiastes is nowhere quoted in the New Testament, and as far as direct, formal quotations are concerned the assertion is strictly true. It was not strange that it should thus be passed over. The controversy already referred to (Ch. III.) between the schools of Hillel and Shammai as to its reception into the Canon, the doubts that hung over the drift of its teaching, would naturally throw it into the background of the studies of devout Israelites. It would not be taught in schools. It was not read in Synagogues. It was out of harmony with the glowing hopes of those who were looking for the Christ or were satisfied that they had found Him. Traces of its not being altogether unknown to the writers of the New Testament may, however, be found. When St Paul teaches why "the creation was made subject to *vanity*" (Rom. viii. 20), using the same Greek word as that employed by the LXX. translators, we may recognise a reference to the dominant burden of the book. When St James writes "What is your life? It is even a vapour, that appeareth for a little time, and then vanisheth away" (James iv. 14) we may hear something like an echo of Eccles. vi. 12.

The earlier Christian writers followed in the same track and the only trace of the book in the Apostolic Fathers is the quotation of Eccles. xii. 13 ("Fear God and keep His commandments") in the *Shepherd* of Hermas (*Mand.* VII.). Justin quotes the Wisdom of Solomon but not Ecclesiastes. Irenæus neither names nor quotes it. Clement of Alexandria, who makes no less than twenty-six quotations from the Wisdom of Solomon, quotes in one solitary passage (*Strom.* I. 13) from Eccles. i. 16— 18, vii. 13. In Origen, though the quotations from Wisdom are still far more numerous, we have more traces of a thoughtful study. The *vanitas vanitatum* is connected with Rom. viii. 20 as above (*de Princ.* I. 7, *c. Cels.* I. 7). He supposes Eccles. i. 6 to have given occasion to the contemptuous language in which Celsus had spoken of Christians as talking of "circles upon circles" (*c. Cels.* VI. 34, 35). In Eccles. i. 9 he finds a confirmation of his belief that there have been worlds before the present world and that there will be others after it (*de Princ.* III. 5, *c. Cels.* IV. 12). The "Spirit of the ruler" (Eccles. x. 4) is interpreted of the evil Spirit (*de Princ.* III. 2). In the words "the earth abideth for ever" (Eccles. i. 4) he finds an instance of the use of the word "eternity" with a secondary and limited connotation (*Comm. in Rom.* B. VI.). He gives a mystical interpretation of Eccles. iv. 2 as meaning that those who are crucified with Christ are better than those that are living to the flesh; of the "untimely birth" of Eccles. vi. 3 as meaning Christ whose human nature never developed, as that of other men develops, into sin (*Hom.* VII. *in Num.*), and cites Eccles vii. 20, with Rom. xi. 33 as a confession that the ways of God are past finding out (*de Princ.* IV. 2).

The passages now cited are enough to shew that it was probable that those who had studied in the school of Origen would not entirely neglect a book to which he had thus directed their attention. His treatment of them indicates that they were likely to seek an escape from its real or seeming difficulties in an allegorizing, or, to use the Jewish phrase, a Haggadistic interpretation. And this accordingly is what we find. The earliest systematic treatment of Ecclesiastes is found in the *Metaphrasis* or Paraphrase of Gregory Thaumaturgus, who had studied under the great Alexandrian teacher. Of all patristic commentaries it is the simplest and most natural. From first to last there is no strained allegorism or mysticism, finding in the text quite another meaning than that which was in the mind of the writer. The scepticism of Eccles. iii. 20, 21 is freely rendered, "The other kind of creatures have all the same breath of life and men have nothing more...For it is uncertain regarding the souls of men, whether they shall fly upwards; and regarding the others which the unreasoning creatures possess whether they shall fall downwards." The Epicurean counsel of Eccles. ix. 7—9 is stated without reserve, but is represented as the error of "men of vanity," which the writer rejects. The final close of the writer's thought (Eccles. xii. 7) is given without exaggeration, "For men who be on the earth there is but one salvation, that their souls acknowledge and wing their way to Him by whom they have been made." Perhaps the most remarkable passage of the Commentary is the way in which the paraphrase of Eccles. xii. 1—6 represents the original as depicting the approach of a great storm filling men with terror, anticipating in this the interpretation which Dr Ginsburg and Mr Cox have worked out with an elaborate fulness :

"Moreover it is right that thou shouldest fear God, while thou art yet young, before thou givest thyself over to evil things, and before the great and terrible day of God cometh, when the sun shall no longer shine, neither the moon, nor the other stars, but when in that storm and commotion of all things, the powers above shall be moved, that is, the angels who guard the world; so that the mighty men shall cease, and the women shall cease their labours, and shall flee into the dark places of their dwellings, and shall have all the doors shut; and a woman shall be restrained from grinding by fear, and shall speak with the weakest voice, like the tiniest bird; and all impure women shall sink into the earth, and cities and their blood-stained governments shall wait for the vengeance that comes from above, while the most bitter and bloody of all times hangs over them like a blossoming almond, and continuous punishments impend over them like a multitude of flying locusts and the transgressors are cast out of the way like a black and despicable caper plant. And the good man shall depart with rejoicing to his own everlasting habitation; but the vile shall fill all their places with wailing, and neither silver laid up in store, nor tried gold, shall be of use any more. For a mighty stroke shall fall upon all things, even to the pitcher that standeth by the well, and the wheel of the vessel which may chance to have been left in the hollow, when the course of time comes to an end and the ablution-bearing period of a life that is like water has passed away[1]."

A more ambitious but less complete treatment of Ecclesiastes is found in eight homilies by Gregory of Nyssa, which cover however only the first three chapters. Like his other writings it breathes the spirit of a devout thinker trained in the school of Origen, alike in his allegorizing method of interpretation and in his utterance of the wider hope. At every step he diverges from the true work of the interpreter to some edifying and spiritual reflection. The Greek title of the book suggests its connexion with the work and life of the *Ecclesia* of Christ. Christ himself was the true *Ecclesiastes* gathering together those that had been scattered into the unity of His fulness. The true son of David was none other than the incarnate Word. In the language of Eccles. i. 11, "neither shall there be any remembrance of things that are to come," Gregory finds an indication of his deeply-cherished conviction that the final restitution of all things will work out an entire obliteration even of the memory of evil (*Hom.* I.). The words "that which is lost cannot be numbered" seem to him connected with the fall of Judas as the son of perdition, with the wandering sheep who reduces the complete hundred to the incompleteness of the ninety and nine (*Hom.* II.). The description of the magnificence of Solomon in Eccles. ii. 1—8 leads to a whole train of half-mystical reflections. The true palace is that of Wisdom and its pillars are the virtues that sustain the soul. What need is there of gardens for one who was in the true Paradise of contemplation? (*Hom.* III.). Is not the true fountain

---

[1] The original is obscure and probably corrupt. The meaning of the commentator may be that the period of life in which a man may receive the "washing of regeneration" will in that day come to a sudden end.

the teaching that leads to virtue? The mention of servants and handmaids leads him to protest against the evil of slavery (*Hom.* IV.). In the counsel to eat and drink he finds a reference not to the bread which nourishes the body but to the food which sustains the soul (*Hom.* V.). The catalogue of Times and Seasons in Eccles. iii. 1—8 suggests, as might be expected, a copious variety of like reflections. He cannot speak of the "time to plant" without thinking of the field of which the Father is the husbandman, of "the time to pluck up" without dwelling on the duty of rooting out the evil tares of sin (*Hom.* VI.). The "time to kill" can refer only to the vices which we are called on to strangle and destroy. The "time to weep" recalls to his mind the beatitudes of the Sermon on the Mount (Matt. v. 4) and the parable of the children sitting in the market-place (Matt. xi. 16, 17) (*Hom.* VII.). So "the time to gather stones" is applied to the stones of temperance and fortitude by which we destroy vice. The "time to keep silence" reminds him of St Paul's rule bidding women be silent in the Church, and the "time for war" of the Christian warfare and the whole armour of God (*Hom.* VIII.). Beyond this point he does not go, and perhaps it is well that he stopped where he did. Interesting and even edifying as such homiletic treatment may be as the expression of a refined and devout and noble character, it is obvious that it hardly contributes one jot or tittle to the right understanding of the book which it professes to expound. With the exception of the hints given by Gregory Thaumaturgus, the Greek Fathers of the Church have contributed almost as little to the exegesis of Ecclesiastes as the Rabbis of the *Midrash Koheleth.*

The history of the interpretation of Ecclesiastes among the Latin Fathers runs more or less on parallel lines with that which has just been traced. The earlier writers knew the book, and this or that proverbial sentence dwells in their memories, but they have not studied it and do not venture on any systematic interpretation. Thus Tertullian simply quotes three times the maxim of Eccles. iii. 1, that "there is a time for all things" (*adv. Marc.* V. 4, *de Monog.* III., *de Virg. Vel.* III.). Cyprian cites Eccles. i. 14, v. 4, 10, vii. 17, x. 9 in his *Testimonia adversus*

Judæos (c. 11, 30, 61, 53, 86) but with no indication that the book as a whole had been thought over, and no trace of any mystical interpretation. When we come to Augustine the case is widely different. The allegorizing method which had been fostered by Origen had taken root, and the facility with which it ministered to spiritual meditation and turned what had been stumblingblocks into sources of edification, commended it to devout interpreters. He does not write a Commentary on the book, but he quotes it in a way which shews that it was often in his hands and is always ready with an interpretation that brings an edifying thought out of the least promising materials. Thus he fastens on the "*vanitas vanitantium*" of the old Latin Version as shewing that it is only for the "*vanitantes*," the men who are without God, that the world is vanity (*de Ver. Relig.* c. 41). The "portion to seven and also to eight" of Eccles. xi. 2 is for him "*ad duorum Testamentorum significationem*," the one resting on the sabbath, the other "on the eighth day, which is also the first, the day of the Lord's Resurrection" (*ad Inqu. Jan.* c. 23). In the words that "the Spirit returns to God who gave it" (Eccles. xii. 7) he finds a proof that each single soul is created by an individual divine act and not engendered as was the bodily frame in which it dwelt. He connects Rom. viii. 20 ("the creature was made subject to vanity") with the main thesis of the book, as shewing that the sentence "vanity of vanities" is temporary and remedial in its nature and will one day be removed (*Expos. Epist. Rom.* c. 53), and dwells on the fact that it applies only to the things that are "under the sun," to the visible things which are temporal, and not to the invisible which are eternal (*Enarr. in Ps. xxxviii.*). His controversy with Pelagianism leads him to recognise in the "righteous overmuch" of Eccles. vii. 16 the character of the man who wraps himself up in the garments of his own "righteousness of works" (*Tract. in Joann.* XCV.). He contrasts the "one generation goeth and another generation cometh" with the permanence of the eternal Word (*Enarr. in Ps. ci.*). The maxim that "he that increaseth knowledge increaseth sorrow" (Eccles. i. 18) is for him true even of the wisdom of charity, seeing that we cannot love men with-

out a fresh pang of sorrow for their sufferings and their sins
(*Enarr. in Ps. xcviii.*). On the "many inventions" of Eccles.
vii. 30 he characteristically preaches "*Mane apud unum, Noli
ire in multa, Ibi beatitudo*" (*Serm.* XCVI.). In his later treatment
of the book the allegorical method is more fully developed and
the "eating and drinking," the "bread and wine" of Eccles. viii.
15, ix. 7 are interpreted as pointing not even to the most innocent forms of sensuous enjoyment, but to that which is represented by the symbols of the Eucharistic feast (*de Civ. Dei*,
XVII. 20). The "dead flies" that mar the fragrant "ointment
of the apothecary" (Eccles. x. 1) are the post-baptismal sins
which taint the good fame of professing Christians (*c. Epist.
Parmen.*). The Haggadistic style of interpretation culminates in
his explanation of Eccles. x. 16, 17. He finds there the "*duæ
civitates*" which are the subject of his great work, the land
whose "king is a child" is the evil city of the world, and the devil
is the young king who is wilful and rebellious, and the princes
who "eat in the morning" are the men of the world, who find
their pleasures in this earthly life which is but the dawn of their
existence, and the "son of nobles" is none other but the Christ,
the heir, according to the flesh, of patriarchs and kings, and
the "princes who eat in due season" are the believers who are
content to wait for their future blessedness in the heavenly city
(*De Civ. Dei*, XVII. 20).

In Jerome's treatment of the book we have, as was to be
expected from his student character, a more systematic exposition. It takes the form of a Commentary, is fuller than
the *Metaphrase* of Gregory Thaumaturgus, less merely homiletic
and fragmentary than the *Discourses* of Gregory of Nyssa.
He had compared the translations of Aquila and Symmachus
and Theodotion with that of the LXX. and discusses criti-
cally the two renderings of the 'burden' of the book which he
found in them, the ματαιότης ματαιοτήτων ("vanity of vanities")
of the LXX., the ἀτμὶς ἀτμίδων ("vapour of vapours") of all the
others. He compares, in dealing with the companion phrase,
the προαίρεσις πνεύματος (a deliberate choice of wind) with the
νομὴ of Aquila and Theodotion, the βόσκησις πνεύματος of Sym-

machus (both = feeding upon wind). Perhaps the chief interest
of the Commentary lies in the traces which it preserves of the
divided counsels of the earlier Rabbis as to the drift and authority of the book. "Some," he says, "affirms that it came from
Solomon as a penitent confessing his transgressions." Some
had rejected the book because it seemed inconsistent with itself,
now bidding men go to the house of mourning as better than
the house of feasting, now telling them that there was nothing
better than to eat bread and drink wine and live with the
woman they love, and perfume themselves with costly unguents,
the latter precepts being those of Epicurus and not of Israel.
His knowledge of Hebrew led him to connect the "dead flies"
of Eccles. x. 1 with Baal-zebub, the Lord of flies, and also the
prince of the devils, and so to find in them the evil thoughts which
do the devil's work. He, almost alone among commentators,
connects the "almond tree" of Eccles. xii. with its figurative use
as the "early waking" tree in Jer. i. 11, and therefore as the
symbol of the old man's wakefulness. He discusses the various
meanings of the words which we render "grasshopper" and "desire" in the same passage. His view of the drift of the book may
be inferred partly from his having read it with Blæsilla, one of
the many female disciples to whom he acted as director, when he
sought to lead her to enter on the life of the convent at Bethlehem (*Præf. in Eccles.*), partly from his assigning, on the traditional theory of the authorship of the three books, Proverbs to
the youth of Solomon, Ecclesiastes to his middle age, the Song
of Songs to his old age, first the maxims of prudence, then the
experience of the world's vanities, lastly, as the crown of life's
teaching, the mystical passion of the bride and bridegroom, of
the soul and Christ. He starts, as Gregory of Nyssa had
done, with the thought that "*Ecclesiastes noster est Chris-
tus,*" and taking this as his key-note he finds suggestions of
devout thoughts where we see only the maxims of prudential or
even Epicurean wisdom. Thus the "one alone" that "hath not a
second" of Eccles. iv. 8 is referred to Christ as the one Media-
tor saving men by His one sacrifice, and the teaching as to
friendship of Eccles. iv. 9—11 is applied to Christ as the Friend

who raises us when we fall, and will warm us when we lie cold in the grave to everlasting life, and, like Augustine, he finds in the "bread and wine" which man is to enjoy (Eccles. ix. 7), the symbols of the body and blood of Christ; but these are given obviously rather as homiletic reflections than as direct interpretations. A trace of early tendencies to the characteristic teaching of Origen is found in his suggesting as a tenable interpretation of Eccles. i. 15 that "*omnibus per pœnitentiam in integrum restitutis solus diabolus in suo permanebit errore.*" On the whole, we may say that Jerome's style of commenting might have been followed with advantage by many of his successors.

As it was, however, the ascetic and the allegorizing interpretations which had thus been started developed with a marvellous rapidity. Ambrose reproduces what we have seen in Jerome and, in addition, finds the Christ as the second Adam in the "second child" of Eccles. iv. 15 and the doctrine of the Trinity in Unity in the "threefold cord" of Eccles. iv. 12. The allegorizing, mystical method is found yet further expanded in Gregory the Great (*Commentary on Job*), and after the marvellous interpretations of that book nothing seems impossible. In the application of that method to Ecclesiastes the two leaders of the mystic school, Richard and Hugo of St Victor, holds a foremost place. In "the rivers that run into the sea" (Eccles. i. 7) the former finds the fleshly lusts that seem sweet and pleasant, yet end in bitterness. In the "casting away of stones" (Eccles. iii. 5) the latter sees the multiplication of good works, in the "gathering stones" the reward of those works. The Haggadistic method, however, culminates in Peter Lombard, and his exposition of Eccles. xii. 5 presents, perhaps, the *ultima Thule* of this style of interpretation. The "almond," with its rind, shell and kernel, answers to the tripartite nature of Christ, body, soul, and Deity. It flowered when He rose from the dead. The fattening of the "grasshopper" (so the Vulg. *impinguabitur locusta*) represents the admission of the Gentiles, leaping, as leaps the grasshopper, into the Church of Christ. In the Vulg. for "desire shall fail" (*dissipabitur capparis*) he sees the dispersion of the unbelieving.

The continuity of succession in this method was broken by Nicholas de Lyra, who, having been born and educated in the Jewish schools that had felt the influence of the more critical spirit of Maimonides, laid stress on the necessity of first settling the literal meaning of the text before entering into speculation on its allegorical, moral, and anagogical or mystical meanings, and so led the way to the enquiries of later students. In this he was followed by Luther whose views as to the authorship of the Book have been already noticed (chap. II.) and who maintains in his *Commentary on Ecclesiastes* that its aim was to reject the ascetic, gloomy view of life of which monasticism was the development, and to commend a life of active industry and simple innocent enjoyment. Luther was followed in his turn by Melancthon, and so we enter on the line of individual commentators, Grotius and his followers, each thinking for himself, and working out his own conclusion as to the meaning of individual passages and the drift of the whole book. The limits of the present volume do not admit of our tracing the varying opinions thus arrived at. Those who wish to follow them through their many windings will find them analysed in Dr Ginsburg's exhaustive, *Introduction* to his *Commentary on Koheleth*.

CHAPTER VIII.

ANALYSIS OF ECCLESIASTES.

It follows from what has been already said (chap. III.) that the Book before us is very far removed from the character of a systematic treatise and therefore does not readily admit of a formal analysis. What will now be attempted accordingly is rather to prepare the reader for the study of the book itself by tracking, as far as the conditions of the case admit, the oscillations and wanderings of thought by which the writer makes his way to his final conclusion. It will be convenient, as in the ideal biography given in chap. III., to use the name Koheleth as that by which the writer wished himself to be known.

(1) I. **1—11**. The book opens with reproducing the phase of despair and weariness in which it had originated. All things are "vanity" and "vapour." There was no gain in living (1—3). The monotony of succession in nature, and in human life, was absolutely oppressing. It was made even more so by the feeling of the oblivion that sooner or later falls over all human activities. There was nothing new in the world, nothing permanent (4—11).

(2) I. 12—II. **23**. Koheleth appears in the personated character of the son of David, and as such retraces his experience. He had found the search after wisdom wearisome and unsatisfying. It was all "vapour and feeding upon wind." Increase of knowledge was but increase of sorrow (i. 12—18). From wisdom he had turned to kingly state, and magnificence, and luxury, and had found that this also was vanity, and without profit (ii. 1—11). Then came the study of human nature in its manifold phases of sanity and insanity, and something was gained in the conviction that the former was better than the latter (ii. 12, 13). This was soon traversed, however, by the thought that the advantage lasted but for the little span of life, and that death, the great leveller, placed the wise man and the fool on the same footing, and that thought made life more hateful than before, and deepened the feeling that all was vanity and "feeding upon wind" (ii. 14—23). He fell back from all this profitless endeavour upon a less ambitious yet more practical and attainable ideal. To eat and drink, not with the license of the sensualist, but as the condition of a healthy activity, accepting the limitations of man's earthly life, this was at least safe, and if received as from the hand of God, not otherwise than religious.

III. **1—17**. Another thought helps to restore the mind of Koheleth to equilibrium. Wisdom lies in opportuneness. The chances and changes of life have each their appointed season in a divine order. Man's wisdom is to take each of them in its season, not to strive restlessly after that which is not given him (1—8). And yet there is a disturbing element in man's very nature which hinders this conformity to circumstances. He is a "being of large discourse, looking before and after," and craves to find beauty and order throughout the universe (9—11). Yet he must repress, or at least limit that craving, and fall back as before upon the practicable union of honest labour and innocent enjoyment. Such a life was consistent with that "fear of God" which was the beginning of wisdom (iii. 12—14). And that fear of God led on to the thought of a law of retribution working through the disorders of the world (15—17). It was a thought, a fear, a hope. Could he say that it was more? Who could answer the question as to the "whither" of man's spirit after death? Was not his life subject to the same conditions as that of beasts? That doubt might be painful, but it did not affect the practical ideal to which he had before been led. It need not lead to despair, or madness, or reckless profligacy. Reasonable labour, reasonable enjoyment, that was still within his reach.

(3) IV. **1—16.** New phases of thought are indicated by the words "I returned," "I considered." The wrongs and miseries of the world, the sufferings of others rather than his own, these weighed on his spirit. How could he account for them? (iv. 1—3). Was it worth while labouring when the success of his labour did but expose a man to envy? Was it better not to labour when indolence led on to poverty? (iv. 4). The extremes of wealth and poverty brought the risk of isolation, and cut a man off from that companionship which was at least an unquestioned good (iv. 7—12). His survey of life, alike in the vicissitudes of national and individual life, oppresses him once more with the thought that all is vanity and "feeding upon wind" (iv. 13—16).

(4) V. **1—VI. 12.** There was one phase of human life which yet remained to be examined. Koheleth turned to the religionists of his time. Did he find anything more satisfying there? The answer was that he found hollowness, formalism, hypocrisy, frivolous excuses and dreams taken for realities (v. 1—7). From the religious life he turned to the political, and there also all was anomalous and disheartening, rulers oppressing the tillers of the soil, yet less happy in their wealth than the labourers in their poverty, heaping up riches and not knowing who should gather them (v. 8—17). What remained but to make the best of life under such conditions, seeking neither poverty nor riches, rejoicing in God's gifts of wealth and honour within the same limitations as before? (v. 13—20). Yes, but then there comes once more the depressing thought that we must leave all this, often before we have had any real enjoyment of it. Another comes and reaps what we have sown. Would it not be better that we had not been born? Is not even this moderated aim, this lower ideal, a delusion and a dream, subject, as the higher aim was, to the doom of vanity? (vi. 1—12).

(5) VII. **1—22.** The succession of thoughts becomes less con-secutive and systematic, and we have the lessons on many things which Koheleth had been taught by his experience. Reputation, the

7—2

fair name that is fragrant in the memories of men, this is better than riches or pleasure. It is worth dying to get that posthumous immortality (vii. 1). It is worth while to visit the sorrowing and the sick, for so we learn to sympathize and correct the flattering deceits of false hopes, and learn the calmness of wisdom (vii. 2—6). The root-evil in life is impatience, the wish to have lived in a former age, under different conditions (vii. 7—10). Prosperity and adversity have each their lessons, and in each we need the spirit which accepts what comes to us as part of God's order, and avoids the falsehood of extremes (vii. 11—18). This was wisdom, but then how few were wise, how far fewer still were righteous? One among a thousand might be found among men: not one among all the women whom Koheleth had ever known. The conclusion to which he was led was that man's freedom had marred God's order as it was when He looked on all that He had made and saw that it was very good (vii. 19—29).

(6) VIII. 1—IX. 10. The same weary round is trodden over again. The experience of Koheleth throws his mind upon the wisdom that is needed by those who live in the courts of kings (viii. 1—5). But that life, with its unequal distribution of rewards and honours, ambition cut short by death, power hurting its possessor, the unrighteous ruler exulting in his impunity, these were fresh elements of disorder and vanity. He retired once more from the life of courts to that of a tranquil seclusion and calm enjoyment (viii. 6—15). What profit was there in speculating on the problems presented by history any more than on those of individual men? Here also there was that which was inscrutable. Men might talk of the law of retribution, might feel that there must be such a law, but facts were against them. There was one event to the righteous and the wicked (viii. 16—ix. 3). Before, that thought had almost driven him to despair. Now, the path by which he has travelled has led him to a truer solution of the problem. Make life worth living. Work, rest, rejoice, lay aside the vexing questions which make life miserable. All beyond is darkness (ix. 4—10).

(7) IX. 11—X. 20. As before, the phrase "I returned" indicates a fresh start of thought. Koheleth looks on life and is struck by the want of proportion in the distribution of its rewards. The race is not to the swift. Time and chance seem to order all things. The sons of men are ensnared in an evil net. Wisdom does more than strength, and yet the wise man is forgotten and wealth carries off the world's honours (ix. 11—18). Even in the wise there are follies that

mar their wisdom, and though we despise the fool, we see him sitting in high places (x. 1—7). The labour of the reformer, who seeks to set things right, ends too often in his own ruin and disgrace, and the empty-headed babbler gains the day (x. 8—15). The evils of mis-government, the caprice of a boy king, the oppressions of his ministers, were patent evils, and yet there was no remedy for them without peril and no course open except silent acquiescence (x. 16—20).

(8) XI. 1—XII. 7. Koheleth feels that it is time these many wan-derings should end, and that his book, perhaps his life also, is drawing to a close. He passes therefore to more direct teaching. Whatever else was doubtful, it was clear that to do good must be right. To use opportunities for a wide charity, without over-anxious care as to immediate results, this was the path of wisdom (xi. 1—6). This at least made life worth living, even though darkness lay beyond it. And with this clearer insight into the true law of life there came a clearer faith. Joy and pleasure were not in themselves evil, but they might easily become so, and the young man in the midst of the glow of life, must remember that the Creator is also the Judge. We see tokens of that judgment now in the evil days which follow on a life of sensuous pleasure—the decay of strength, and health, and faculties of perception and of thought (xi. 7—xii. 6). Soon the goal is reached, and death closes all, and the spirit returns to God who gave it (xii.). Are there not grounds for believing that the judgment which we see here working partially, the education which here so often ends in seeming failure, will then work out their tendencies into results? Is not that a conclusion in which the spirit of man may rest? It was, at all events, Koheleth's last word on the great problem.

(9) XII. 8—14. The closing verses of the book are in the nature of an epilogue, added, it is almost certain, by another writer. The book is commended to the reader as written by a seeker after wisdom, who had sought to make the words of truth acceptable, whose incisive maxims were as goads and nails. Such a book, short and incomplete as it might seem, was better in its pregnant truthfulness than the tomes of elaborate system-builders. As a guide to the reader in tracking his path through the somewhat labyrinthine structure of the book, the editor sums up what seemed to him, as it seems to us, the outcome of the whole. It was man's wisdom to fear God, and keep His commandments and live in the expectation of His judgment.

ECCLESIASTES,

OR,

THE PREACHER.

THE words of the Preacher, the son of David, king in **1**
Jerusalem.

Vanity of vanities, saith the Preacher, vanity of vanities; **2**

1. *The words of the Preacher*] For the title of the Book and the
meaning of the word translated "Preacher" (better, **Debater**, or, perhaps, as the Hebrew noun has no article, Koheleth, as a proper name,
carrying with it the meaning of **Debater**), see *Introduction*. The description "king in Jerusalem" is in apposition with "the Preacher"
not with "David." It is noticeable that the name of Solomon is not
mentioned as it is in the titles of the other two books ascribed to him
(Prov. i. 1; Song of Sol. i. 1).

2. *Vanity of vanities*] The form is the highest type (as in the "servant of servants" of Gen. ix. 25, the "chief over the chief" of Num. iii.
32) of the Hebrew superlative. The word translated "vanity," identical with the name Abel or *Hebel* (Gen. iv. 2) means primarily a "breath,"
or "vapour," and as such becomes the type of all that is fleeting and
perishable (Ps. lxii. 9, cxliv. 4). It is uniformily translated by "vanity"
in the English Version of this book, which is moulded on the Vulgate
as that was upon the LXX. The other Greek versions gave "vapour
of vapours" (Hieron. *in loc.*) and this may perhaps be regarded as, in
some respects, a preferable rendering. The watchword of the book,
the key-note of its melancholy music, meeting us not less than thirty-
nine times, is therefore, whether we take it as a proposition or an
exclamation, like that of the Epicurean poet "*Pulvis et umbra
sumus*" (Hor. *Od.* IV. 7. 9), like that also, we may add, of St James
(Jas. iii. 14) and the Psalmist (Ps. xc. 3—10). In the *Wisdom of
Solomon* apparently written (see *Introduction*, chap. v.) as a corrective
complement to Ecclesiastes we have a like series of comparisons,
the "dust," the "thin froth," the "smoke," but there the idea of
'vanity' is limited to the "hope of the ungodly" and the writer, as

3 all *is* vanity.   What profit hath a man of all his labour
which he taketh under the sun?

4   *One* generation passeth away, and *another* generation

if of set purpose, avoids the sweeping generalizations of the **Debater**,
who extends the assertion to the "all" of human life, and human aims.
It is not without significance that St Paul, in what is, perhaps, the
solitary reference in his writings to this book, uses the word which the
LXX. employs here, when he affirms that "the creature was made
subject to *vanity*" and seeks to place that fact in its right relation to
the future restitution of the Universe (Rom. viii. 20).

   3.   *What profit hath a man*]   The question is, it is obvious, as in
the analogous question of Matt. xvi. 26, the most emphatic form of a
negation.   For "all his labour which he taketh" read **all his toil
which he toileth**, the Hebrew giving the emphasis of the combination
of the verb with its cognate substantive.   The **Debater** sums up his
experience of life in this, "There is toil, and the toil is profitless."
The word for "profit," not meeting us elsewhere in the Hebrew of the
O. T., occurs ten times in Ecclesiastes.   Its strict meaning is "that
which remains,"—the surplus, if any, of the balance-sheet of life.   It
was, probably, one of the words which the commerce of the Jews, after
the Captivity, had brought into common use.   The question is in
substance, almost in form, identical with that of our times "Is life
worth living?"

   under the sun]   The phrase thus used, occurring 29 times in *Ecclesi-
astes*, has nothing like it in the language of other books of the Old
Testament.   It is essentially Greek in character.   Thus we have in
Euripides, *Hippol.* 1220,

ὅσα τε γᾶ τρέφει
τὰν "Αλιος αἰθομέναν δέρκεται
ἄνδρας τε.

"All creatures that the wide earth nourisheth
Which the sun looks on radiant, and mankind."

And Theognis, 168,

τὸ δ' ἀτρεκές, ὄλβιος οὐδεὶς
ἀνθρώπων, ὁπόσους ἤελιος καθορᾷ.

"One thing is certain, none of all mankind,
On whom the sun looks down, gains happiness."

   Our English "sublunary" may be noted as conveying an analogous
idea.

   4.   *One generation passeth away, and another generation cometh*]   The
sentence loses in strength by the words inserted in italics.   Better,
generation passeth and generation cometh.   This is, as it were,
the first note of vanity.   Man, in idea the lord of the earth, is but as a
stranger tarrying for a day.   As in the touching parable of the Saxon
chief, he comes from the darkness as into the light of a festive hall, and
then passes into the darkness once again (Bede, *Eccl. Hist.* II. c. 14),

cometh: but the earth abideth for ever.   The sun also 5
ariseth, and the sun goeth down, and hasteth to his place

but the earth which is in idea subject to him boasts a permanence which
he cannot claim.   In the Hebrew word which answers to "for ever"
we have, as elsewhere, an undefined rather than an absolutely infinite
duration.

Parallelisms of thought present themselves in Ecclus. xiv. 19; Job
x. 21; Ps. xxxix. 13, and, we may add, in Homer, *Il.* VI. 146,

> οἵη περ φύλλων γενεή, τοιήδε καὶ ἀνδρῶν.
> φύλλα τὰ μέν τ' ἄνεμος χαμάδις χέει, ἄλλα δέ θ' ὕλη
> τηλεθόωσα φύει, ἔαρος δ' ἐπιγίγνεται ὥρη·
> ὡς ἀνδρῶν γενεὴ ἡ μὲν φύει, ἡ δ' ἀπολήγει.

> "As are the leaves, so is the race of men;
>   Some the wind scatters on the ground, and some
>   The fruitful forest, when the springtide comes,
>   Puts forth; so note we also with mankind;
>   One comes to life, another falls away."

It is significant that these lines were ever in the mouth of Pyrrho,
the founder of the Greek school of Sceptics (Diog. Laert. IX. 11. 6).

5.   *The sun also ariseth*]   From the standpoint of modern thought
the sun might seem even more than the earth to be the type of permanent existence, but with the Hebrew, who looked on it in its phe-
nomenal aspect, it was not so, and the sun accordingly appears as
presenting not a contrast, but a parallel, to human mutability and
resultless labour.   We are reminded of the Rabbinic legend of Abraham's looking on the sun, and, when half tempted to adore it, repressing
the temptation by watching its going down and saying "The God
whom I worship must be a God that does not set."   Koran, *Sur.* 6.
Stanley's *Jewish Church*, I. Lect. I.

hasteth to his place where he arose]   The primary meaning of the first
of the two verbs is that of the panting of one who travels quickly.
Here again we have to think of the belief that, between the sunset and
the sunrise, the sun had a long journey to perform, as the Greeks
thought, by the great Ocean river, till it returned to the point where
it had risen the day before.   Possibly the clouds and mists of the
morning were thought of as the panting of the sun, as of "the strong
man" who "runs his race" (Ps. xix. 5).

Parallels present themselves in Ps. xix. 5 ("rejoiceth as a strong man
to run a race") and yet more strikingly in Virgil, *Georg.* I. 250,

> Nosque ubi primus equis Oriens adflavit anhelis,
> Illic sera rubens accendit lumina Vesper.

> "And when to us the sun with panting steeds
>   Hastens at dawn, far off the star of eve
>   There lights her glowing lamp."

Comp. also *Æn.* XII. 113.

6 where he arose. The wind goeth toward the south, and turneth about unto the north; it whirleth about continually, 7 and the wind returneth *again* according to his circuits. All the rivers run into the sea; yet the sea *is* not full; unto the place from whence the rivers come, thither they return

6. *The wind goeth toward the south*] This comes after the sun as exhibiting a like, though more irregular, law of mutability. "South and north" only are named, partly, perhaps, because east and west were implied in the sunrise and sunset of the previous verse, more probably because these were the prevailing currents of air in Palestine. Comp. "Awake, O north wind; blow, O south," in Song of Sol. iv. 16; Ecclus. xliii. 20; Luke xii. 55.

It whirleth about continually] The whole verse gains in poetic emphasis by a more literal rendering, **It goeth to the south, and it circleth to the north, circling, circling goeth the wind, and on its circlings returneth the wind.** The iteration and order of the words seem to breathe the languor of one who was weary with watching the endless and yet monotonous changes. (Comp. the illustration in *Introduction*, chap. III.)

7. *All the rivers run into the sea; yet the sea is not full*] The words express the wonder of the earliest observers of the phenomena of nature: as they observed, the poet described.

So we have in Aristophanes (*Clouds*, 1248),

αὕτη μὲν (ἡ θάλαττα) οὐδὲν γίγνεται
ἐπιρρεόντων τῶν ποταμῶν, πλείων.

"The sea, though all the rivers flow to it,
Increaseth not in volume."

Lucretius, representing the physical science of the school of Epicurus, thought it worth his while to give a scientific explanation of the fact:

"Principio, mare mirantur non reddere majus
Naturam, quo sit tantus decursus aquarum."

"And first men wonder Nature leaves the sea
Not greater than before, though to it flows
So great a rush of waters."
                                        LUCRET. VI. 608.

thither they return again] We are apt to read into the words the theories of modern science as to the evaporation from the sea, the clouds formed by evaporation, the rain falling from the clouds and replenishing the streams. It may be questioned, however, whether that theory, which Lucretius states almost as if it were a discovery, were present to the mind of the **Debater** and whether he did not rather think of the waters of the ocean filtering through the crevices of the earth and so feeding its wells and fountains. The Epicurean poet himself accepts this as a partial solution of phenomena, and on the view taken in the *Introduction* as to the date of *Ecclesiastes* it may well have been known

again.   All things *are* full of labour; man cannot utter *it:* 8
the eye is not satisfied with seeing, nor the ear filled with

to the author as one of the physical theories of the school of Epicurus.
We can scarcely fail, at any rate, to be struck with the close parallelism
of expression.

> "Postremo quoniam raro cum corpore tellus
> Est, et conjuncta est, oras maris undique cingens,
> Debet, ut in mare de terris venit umor aquai,
> In terras itidem manare ex aequore salso;
> Percolatur enim virus, retroque remanat
> Materies humoris, et ad caput amnibus omnis
> Confluit; inde super terras redit agmine dulci."

> "Lastly since earth has open pores and rare,
> And borders on the sea, and girds its shores,
> Need must its waters, as from earth to sea
> They flow, flow back again from sea to earth,
> And so the brackish taint is filtered off
> And to the source the water back distils,
> And from fresh fountains streams o'er all the fields."
>
> LUCRET. VI. 631—637.

The same thought is found in Homer, *Il.* XXI. 196,

> "Ocean's strength
> From which all rivers flow,"

and is definitely stated in the Chaldee paraphrase of the verse now
before us.   Comp. also Lucret. v. 270—273.   An alternative rendering
gives "to the place whither the rivers go, thither they return again"
or "thence they return again."

8.   *All things are full of labour*]   The Hebrew *dabar* may mean
either "word" or "thing," and so the sentence admits equally of this
or the nearly equivalent rendering, **All things are weary with toil**
and **All words are feeble,** and each gives, it is obvious, a fairly tenable
meaning.   The first generalizes as by an induction from the previous
instances, that all things (especially, *i. e.* all human affairs) are alike
"stale, flat and unprofitable."   The latter stops in the induction to say
that all speech is feeble, that time and strength would fail to go through
the catalogue.   On the whole, looking to the fact that the verb "utter"
is cognate in form with the word translated "things," the latter seems
more closely in harmony with the context.   We might fairly express
the force of the Hebrew by saying **All speech fails; man cannot
speak it.**   The seeming tautology gives the sentence the emphasis of
iteration.   So the LXX. and the Targum.

the eye is not satisfied with seeing]   The thought is limited by the
context.   It is not that the **Debater** speaks of the cravings of sight and
hearing for ever-new objects, true as that might be; but that wherever
the eye or the ear turn, the same sad tale meets them, the same paradox
of an unvarying record of endless yet monotonous variation.   The state
which Lucretius (II. 1037) describes, probably as echoing Epicurus, that

9 hearing. The thing that hath been, *it is* that which shall be; and that which is done *is* that which shall be done: 10 and *there is* no new *thing* under the sun. Is there *any* thing whereof it may be said, See, this *is* new? it hath been 11 already of old time, which was before us. *There is* no

of one "*fessus satiate videndi*," presents a parallelism too striking to be passed over.

9. *The thing that hath been*] What has been affirmed of natural phenomena is now repeated of the events of human life. The writer reproduces or anticipates the Stoic doctrine of a recurring cycle of events which we find reproduced in Virgil:

"Magnus ab integro sæclorum nascitur ordo.
Alter erit tum Tiphys, et altera quæ vehat Argo
Delectos heroas; erunt etiam altera bella,
Atque iterum ad Troiam magnus mittetur Achilles."

"Lo! the great cycle runs its course anew:
A second Tiphys springs to life, and steers
A second Argo with its warrior freight
Of chosen heroes, and new wars arise,
And once again Achilles sails for Troy."

VIRG. *Ecl.* IV. 5, 34—36.

10. *Is there any thing*] A man may challenge, the writer seems to say, the sweeping assertion just uttered. He may point to some new phenomenon, some new empire, some invention of art, or discovery of science. It is all to no purpose. It has been before in the vast æons (the Hebrew word for "of old time" is the plural of that commonly translated "age" or "eternity") of the recorded or unrecorded past. It is but an oblivion of what has been that makes us look to that which is to be as introducing a new element in the world's history. The thought was a favourite one with the Stoics. For a full account of their doctrine on this point see Zeller's *Stoics and Epicureans*, ch. VII. Aurelius does but sum up the teaching of the school, where he says, almost in the very words of Ecclesiastes, that "they that come after us will see nothing new, and that they who went before us saw nothing more than we have seen" (*Meditt.* XI. 1). "There is nothing new" (*Ibid.* VII. 1). "All things that come to pass now have come to pass before and will come to pass hereafter" (*Ibid.* VII. 26). So Seneca (*Ep.* XXIV.), "*Omnia transeunt ut revertantur; Nil novi video, nil novi facio.*" ("All things pass away that they may return again; I see nothing new, I do nothing new.")

11. *There is no remembrance of former things*] Better, **of former men**, or **of those of old time**, and so in the next clause **of those that shall come after.** The thought of the oblivion of the past, suggested in the previous verse, as explaining the fact that some things seem new to us which are not so, is reproduced in another aspect as yet a new element in the pessimism into which the writer has fallen.

remembrance of former *things;* neither shall there be *any*
remembrance of *things* that are to come with *those* that shall
come after.

I the Preacher was king over Israel in Jerusalem. And ¹²
I gave my heart to seek and search out by wisdom concern- ¹³

Men dream of a fame that shall outlive them. How few of those that
went before them do they remember even by name? How little do
they know even of those whose names have survived amid the wreck
that has engulfed others? What does it profit to be famous now, just
known by name to the generation that follows, and then forgotten altogether? Comp. a striking passage to the same effect in Jeremy Taylor's
Contemplations of the State of Man, ch. III., " The name of Echebar
was thought by his subjects to be eternal, and that all the world did
not only know but fear him ; but ask here in Europe who he was, and
no man hath heard of him ; demand of the most learned, and few shall
resolve you that he reigned in Magor," and Marc. Aurel. *Meditt.* II. 17,
ἡ ὑστεροφημία, λήθη, " posthumous fame is but oblivion."   So ends
the prologue of the book, sounding its terrible sentence of despair on
life and all its interests. It is hardly possible to turn to the later work,
which also purports to represent the *Wisdom of Solomon,* without feeling
that its author deliberately aimed at setting forth another aspect of
things. He reproduces well nigh the very words of the prologue, "the
breath of our nostrils is as smoke"..."our name shall be forgotten in
time: our life shall pass away as the trace of a cloud"...but he puts all
this into the mouth not of his ideal Solomon but of "ungodly men,...
reasoning with themselves but not aright," Wisd. ii. 1—5, and shews
how it leads first to sensuous self-indulgence, and then to deliberate
oppression, and persistent antagonism to God. (See *Introduction,*
chap. V.)

12. *I the Preacher was king over Israel*] Better, "I...**have been**
king." It would, perhaps, be too much to say that this mode of introducing himself, is so artificial as to exclude, as some have thought, the
authorship of the historical Solomon. Louis XIV.'s way of speaking
of himself *"Quand j'etois roi"* may well have had its parallel, as Mr
Bullock suggests in the *Speaker's Commentary,* in the old age of another
king weary of the trappings and the garb of Majesty. As little, however, can they be held to prove that authorship. A writer aiming at a
dramatic impersonation of his idea of Solomon would naturally adopt
some such form as this and might, perhaps, adopt it in order to indicate
that it was an impersonation. The manner in which the son of David
appears in Wisd. vii. 1—15 presents at once a parallel and a contrast.

13. *I gave my heart*] The phrase, so expressive of the spirit of an
earnest seeker, is eminently characteristic of this book and meets us
again in ver. 17, chaps. vii. 25, viii. 9, 16. Like forms are found in Isai.
xli. 42 ; Ps. xlviii. 14. "Heart" with the Hebrews, it may be noticed,
is the seat of the intellect as well as the affections, and "to give the heart"
is therefore specially expressive of an act of concentrated mental energy.
The **all that is done under heaven** (we note the variation of phrase

ing all *things* that are done under heaven: this sore travail
hath God given to the sons of man to be exercised there-
14 with.   I have seen all the works that are done under the
15 sun; and behold, all *is* vanity and vexation of spirit.   *That*
which is crooked cannot be made straight: and that which
16 is wanting cannot be numbered.   I communed with mine

from the "under the sun" of verse 9) takes in the whole range of human
action as distinct from the cosmical phenomena of verses 5—7.   The
enquiry of the seeker was throughout one of ethical rather than physical
investigation.

this sore travail]   The words express the feeling with which the
writer looked back on his inquiry.   It had led to no satisfying result,
and the first occurrence of the name of God in the book is coupled with
the thought that this profitless search was His appointment.   He gave
the desire but, so the preacher murmurs in his real or seeming pessimism, not the full Truth in which only the desire can rest.   The word
for "travail" is peculiar to this book.   That for "exercised" is formed
from the same root.

14.   *all is vanity and vexation of spirit*]   The familiar words, though
they fall in with the **Debater's** tone and have the support of the Vulg.
"*afflictio spiritus,*" hardly express the meaning of the Hebrew and we
must read "**vanity and feeding upon wind.**"   The phrase has its parallel
in Hos. xii. 2 ("Ephraim feedeth on wind") and Isai. xliv. 20 ("feedeth
on ashes") and expresses, with a bold vividness, the sense of emptiness
which accompanies unsatisfied desire.   Most commentators, however,
prefer the rendering "striving after the wind" or "windy effort," but
"feeding" expresses, it is believed, the meaning of the Hebrew more
closely.   The LXX. gives προαίρεσις πνεύματος (= resolve of wind, *i.e.*
fleeting and unsubstantial).   Symmachus gives βόσκησις and Aquila
νομή (= feeding).   The word in question occurs seven times in Ecclesiastes but is not found elsewhere.   The rendering "vexation" rests
apparently on a false etymology.

15.   *That which is crooked*]   The words are apparently a proverbial
saying quoted as already current.   The complaint is that the search
after wisdom brings the seeker face to face with anomalies and defects,
which yet he cannot rectify.   The Hebrew words are not the same, but
we may, perhaps, trace an allusive reference to the promise of Isai. xl.
4 that "the crooked shall be made straight," and the **Debater** in his
present mood looks on this also as a delusive dream.   There is nothing
left but to take things as they are and "accept the inevitable."   Comp.
chap. vii. 13, as expressing the same thought.

that which is wanting]   The second clause presents the negative
aspect of the world's defects as "crooked" did the positive.   Everywhere, if there is nothing absolutely evil, there is an "incompleteness"
which we cannot remedy, any more than our skill in arithmetic can
make up for a deficit which stares us in the face when we look into an
account, and the seeker had not as yet attained to the faith which sees

own heart, saying, Lo, I am come to great estate, and have
gotten more wisdom than all *they* that have been before me
in Jerusalem: yea, my heart had great experience of wisdom and knowledge. And I gave my heart to know wis- 17

beyond that incompleteness the ultimate completeness of the Divine
order.

16. *Lo, I am come to great estate*] The pronoun is used emphatically. The verb in the Hebrew is connected closely with what follows
and speaks not of outward majesty but of "becoming great," in
wisdom. So taken we may read, **"I became great and increased in
wisdom more than all."** We note again, as in verse 13, the kind of
dialogue which the **Debater** holds with his inner consciousness. He
"communes with his heart" (comp. Ps. iv. 4, lxxvii. 6). So Marcus
Aurelius gave to the book which we call his *Meditations*, the title τὰ εἰς
ἑαυτόν—literally, "Things for myself" or "Self-communings."

they that have been before me in Jerusalem] Better, **"over Jerusalem."**
Those who maintain the late origin of the book point to this apparent
retrospect over a long series of predecessors as betraying, or possibly
as intended to indicate, the pseudonymous authorship. The historical
Solomon, it is said, had but one predecessor over Jerusalem. The
inference is, however, scarcely conclusive. Even on the theory of
personated authorship, the writer would scarcely have slipped into
so glaring an anachronism, and the words admit of being referred, on
either view, either to the line of unknown Jebusite rulers, including
perhaps Melchizedek (Gen. xiv. 18), Adonizedek (Josh. xv. 63; 2 Sam.
v. 7) and others, or to the sages "Ethan the Ezrahite and Heman and
Chalcol and Darda the sons of Mahol," who are named in 1 Kings
iv. 31, and who may, in some sense, as teachers and guides, have been
"over" as well as "in" Jerusalem. Some MSS. indeed give the
preposition "in" instead of "over."

my heart had great experience] More literally, and at the same time
more poetically, **my heart hath seen much wisdom and knowledge.**
The two nouns are related, like the Greek σοφία and ἐπιστήμή, the
former expressing the ethical, the latter the speculative, scientific side
of knowledge.

17. *And I gave my heart*] The apparent iteration of the phrase
of verse 13 expresses the concentration of purpose. The writer adds
that his search took a yet wider range. He sought to know wisdom
through its opposite, to enlarge his experience of the diseases of
human thought. He had fathomed the depths of the "madness and
folly;" the former word expressing in Hebrew as in English the wilder
forms of unwisdom. There is, perhaps, a touch of self mockery in the
fact that the latter word in the Hebrew is all but identical in sound
with a word which means "prudence." One, the writer seems to say,
has the same issue as the other. Some critics, indeed (*e.g.* Ginsburg),
think that the present text originated in an error of transcription and
that we ought to read "to know wisdom and knowledge." It has

dom, and to know madness and folly: I perceived that
18 this also *is* vexation of spirit.   For in much wisdom *is*
much grief: and he that increaseth knowledge increaseth
sorrow.

been thought and, as stated in the *Introduction* (chap. II.), with some
reason, that in the use of the stronger word we have an echo of the
current language of the Stoics who looked on all the weaknesses of
mankind as so many forms of insanity. So Horace (*Sat.* II. 3. 43),

> "Quem mala stultitia et quemcunque inscitia veri
> Cæcum agit, insanum Chrysippi porticus et grex
> Autumat. Hæc populos, hæc magnos formula reges,
> Excepto sapiente, tenet."

> "Him, whom weak folly leads in blindness on,
> Unknowing of the Truth, the Porch and tribe
> Who call Chrysippus Master, treat as mad.
> Peoples and mighty kings, all but the wise
> This formula embraces."

So also Diog. Laert. VII. 124,

> λέγουσι πάντας τοὺς ἄφρονας μαίνεσθαι.

> "All that are foolish they pronounce insane."

vexation of spirit] Better, **feeding on wind**, as before. See note
on ver. 14. The word is, however, not identical in form, but expresses
a more concrete idea. By some it is rendered "meditation." The
fact that the writer uses a word not found elsewhere in the Old Testament, suggests the thought that he wanted a new word for the expression
of a new thought.

18. *in much wisdom is much grief*] The same sad sentence was
written on the study of man's nature in its greatness and its littleness,
its sanity and insanity. The words have passed into a proverb, and
were, perhaps, proverbial when the **Debater** wrote them. The mere
widening of the horizon, whether of ethical or of physical knowledge,
brought no satisfaction. In the former case men became more conscious
of their distance from the true ideal. They ate of the fruit of the tree
of knowledge of good and evil, and the only result was that they knew
that "they were naked" (Gen. iii. 7). In the latter, the more they
knew of the phenomena of nature or of human life the more they felt
that the "most part of God's works were hid." Add to this the brain-
weariness, the laborious days, the sleepless nights, the frustrated ambitions of the student, and we can understand the confession of the
Debater. It has naturally been often echoed. So Cicero (*Tusc. Disp.*
III. 4) discusses the thesis, "*Videtur mihi cadere in sapientem
ægritudo*" ("Sickness seems to me to be the lot of the wise of heart").

I said in mine heart, Go to now, I will prove thee with 2
mirth, therefore enjoy pleasure: and behold, this also *is*
vanity.   I said of laughter, *It is* mad: and of mirth, What 2
doeth it?   I sought in mine heart to give myself unto wine, 3

CHAPTER II.

1. *I will prove thee with mirth*] The self-communing of the man
talking to his soul, like the rich man in Luke xii. 18, 19, in search of
happiness, leads him to yet another experiment.   He will lay aside
philosophy and try what pleasure will do, and live as others live.   The
choice of Faust in Goethe's great drama, presents a striking parallel in
the world of creative Art.   The fall of Abelard is hardly a less striking
parallel in the history of an actual life.   Consciously or unconsciously
(probably the former) the **Debater** had passed from the Hebrew and the
Stoic ideals of wisdom to that of the school of Epicurus.   The choice of
the Hebrew word for "pleasure" (literally "good") implies that this now
appeared the *summum bonum* of existence.   But this experiment also
failed.   The doom of "vanity" was on this also.   The "laughter" was
like the crackling of burning thorns (chap. vii. 6) and left nothing but
the cold grey ashes of a cynical satiety.   In the "Go to now" with
which the self-communing begins we trace the tone of the irony of
disappointment.

2. *I said of laughter, It is mad*] The choice of a word cognate
with the madness of chap. i. 17, gives a special emphasis to the judgment which the man thus passes on himself.   There was as much insanity in this form of life as in the other.   He was plunging into madness with his eyes open and might say,

> "Video meliora proboque,
> Deteriora sequor."

> "I see the better, yet the worse pursue."

> OVID, *Metamorph.* VII. 20.

In each case the question might be asked "What does it work?   What
is its outcome?"   And the implied answer is "Absolutely nothing."

3. *to give myself unto wine*] Literally, and more vividly, **to cherish
my flesh with wine.**   The Hebrew word for "give" is unusual and
obscure.   The primary meaning is "to draw out," that of the word for
"acquainting" is "to guide" or "drive," as in Exod. iii. 1 ; 2 Sam. vi. 3.
Possibly, as Lewis suggests in Lange's *Commentary*, the idea is like that
of the parable in the *Phædrus* of Plato (p. 54) and the seeker gives the
rein to pleasure, yet seeks to guide or drive the steed with his wisdom.
The words point to the next stage in the progress of the pleasure seeker.
Pleasure as such, in its graceful, lighter forms, soon palls, and he seeks
the lower, fiercer stimulation of the wine cup.   But he did this, he
is careful to state, not as most men do, drifting along the current of
lower pleasures

> "Till the seared taste, from foulest wells
> Is fain to quench its fires,"

(yet acquainting mine heart with wisdom) and to lay
hold on folly, till I might see what *was* that good for the
sons of men, which they should do under the heaven all
4 the days of their life. I made me great works; I builded
5 me houses; I planted me vineyards: I made me gardens

but deliberately, "yet **guiding** mine heart with wisdom." This also
was an experiment, and he retained, or tried to retain, his self-analysing
introspection even in the midst of his revelry. All paths must be tried,
seeming folly as well as seeming wisdom, to see if they gave any
adequate standard by which the "sons of men" might guide their
conduct, any pathway to the "chief good" which was the object of
the seeker's quest.

4. *I made me great works*] The verse may be either a retrospect of
the details of the life of the pleasure-seeker as sketched in the previous
verse, or, as seems more probable, the account of a new experiment in
which the man passed from purely sensual pleasures to the life of what
we know as 'culture,' the pursuit of beauty and magnificence in Art.
Here the writer throws himself into the surroundings of the historical
Solomon. We may venture to refer to Tennyson's *Palace of Art* as
tracing the working out of a like experiment to its inevitable issue. See
Appendix II.

I builded me houses] We think of David's house of cedar (2 Chron.
ii. 3) and the storehouses, oliveyards and vineyards (1 Chron. xxvii.
25—31) which Solomon had inherited, of his own palace, and the house
of the forest of Lebanon and the house for Pharaoh's daughter, which he
built (1 Kings vii. 1—9), of Tadmor and Hamath and Beth-horon and
Baalath, the cities in far off lands which owned him as their founder
(2 Chron. viii. 3—6). It is significant, on any theory of authorship,
that we find no reference to Solomon's work in building "the house of
the Lord." That was naturally outside the range of the experiments in
search of happiness and too sacred to be mentioned in connexion with
them here, either by the king himself or by the writer who personates
him. On the assumption of personation the writer may have drawn his
pictures of kingly state from the palaces and parks of the Ptolemies, including the botanical and zoological gardens connected with the Museum
at Alexandria, or from those of the Persian kings at Susa or Persepolis.

I planted me vineyards] Of these one, that of Baal-hamon, has been
immortalised by its mention in the Song of Solomon (viii. 11). It
was planted with the choicest vine, and the value of its produce esti-
mated at a thousand pieces of silver. Engedi seems also to have been
famous for its vineyards (Song Sol. i. 14).

5. *I made me gardens and orchards*] The latter word, originally
Persian, and found only in the O. T. in this book, in Song Sol. iv. 13,
and Nehem. ii. 8, is the "paradise" of Xenophon, of later Rabbinic
writings and of the New Testament (Luke xxiii. 43; 2 Cor. xii. 4). It
indicates what we call a park, with flowing streams and shady groves and
fruit trees, and deer feeding on the fresh green grass, and doves flitting
through the trees, such as seemed to the Eastern imagination the fittest

and orchards, and I planted trees in them of all *kind of* fruits: I made me pools of water, to water therewith the 6 wood that bringeth forth trees: I got *me* servants and 7 maidens, and had servants born in *my* house; also I had

type of the highest blessedness. The whole scenery of the Song of Solomon is such a garden, planted with pomegranates and pleasant fruits, spikenards and camphire, calamus and cinnamon, and trees of frankincense, and lilies (Song Sol. iv. 13—15, vi. 2). The pools of Solomon at Etam, on the south-west of Bethlehem, described by Josephus (*Ant.* VIII. 7. 3) still preserve the memory of such a "paradise." Other traces of these surroundings of the palaces of Jewish kings are found in the history of Naboth's vineyard, where the "garden of herbs" can hardly be thought of as merely a "kitchen garden" (1 Kings xxi. 2) and in the garden of Zedekiah (Jer. lii. 7).

all kind of fruits] The horticulture of Palestine included the apple, the fig, the pomegranate, the date, the caper-tree, nuts, almonds, raisins and mandrakes. The account is in strict keeping with the character of the king who spake of trees "from the cedar that is in Lebanon to the hyssop on the wall" (1 Kings iv. 33).

6. *I made me pools of water*] Those at Etam have been mentioned above. Besides these we have the fish-pools of Heshbon (Song Sol. vii. 4), the pool of the king (Neh. ii. 14), possibly also, the pools of Siloam (John ix. 7), and Beth-esda (John v. 2). In Palestine, as in India, these large tanks or reservoirs of water, as meeting the necessities of the climate, were among the favourite works of kingly munificence. Stress is laid on the fact that they were not for beauty only, but for service in irrigating the extensive park.

the wood that bringeth forth trees] Better, "**a grove making trees to bud**," *i.e.* in the language of modern gardening, a "nursery" for young trees.

7. *I got me servants and maidens*] Better, **I bought.** The picture of Oriental state was incomplete without this element, and the slave trade, of which the Midianites were the chief representatives in the patriarchal history (Gen. xxxvii. 28), had probably been carried on without intermission, and supplied both the household and the harem of Solomon. In the Cushi of 2 Sam. xviii. 21, in his namesake of Jer. xxxvi. 14, in Ebedmelech, the Cushite, or Ethiopian, of Jer. xxxviii. 7, we have instances of the presence of such slaves in the royal households. The history of every ancient nation shews the universality of the traffic. Of these slaves each great household had two classes: (1) those "bought with money," men of other races, captives in war, often, probably, negroes (Jer. xxxviii. 7) who were employed in the more menial offices (Gen. xi. 11, 12, 23), and (2) those born in the house (Gen. xiv. 14, xv. 3; Jer. ii. 14), the 'sons of the handmaids' (Exod. xxiii. 12), who rose into more confidential service, the οἰκογενεῖς of the Greeks, the *vernae* of the Latins. On the assumption that the book was written under the Ptolemies, their court would present the same features in an even more conspicuous manner.

8—2

great possessions of great and small cattle above all that
8 were in Jerusalem before me: I gathered me also silver
and gold, and the peculiar treasure of kings and of the
provinces: I gat me *men* singers and *women* singers, and
the delights of the sons of men, *as* musical instruments,

great and small cattle] Better, **oxen and sheep**. The daily provision
for Solomon's household (1 Kings iv. 22) gives some idea of the mag-
nitude of his flocks and herds. See also 1 Chron. xxvii. 29; 1 Kings
v. 3.

8. *I gathered me also silver and gold*] Here also we find a counterpart in what is recorded of the wealth of Solomon, the ships of Hiram
that brought gold from Ophir, to the amount of 420 talents (1 Kings
ix. 28), the gifts from the queen of Sheba (1 Kings x. 1), the total
revenue of 666 talents (1 Kings x. 15), the 200 targets and 300 shields
of beaten gold, and the throne of gold and ivory and the drinking vessels
of the house of the forest of Lebanon, and the silver that was in Jerusalem as stones (1 Kings x. 16—27).

the peculiar treasure of kings and of the provinces] The words may point
to the special gifts which came to Solomon by way of tribute from other
lands, from Seba and Sheba (Ps. lxxii. 10), from the "kings of Arabia
and the governors of the country" (1 Kings ix. 15, x. 27). Many commentators, however, see in the phrase a description of the treasures of
Solomon as being such as were the special possessions of sovereign
rulers and sovereign states as distinct from the wealth of private citizens.
The word for "province" may be noted as a comparatively late word,
hardly coming into use till the time of the Captivity (Lam. i. 1 ; Ezek.
xix. 8), and prominent chiefly in the books of the Persian period,
Ezra, Nehemiah, Esther and Daniel. It probably designates here the
twelve districts into which Solomon divided his empire (1 Kings iv.
7—19).

men singers and women singers] The mention of women shews that
the singers meant are not those connected with the choir of the Temple,
but those who, as in the speech of Barzillai (2 Sam. xix. 35), figured at
state banquets. These women, as in Isai. xxiii. 6, were commonly taken
from the class of harlot aliens, and as such were condemned by the
counsel of the wise of heart (Ecclus. ix. 4). For the general use of
music at feasts, comp. Isai. v. 11, 12; Amos vi. 5; Ecclus. xxxii. 5, 6,
xlix. 1.

the delights of the sons of men] The use of the word in Song Sol.
vii. 6 leaves little doubt that the phrase is an euphemism for sensual
pleasures, and as such it helps to determine the meaning of the words
that follow.

musical instruments, and that of all sorts] The Hebrew substantive,
which is not found elsewhere, is first given in the singular and then in
the plural, as an emphatic way of expressing multitude, and has been
very variously interpreted, as meaning, with the A.V., following Luther,

and that of all sorts. So I was great, and increased more 9
than all that were before me in Jerusalem: also my wisdom remained with me. And whatsoever mine eyes de- 10
sired I kept not from them, I withheld not my heart from
any joy; for my heart rejoiced in all my labour: and this
was my portion of all my labour. Then I looked on all the 11

---

a "musical instrument," or with the Vulgate "cups," or with the LXX.
"cup-bearers," or a "bath," or "heaps" of treasure, or a "chariot," or
a "palanquin," or even "male and female demons." Most modern
scholars however agree, though differing as to its etymology, some finding
its root-meaning in "couch," and some in the "female breast," and
others in "captives taken in war," in rendering it as a "concubine."
This agrees, it is obvious, with the context and with what is recorded of
Solomon's seraglio with its thousand inmates (Song Sol. vi. 8; 1 Kings
xi. 3). It was not likely, we may add, that so characteristic a feature
in that monarch's prodigal excesses should have been altogether passed
over in a picture so elaborate. "Musical instruments," it may be added,
would have formed a somewhat poor climax to the long catalogue of
kingly luxuries. The interpolated *"as"* should be omitted.

9. *I was great, and increased*] There is something significant in
the repetition of the formula of ch. i. 16. The king had surpassed
all others in wisdom, he was now surpassing all others in magnificence.

also my wisdom remained with me] The thought expressed seems
to be, as in verse 3, that the seeker, though he plunged into the pleasures
of a sensual life, was never altogether their slave. They were for him
experiments which he watched as with an intellectual impartiality. Like
Goethe, he analysed his voluptuousness, and studied his own faculties
of enjoyment.

10. *whatsoever mine eyes desired*] From such a life the idea of self-
denial, even of self-control, was absolutely excluded. Money and
power were but means to the end, and the end proposed was the
gratification of the "desire of the eyes," not identified with the "lust of
the flesh," but closely allied to it (1 John ii. 16), in all its restless cravings.
It was not altogether a fruitless effort. Such joy as these things could
bring he had in abundant measure. It was for a time his "portion."
Like the rich man in the parable of Luke xvi. 25 he had his "good
things," and could not complain that the experiment failed as through
imperfect apparatus. He also was tasting of the "tree of knowledge
of good and evil," and found that it was "good for food, and pleasant
to the eyes, and a tree to be desired to make one wise" (Gen.
iii. 6).

11. *Then I looked*] Here also, however, the result was as before.
There came the afterthought which scrutinised the enjoyments and found
them wanting. The pursuit of pleasure was as unsatisfying as the
pursuit of knowledge. Like others who have trodden the same path,
he had to confess that

works that my hands had wrought, and on the labour that I
had laboured to do: and behold, all *was* vanity and vexation of spirit, and *there was* no profit under the sun.

12   And I turned myself to behold wisdom, and madness,
and folly: for what *can* the man *do* that cometh after
13 the king? *even* that which hath been already done.   Then
I saw that wisdom excelleth folly, as far as light excelleth

> "Medio de fonte leporum
> Surgit amari aliquid."

> " E'en from the centre of the fount of joys
> There springs an element of bitterness."
> LUCRET., *De Rer. Nat.* IV. 1127.

All was vanity and **feeding on the wind.**   There was no real "profit"
(see note on chap. i. 3) that could take its place among his permanent
possessions, no surplus to his credit on the balance-sheet of life.   In the
more solemn words of Matt. xvi. 26, "What is a man profited if he
shall gain the whole world, and lose his own soul?" we have substantially
the same teaching.

12.   *I turned myself to behold wisdom, and madness, and folly*]   We
enter on yet another phase of the life of the seeker after happiness.   He
falls back with a cynical despair, when mere pleasure left him a prey to
satiety and ennui, upon his former study of human nature in its contrasted developments of wisdom, and madness, and folly (see note on
chap. i. 17).

what can the man do that cometh after the king?]   Literally, **What is
the man**......The words are apparently a kind of proverb.   No other
child of man could try the experiment under more promising conditions
than a king like the Solomon of history, and therefore the answer to the
question, What can such a man be or do? is simply (if we follow the
construction of the A. V.) **"Even that which men did before."**   He
shall tread the same weary round with the same unsatisfying results.
The verse is, however, obscure, and has been very variously rendered.
So (1) the LXX., following another text, gives "What man will follow
after counsel in whatsoever things they wrought it;" (2) the Vulgate,
" What is man, said I, that he can follow the King, his Maker;" and
(3) many modern interpreters. "What can the man do that comes after
the king, whom they made long ago?" *i.e.* Who can equal the time-
honoured fame of Solomon?

13.   *I saw that wisdom excelleth folly*]   Better, as keeping up, in the
English as in the Hebrew, the characteristic word of the book, **There
is profit in wisdom more than in folly,** and so in the second clause.
Something then had been gained by the experience.   In language like
that of the Stoics he sings the praises of wisdom.   Even the wisdom
that brings sorrow (ch. i. 13) is better than the mirth of fools.   A man
is conscious of being more truly man when he looks before and after,
and knows how to observe.   Light is, after all, better than darkness,

darkness. The wise *man*'s eyes *are* in his head; but the 14
fool walketh in darkness: and I myself perceived also
that one event happeneth to them all. Then said I in my 15
heart, As it happeneth to the fool, so it happeneth even to
me; and why was I then more wise? Then I said in my

even if it only shews us that we are treading the path that leads to
nothingness. The human heart obeys its instincts when it cries out with
Aias,

ἐν δὲ φάει καὶ ὄλεσσον.

"And if our fate be death, give light, and let us die."

HOM. *Il.* XVII. 647.

14. *The wise man's eyes are in his head*] The figurative language is
so much of the nature of an universal parable that we need hardly look
to any special source for it, but we are at least reminded of those that
"walk on still in darkness," who have eyes and yet "see not" in any
true sense of seeing (Isai. vi. 10). In Prov. xvii. 24 we have the opposite form of the same thought: "The eyes of a fool are in the ends of
the earth." Comp. also John xi. 10, xii. 33.

and I myself perceived also] Better, **And yet I myself perceived.**
The thought of verse 13 which had given an apparent resting-place for
the seeker, is traversed by another which sends him once more adrift.
Wisdom is better than folly. True, but for how long? With an emphasized stress on his own personal reflections, he goes on, "Yes, I
myself, learning it for myself, and not as a topic of the schools, saw
that there is one event for the wise and for the fool." In a few short
years the difference in which the former exults will vanish, and both
will be on the same level. So sang the Epicurean poet:

"Omnes una manet nox,
Et calcanda semel via lethi."

"One dark black night awaits us all;
One path of death we all must tread."

HOR. *Od.* I. 28. 15.

15. *why was I then more wise?*] Better, **Why have I been wise now
overmuch?** The very wisdom of the seeker might lead him to see
that he has not only been wiser than others, but wiser than it was
wise to be. The last word is almost identical with the "profit" which
occurs so frequently. He found that he had a surplus of wisdom, and
that it was but surplusage. We seem to hear an echo of the Μηδὲν
ἀγὰν, the *Ne quid nimis* ("Nothing in excess") of Greek and Roman
sages. So, with the same Hebrew word, we have in chap. vii. 16, "Be
not righteous over much." So it was that the sentence of 'Vanity' was
once more written on wisdom as well as folly. It is not without significance that the man feels the bitterness of the sentence, because, even
in his wisdom, he, like the Stoics, had been egoistic. That he and the
fool, the man of large discourse, and the man to whom culture was an

16 heart, that this also *is* vanity. For *there is* no remembrance of the wise more than of the fool for ever; seeing *that* which now *is, in* the days to come shall all be forgotten.
17 And how dieth the wise *man?* as the fool. Therefore I hated life; because the work that is wrought under the sun

unknown word, should die the same death, this made him curse his destiny.

16. *there is no remembrance of the wise*] More accurately, **For the wise man as for the fool there is no remembrance for ever**, the last two words being emphatic, almost as if intentionally calling in question the teaching of Ps. cxii. 6, that "the righteous shall be had in everlasting remembrance." The assertion seems at first too sweeping. There are sages, we say, who live yet in the memory of men whose names the world will not willingly let die. Practically, however, as regards the influence of the desire for posthumous fame as a motive, the number of such names is inappreciably small, even with the manifold resources of monuments and written records. The scribes and doctors, the artists and the poets of one age are forgotten in the next, and only here or there can any man be bold to say with Bacon that he commits his memory "to the care of future ages." (See note on ch. i. 11.) Even a biographical dictionary is often but as the sepulchre of the mouldering remains of reputations that have been long since dead, and their place knoweth them no more. Then, as in later days, there were those who substituted the permanence of fame for that of personal being, and the **Debater,** with his incisive question shatters the unsubstantial fabric.

And how dieth the wise man? As the fool] Literally, "**with the fool,**" as if in partnership with him, sharing the same lot. Better, perhaps, as an exclamation, not a question, "**How dieth the wise man with** (= as) **the fool.** The absence of any hope of an immortality beyond that of fame has been already implied. The present clause brings before us the manner and circumstances of death. We stand, as it were, by the two death-beds, of the wise and of the fool, and note the same signs of the end, the same glazed eye, the same death-dew on the brow, the same failing power of thought. The picture of chap. xii. 1—6 is true of both. The seeker had apparently never stood by the death-bed of one whose face was lit up, and, as it were, transfigured by a "hope full of immortality." Here also we may trace in the later personator of Solomon a deliberate protest against what seemed to him the teaching of Ecclesiastes (Wisd. ii. 1—9).

17. *Therefore I hated life*] Better, **And I hated.** Of such a temper, the extremest form of pessimism, suicide would seem the natural and logical outcome. In practice, however, the sages who have thus moralized, from Koheleth to Schopenhauer, have found life worth living for, even when they were proving that it was hateful. Even the very utterance of the thought has been a relief, or, like Hamlet, they have been deterred by the vague terror of the "something after death"

is grievous unto me: for all *is* vanity and vexation of spirit. Yea, I hated all my labour which I *had* taken under the 18 sun: because I should leave it unto the man that shall be after me. And who knoweth whether he shall be a wise 19 *man* or a fool? yet shall he have rule over all my labour where*in* I have laboured, and where*in* I have shewed myself wise under the sun. This *is* also vanity. Therefore I went 20 about to cause my heart to despair of all the labour which I

which their scepticism cannot quite shake off. The actual self-murderers are those who cannot weave their experiences into poems and confessions, and find the burden of life, including its sin and shame, more than they can bear. It may be questioned whether mere weariness of life, able to find vent for itself in verse or prose, has ever led to suicide. The man, as here, seems to come to the very verge of it, and then draws back. It is suggestive that in the history of Greek and Roman philosophy suicide was more frequent and more honoured among the Stoics than the Epicureans (Zeller, *Stoics and Epic.* 'c. xii.). The recurrence of the burden "vanity and **feeding upon wind**" rings, as it were, the death-knell of life and hope.

18. *because I should leave it unto the man that shall be after me*] The history of the great ones of the earth presents not a few parallel utterances. Mazarin walks through the galleries of his palace and says to himself, "*Il faut quitter tout cela*." Frederick William IV. of Prussia turns to his friend Bunsen as they stand on the terrace at Potsdam, and says, as they look out on the garden, "*Das auch, das soll ich lassen*," ("This too I must leave behind me".) The thought recurs again and again (chs. iv. 8, v. 14, vi. 2).

19. *who knoweth whether he shall be a wise man*] We note in this rather the utterance of a generalized experience than, as some have thought, the special thought of the historical Solomon watching the growth of a character like Rehoboam. No man, whatever care he may take to entail his possessions, can secure an entail of character. And there is something irritating at times,—the writer seems to hint, almost maddening,—in the thought that whatever may be the character of the heir, he will have power to scatter in random waste what has been brought together, as with a purpose and a policy. Lands, libraries, galleries are all liable to be scattered and broken up. So in Ps. xxxix. 6 we have as the doom of the mammon-worshipper, "He heapeth up riches, and cannot tell who shall gather them." So the sting of the message that comes to the Rich Fool of the parable is "Then whose shall those things be which thou hast provided?" Luke xii. 20.

20. *I went about to cause my heart to despair*] The verb for despair is not a common one. Another form of it meets us in the emphatic cry, "There is no hope" of Jer. ii. 25, xviii. 12. What he had felt had made the seeker renounce the very impulse that led to labour. In the phrase "I went about," literally, "**I turned**," we have, as it were, the

21 took under the sun. For there is a man whose labour *is* in wisdom, and in knowledge, and in equity; yet to a man that hath not laboured therein shall he leave it *for* his por-
22 tion. This also *is* vanity and a great evil. For what hath man of all his labour, and of the vexation of his heart, wherein he *hath* laboured under the sun?
23 For all his days *are* sorrows, and his travail grief; yea, his heart taketh not rest in the night. This *is* also vanity.
24 *There is* nothing better for a man, *than* that he should

attitude of one who looks behind him on the road on which so far he has travelled. The retrospect was so dreary that it made the prospect drearier still.

21. *For there is a man*] It is characteristic of the **Debater** that he broods over the same thought, and contemplates it as in a variety of aspects. It is not merely, as in verse 19, that another possessed his heaped up riches who may use them quite otherwise than he would have them used, but that the man who by his wisdom has achieved wealth (for "equity" we should rather read here and in chap. iv. 4, v. 11 "**skill**" or "**success**," the moral character of the success not being here in question) has to leave it to one who has not worked at all, it may be to an alien in blood.

22. *the vexation of his heart*] The word differs from that for which "*feeding on wind*" has been suggested, but is akin to it, and has been, as in i. 17, rendered by *meditation*. Here, perhaps, "**corroding care**" would best convey its meaning.

23. *yea, his heart taketh not rest in the night*] The verse speaks out the experience of the men who labour for that which does not profit. There is no real pleasure, even at the time. The "cares of this world" come together with "the pleasures of this life" (Luke viii. 14). We trace the same yearning after the "sweet sleep" that lies in the far-off past as in ch. v. 12, perhaps also in the "almond tree" of ch. xii. 5. So has the great master-poet portrayed the wakefulness of successful ambition, the yearning for the sleep of the "smoky crib," or even of the ship-boy on the mast, the terrible conclusion,

> "Uneasy lies the head that wears a crown."
>
> SHAKESPEARE, *Henry IV*. Part II. Act III. 1.

No "poppies" or "mandragora" can restore that sleep to the slave of mammon or the worn-out sensualist.

24. *There is nothing better for a man*] The Hebrew, as it stands, gives a meaning which is partly represented by the LXX., "There is no good for a man which he shall eat and drink," as though the simplest form of bodily pleasure were condemned. Almost all interpreters however are agreed in adopting a conjectural emendation, which again in its turn has given rise to two different renderings: (1) "Is it not better (or "Is it not good") for a man to eat and drink...?" or (2) "there is

eat and drink, and *that* he should make his soul enjoy good

nothing good for a man but to eat and drink ..." The two last are of course substantially the same in their teaching, and both express what we may call the higher type of Epicureanism which forms one element of the book. The pursuit of riches, state, luxury, is abandoned for the simple joys that lie within every man's reach, the *"fallentis semita vitae"* of one who has learnt the lesson of regulating his desires. The words "to eat and drink" are closely connected with "enjoying good *in his labour.*" What is praised is not the life of slothful self-indulgence or æsthetic refinement, but that of a man who, though with higher culture, is content to live as simply as the ploughman, or the vinedresser, or artificer. Λάθε βιώσας, "live in the shade," was the Epicurean rule of wisdom. Pleasure was not found in feasts and sensual excess but in sobriety of mind, and the conquest of prejudice and superstition (Diog. Laert. X. I. 132). The real wants of such a life are few, and there is a joy in working for them. Here again the thought finds multiform echoes in the utterances of men who have found the cares and pleasures and pursuits of a more ambitious life unsatisfying. It is significant that the very words "eat and drink" had been used by Jeremiah in describing the pattern life of a righteous king (Jer. xxii. 15). The type of life described is altogether different from that of the lower Epicureans who said "Let us eat and drink, for to-morrow we die" (1 Cor. xv. 32).

So we have one Epicurean poet singing

> "Si non aurea sunt iuvenum simulacra per aedes
> Lampadas igniferas manibus retinentia dextris,
> Lumina nocturnis epulis ut suppeditentur,
> Nec domus argento fulget auroque renidet
> Nec citharae reboant laqueata aurataque templa,
> Cum tamen inter se prostrati in gramine molli
> Propter aquae rivum sub ramis arboris altae
> Non magnis opibus iucunde corpora curant,
> Praesertim cum tempestas adridet et anni
> Tempora conspergunt viridantis floribus herbas."

> "What though no golden statues of fair boys
> With lamp in hand illumine all the house
> And cast their lustre on the nightly feast;
> Nor does their home with silver or with gold
> Dazzle the eye; nor through the ceilèd roof,
> Bedecked with gold, the harps re-echo loud.
> Yet, while reclining on the soft sweet grass
> They lie in groups along the river's bank,
> Beneath the branches of some lofty tree,
> And at small cost find sweet refreshment there,
> What time the season smiles, and spring-tide weeks
> Re-gem the herbage green with many a flower."

LUCRET. *De Rer. Nat.* II. 24—33.

in his labour.   This also I saw, that it *was* from the hand

So Virgil sang:

> "O fortunatos nimium, sua si bona norint,
>   Agricolas,"

and of these good things dwelt chiefly on

> "At secura quies et nescia fallere vita.
>   Dives opum variarum, at latis otia fundis,
>   Speluncae, vivique lacus, et frigida Tempe,
>   Mugitusque boum, mollesque sub arbore somni
>   Non absunt; illic saltus ac lustra ferarum,
>   Et patiens operum exiguoque adsueta juventus,
>   Sacra deum, sanctique patres; extrema per illos
>   Justitia excedens terris vestigia fecit."

> " Ah ! but too happy, did they know their bliss
>   The tillers of the soil !...
>   Their's the calm peace, and life that knows no fraud,
>   Rich in its varied wealth ; and leisure their's
>   In the broad meadows; caves and living lakes
>   And Tempe cool, and lowing of the kine ;
>   Nor want they slumber sweet beneath the trees ;
>   There are the thickets and the wild beasts' haunts,
>   And youth enduring toil and trained to thrift ;
>   There Gods are worshipped, fathers held in awe,
>   And Justice, when she parted from the earth
>   Left there her latest foot-prints."

Georg. II. 467—474.

So Horace, in the same strain:

> "Beatus ille qui procul negotiis,
>   Ut prisca gens mortalium,
>   Paterna rura bubus exercet suis,
>   Solutus omni foenore."

> "Thrice blest is he who free from care
>   Lives now, as lived our fathers old,
>   And free from weight of honoured gold,
>   With his own oxen drives the share
>   O'er fields he owns as rightful heir."

HORACE, *Epod.* II. I.

So Shakespeare once more makes a king echo the teaching of Eccle-siastes :

> "And to conclude: the shepherd's homely curds,
>   His cold thin drink out of his leather bottle,
>   His wonted sleep under a fresh tree's shade,
>   All which secure and sweetly he enjoys,
>   Is far beyond a prince's delicates,
>   His viands sparkling in a golden cup,

of God.   For who can eat, or who else can hasten *hereunto*, 25
more than I?   For *God* giveth to a man that *is* good in his 26

> His body couched in a curious bed,
> When care, mistrust, and treason wait on him."
>
> *Henry VI.*, Part III. Act II. 5.

This also I saw, that it was from the hand of God] In the thought
which is thus expressed, we find, however, something more than an
echo of Greek Epicureanism. The **Debater** recognises a Divine Will
in this apportionment of happiness, just as he had before recognised
that Will in the toil and travail with which the sons of man were
exercised (ch. i. 13). The apparent inequalities are thus, in part at
least, redressed, and it is shewn as the teaching of experience no less
than of the Divine Master, that "a man's life consisteth not in the
abundance of things which he possesseth" (Luke xii. 15).

25. *For who can eat*] The sequence of thought is obscure, and
many commentators follow the LXX. and the Syriac version, as implying an original text which gives a better meaning, **Who can eat and
who can hasten** (*i.e.* be eager in this pursuit of pleasure), or, as some
take the words, **have enjoyment, without Him,** *i.e.* without God. This,
it is obvious, follows on the thought of the preceding verse, that the
calm enjoyment of which it speaks as "good," is "from the hand of
God." Those who keep to the received text give it very different meanings, of which the two most prominent are : (1) that we have, as it were,
the words of the labourer whose lot the **Debater** here admired, "Who
has a right to eat and enjoy himself, if not I?" the thought being parallel
to that of 2 Tim. ii. 6 ("The husbandman that laboureth must be
first partaker of the fruits"); and (2) that the **Debater** speaks in his own
person, "Who could eat or enjoy more than I? Who therefore can
better attest that it is all in vain without the gift of God." On the assumption that the writer was one who had come into contact with Greek
thought, we may trace in this utterance partly the old faith of Israel
reasserting itself and giving a higher sanction to the life of regulated
enjoyment which the Greek teachers counselled, partly, perhaps, the
mingling of Stoic and Epicurean counsels natural in a mind that had
listened to both and attached himself definitely to neither. So in the
Meditations of Aurelius we have like thoughts : πάντα γὰρ ταῦτα θεῶν
βοηθῶν καὶ τύχης δεῖται ("all these things require the help of the Gods
and of Fortune"); and again τὰ τῶν Θεῶν προνοίας μεστὰ ("the works of
the Gods are full of Providence" (*Meditt.* II. 3). Koheleth, of course,
as an Israelite, used the language of the wiser Stoics, like Cleanthes,
and spoke of one God only.

26. *For God giveth*] The word for God, as the italics shew, is
not in the Hebrew, but it is obviously implied, and its non-appearance
justifies the change in the text of the previous verse, which preserves
the sequence of thought unbroken. What we get here is the recognition of what we have learnt to call the moral government of God in
the distribution of happiness. It is found to depend not on outward
but inward condition, and the chief inward condition is the character

sight wisdom, and knowledge, and joy: but to the sinner he giveth travail, to gather and to heap up, that *he* may give to *him that is* good before God. This also *is* vanity and vexation of spirit.

3 To every *thing there is* a season, and a time to every purpose under the heaven:

that God approves. The **Debater** practically confesses that the life of the pleasure-seeker, or the ambitious, or the philosopher seeking wisdom as an end, was not good before God, and therefore failed to bring contentment.

wisdom, and knowledge, and joy] The combination forms an emphatic contrast with ch. i. 18, and marks a step onward in the seeker's progress. There is a wisdom which is not grief, an increase of knowledge which is not an increase of sorrow. We are reminded of the parallel thought which belongs to a higher region of the spiritual life, "The Kingdom of God...is righteousness and peace and joy in the Holy Ghost" (Rom. xiv. 17). Here the lesson is that the man who seeks great things fails to find them, that he who is content with a little with God's blessing on it, finds in that little much. He becomes αὐτάρκης (= self-sufficing)—and has enough.

but to the sinner he giveth travail] The words point to a further perception of a moral order in the midst of the seeming disorders of the world. The fruitless labour of the sinner in heaping up his often ill-gotten gains is not altogether wasted. His treasure passes into hands that make a better use of it than he has done. So we find a like thought in Prov. xxviii. 8, "He that by usury and unjust gains increaseth his substance, he shall gather it for him that will pity the poor," and in Job xxvii. 16, 17, "Though he heap up silver as the dust, and prepare raiment as the clay; he may prepare it, but the just shall put it on, and the innocent shall divide the silver" (comp. Prov. xiii. 22).

This also is vanity] The question which we have to answer is whether this sentence is passed only on the travail of the sinner, as in verse 11, or whether it includes also the measure of joy attainable by him who is "good" in the sight of God. From one point of view the former interpretation gives a preferable meaning, as more in harmony with what immediately precedes. On the other hand, it is characteristic of the cynical pessimism into which the Preacher has, by his own confession, fallen, that he should fall back into his despondency even after a momentary glimpse of a truth that might have raised him from it. The "Two Voices" utter themselves, as in Tennyson's poem, (see Appendix II.) in a melancholy alternation and there comes a time when the simple joys which God gives to the contented labourer, no less than the satiety of the voluptuous and the rich, seem to him but as "vanity and **feeding upon wind**."

CHAPTER III.

1. *To every thing there is a season, and a time to every purpose*] The

A time to be born, and a time to die;   2
A time to plant, and a time to pluck up *that which is*
  planted;
A time to kill, and a time to heal;   3

two Hebrew nouns stand to each other in much the same relation as the Greek χρόνος and καιρός, the former expressing a period of duration, the latter the appointed time at which an event happens. Accepting this view, the words "season" and "time" in the A.V. ought, perhaps, to change places. The thought is one of which we find an echo in the maxim of Pittacus, Καιρὸν γνῶθι—"Know the right season for everything" (Diog. Laert. I. 4, § 6). It is significant, in connexion with the conclusion maintained in the Introduction, Ch. III., that Demetrius Phalereus, the librarian of Ptolemy Philadelphus, wrote a treatise, περὶ καιροῦ, *of opportuneness* (Diog. Laert. v. 5 § 9). So Theognis, (402), Μηδὲν ἄγαν σπεύδειν, καιρὸς δ' ἐπὶ πᾶσιν ἄριστος, "Do nothing in excess, In all we do is the right season precious." So here the thought with which the new section opens is that it is wisdom to do the right thing at the right time, that inopportuneness is the bane of life. The survey of human occupations and interests that follows has a striking parallel in the *Meditations* of Marcus Aurelius (IV. 32), who, from his Stoic standpoint, sees in their perpetual recurrence, evidence of the monotonous iteration of the phenomena of man's life, analogous to that of the phenomena of Nature.

2.   *A time to be born*] Literally, **a time to bear.** It should be noted that in Hebrew MSS. and printed texts, the list of Times and Seasons appears in two parallel columns, as if forming a kind of rhythmical catalogue, what the Greeks called a συστοιχία, or Table of Contrasts. It seems at first strange that the list should begin with events which are (putting aside the exceptional case of suicide) involuntary. It may be, however, that they were chosen for that very reason as representative instances of the fixed order on which the writer dwells. We shrink from the thought of an untimely birth (ch. vi. 3) or an untimely death; we shudder at the thought of accelerating either, or of hindering the former, and yet the other incidents of life have, not less than these, each of them, their appointed season, if only we could discern it.

a time to plant] Human life in its beginning and its end is seen to have a parallel in that of plants. Here also there is a time for sowing, and after the fruits of the earth have been gathered in (this and not a wanton destruction, which would be a violation of the natural order, is clearly meant) to pluck up that the planting may again come. It is, perhaps, over fanciful to make the words include the "planting" and "uprooting" of nations and kingdoms as in Jerem. i. 10. It is significant, however, that the word for "pluck up" is an unusual word, and, where it occurs elsewhere, in the O. T. is used figuratively of the destruction of cities as in Zeph. ii. 4.

3.   *a time to kill, and a time to heal*] The first group had brought

A time to break down, and a time to build *up;*

4   A time to weep, and a time to laugh;

A time to mourn, and a time to dance;

5   A time to cast away stones, and a time to gather stones together;

together natural death and natural birth. This includes in the induction the death which man inflicts in battle or single combat, in attack or self-defence, or in administering justice, and with it the verb that includes all the resources of the healing art which can raise men from all but actual death. Here also there is an appointed order, and man's wisdom lies in accepting it. This, rather than a fatalistic theory ot Necessity, as being what man cannot, even if he will, resist, seems the thought expressed. The wise man knows when to slay and when to heal.

a time to break down, and a time to build up] The grouping reminds us as before of Jerem. i. 10 and may possibly be extended so as to take in a figurative as well as a literal building. We may perhaps trace an allusive reference, if not to the text, yet to the thought which it expresses, in St Paul's language in Gal. ii. 18, "If I build again the things which I destroyed I make myself a transgressor." His wisdom lay in recognising that the "fulness of time" had come for breaking down the old structure of Judaism and building up the new structure of the kingdom of God. Of the mere literal sense we have a striking illustration in the paraphrase of the words of Elisha to Gehazi (2 Kings v. 26) as given in the *Christian Year.*

"Is this a time to plant and build,
Add house to house and field to field?"

4. *a time to weep*] The two couples are naturally grouped together, the first taking in the natural spontaneous expression of individual feeling, the second the more formal manifestation of the feelings in the mourners and wailers of a funeral (Zech. xii. 10, where the same verb is found) and the dancers at a wedding feast. In the parable of the Children in the Market-place our Lord practically inculcates the lesson of the **Debater.** The Scribes who sneered at the fasts of John's disciples, and condemned the disciples of Jesus for not fasting were as the children whose dramatic funerals and weddings were alike out of place and inopportune, and so the true followers after the Wisdom which "is justified of her children," who recognised that the ascetic and the joyous life had each its true time and season, would not weep to their lamenting or dance to their piping (Matt. xi. 16—19).

5. *A time to cast away stones*] The vagueness of the phrase has naturally given rise to conjectural interpretations. It seems obvious that the words cannot be a mere reproduction of verse 4 and therefore that the "casting away" and the "gathering" of stones must refer to something else than pulling down and building. Possibly we may think, with some interpreters, of the practice of covering fertile lands with

A time to embrace, and a time to refrain from embracing;
A time to get, and a time to lose;   6
A time to keep, and a time to cast away;
A time to rent, and a time to sew;   7

stones as practised by an invading army (2 Kings iii. 19) and clearing out the stones of a field or vineyard before planting it (Isai. v. 2). In this case however we fail to see any link uniting the two clauses in the couplet. A possible explanation may be found (as Delitzsch half suggests) in the old Jewish practice, which has passed into the Christian Church, of flinging stones or earth into the grave at a burial, but this leaves the "gathering" unexplained, except so far as it represents the building of a house, and thus contrasts the close of a man's home life with its beginning. In this case the ceremonial of death would be contrasted with the "embracing" of friends or lovers in the second clause.

6. *A time to get, and a time to lose*] The getting or the losing refer primarily, we can scarcely doubt, to what we call property. There are times when it is better and wiser to risk the loss of all we have rather than to set our minds on acquiring more. Something like this lesson we have in our Lord's paradox "whosoever will (wills to) save his life shall lose it, and whosoever will lose his life for my sake shall find it" (Matt. xvi. 25). In earthly, as in heavenly, things it is the note of a wise man that he knows when to be content to lose. So the Satirist condemns the folly of those who are content,

> "Propter vitam vivendi perdere causas."

> "And for mere life to lose life's noblest ends."
> JUVEN. *Sat.* VIII. 84.

a time to keep, and a time to cast away] The second couplet though closely allied with the foregoing is not identical with it. What is brought before us here is "keeping" as distinct from "getting," and the voluntarily casting away (2 Kings vii. 15) what we know we have, as distinct from the loss of a profit more or less contingent. And here too, as life passes on, it presents occasions when now this, now that, is the choice of wisdom. So the sailor, in danger of shipwreck, casts out his cargo, his tackling, the "furniture" of his ship (Acts xxvii. 18, 19, 38).

7. *A time to rent, and a time to sew*] The words are commonly connected with the practice of rending the garments as a sign of sorrow (Gen. xxxvii. 29, 34, xliv. 13; Job i. 20; 2 Sam. i. 2) and sewing them up again when the season of mourning is past and men return again to the routine of their daily life. It is, however, somewhat against this view that it makes this generalisation practically identical with that of verse 4. The symbolic use of "rending a garment" to represent the division of a kingdom, as in the prophecy of Ahijah the Shilonite (1 Kings xi. 30) and therefore of "sewing" for the restoration of unity (so the "seam-

A time to keep silence, and a time to speak;
8   A time to love, and a time to hate;
A time of war, and a time of peace.

less garment" of John xix. 23 has always been regarded as a type of
the unity of Christ's Church) seems to suggest a more satisfying sense.
There are seasons when it is wise to risk or even to cause discord and
division in families (Matt. x. 34, 35) or schism in Church or State, other
seasons when men should strive to restore unity and to be healers of
the breach (Isai. lviii. 12).   In the parable of the New Patch upon the
old Garment we have an instance of an inopportune sewing which does
but make the rent worse (Matt. ix. 16).

a time to keep silence, and a time to speak] Here again the range of
thought has been needlessly limited by interpreters to the silence which
belongs to deep sorrow, of which we have an example in the conduct of
the friends of Job (Job ii. 12, 13), of the want of which in the sons of
the prophets Elisha complained bitterly (2 Kings ii. 3, 5).   This is, of
course, not excluded, but the range of the law is wider, and takes in on
the one hand, the unseasonable talk of the "prating fool" of Prov. x. 8,
and on the other the "word spoken in due season" (Prov. xv. 23), to one
that is weary (Isai. l. 4), the right word at the right time, in the utterance
of which we rightly see a genius akin to inspiration.   If it is true at times
that speech is silvern and silence golden, there are times when the con-
verse also is true, when the word in season is like "apples of gold (= perhaps, oranges) in a basket of silver" (Prov. xxv. 11).

8.   *A time to love, and a time to hate*] Greek thought again supplies
us with a parallel,

> ἡμεῖς δὲ πῶς οὐ γνωσόμεσθα σωφρονεῖν;
> ἐγὼ δ', ἐπίσταμαι γὰρ ἀρτίως ὅτι
> ὅ τ' ἐχθρὸς ἡμῖν ἐς τοσόνδ' ἐχθαρτέος,
> ὡς καὶ φιλήσων αὖθις, ἔς τε τὸν φίλον
> τοσαῦθ' ὑπουργῶν ὠφελεῖν βουλήσομαι,
> ὡς αἰὲν οὐ μενοῦντα.

> "Shall not we too learn
> Our lesson of true wisdom? I indeed
> Have learnt but now that we should hate a foe
> Only so far as one that yet may love,
> And to a friend just so much help I'll give
> As unto one that will not always stay."
> Soph. *Aias*, 680—686.

a time of war, and a time of peace] The change in the Hebrew, as in
the English, from verbs in the infinitive to substantives is probably intended
to emphasize the completion of the list.   The words are of course closely
connected with the "love" and "hate" of the preceding clause, but differ
in referring to the wider range of national relations.   Here also the
wisdom of a king or statesman lies in discerning the opportuneness of

What profit *hath* he that worketh in *that* where*in* he 9
laboureth?

I have seen the travail, which God hath given to the sons 10
of men to be exercised in it.   He hath made every *thing* 11
beautiful in his time: also he hath set the world in their

war or peace, in seeing when the maxim *"si vis pacem para bellum"*
is applicable or inapplicable.

It may be well to repeat here what was said at the outset in reference
to this list of times and seasons, that the idea of a Necessity, Fate,
Predestination, which many interpreters, bent on finding traces of a
Stoic fatalism, have read into the teaching of the section, is really
foreign to the writer's thoughts.   That which he insists on is the thought
that the circumstances and events of life form part of a Divine Order,
are not things that come at random, and that wisdom, and therefore
such a measure of happiness as is attainable, lies in adapting ourselves
to the order and accepting the guidance of events in great things and
small, while shame and confusion come from resisting it.   The lesson
is in fact identical with one very familiar to us at once in the commonest
of all proverbs, "Take time by the forelock;" "Time and tide wait for
no man," and in a loftier strain,

> "There is a tide in the affairs of men
> Which, taken at the flood, leads on to fortune;
> Omitted, all the remnant of their lives
> Is bound in shallows and in miseries."
>
> SHAKESPEARE, *Julius Caesar*, IV. 3.

It is well to remember such counsels of prudence.   It is well also to
remember that a yet higher wisdom bids us in the highest work "to be
instant, in season, out of season" (εὐκαίρως, ἀκαίρως, 2 Tim. iv. 2).

9.   *What profit hath he that worketh?*]   The long induction is
completed, and yet is followed by the same despairing question as that
of ch. i. 3, asked as from a stand-point that commands a wider
horizon.   Does not this very thought of a right season for every action
increase the difficulty of acting?   Who can be sure that he has found
the season?   The chances of failure are greater than the chances of
success.

10.   *I have seen the travail, which God hath given*]   Better perhaps,
I have seen the labour, or **the business.**   As before, in the preceding
verse, the thinker, once back in the old groove of thought, repeats
himself, and we have the very words of ch. i. 13, but, as before, here
also developed by a wider experience.   In this feeling after the right
"season" for each act, this craving for a harmony between man's will
and the divine order, he recognises a divinely implanted instinct which
yet finds no full satisfaction.

11.   *He hath made every thing beautiful in his time*]   Better, as
removing the ambiguity of the possessive pronoun in modern English
ears, "in **its** time."   The thinker rests for a time in the primeval faith
of Israel that all things were created "very good" (Gen. i. 31), in the

9—2

heart, so that no man can find out the work that God
12 maketh from the beginning to the end. I know that *there
is* no good in them, but for *a man* to rejoice, and to do

Stoic thought of a divine system, a *Cosmos* of order and of beauty, of
a plan, even in the development of human history, in which all things
work together for good. So even in Lucretius,

> "Certa suo quia tempore semina rerum
> Cum confluxerunt, patefit quodcumque creatur."

> "So when the germs of things in season due
> Have met together, all creation's work
> Is to our eyes made open."   *De Rer. Nat.* I. 176.

What hinders it from being a final resting-place of thought is that his
knowledge is confined within narrow limits. He sees but a fragment,
and the "most part" of the Divine Work "is hid."

also he hath set the world in their heart] The Hebrew for "world"
(primarily, "**the hidden**") is that which, in its adverbial or adjectival
use, constantly appears in the English Version as "for ever," "perpetual," "everlasting," "always," "eternal," and the like. No other
meaning but that of a duration, the end or beginning of which is hidden
from us, and which therefore is infinite, or, at least, indefinite, is ever
connected with it in the Hebrew of the Old Testament, and this is its
uniform sense in this book (chs. i. 4, 10, ii. 16, iii. 14, ix. 6, xii. 5).
In post-Biblical Hebrew it passes into the sense of the Greek αἰών, for
the *age*, or the *world* considered in its relation to time and, on the theory
of authorship adopted in the *Introduction* there is, perhaps, an approximation to that sense here. We must however translate, as the nearest
equivalent, **He hath set eternity** (or, **the everlasting**) **in their heart.**
The thought expressed is not that of the hope of an immortality, but
rather the sense of the Infinite which precedes it, and out of which at
last it grows. Man has the sense of an order perfect in its beauty.
He has also the sense of a purpose working through the ages from everlasting to everlasting, but "beginning" and "end" are alike hidden
from him and he fails to grasp it. In modern language he sees not
"the beginning and the end," the whence and the whither, of his own
being, or of that of the *Cosmos*. He is oppressed with what German
thinkers have named the *Welt-Schmerz*, the world-sorrow, the burden
of the problems of the infinite and unfathomable Universe. Here
again we have an echo of Stoic language as reproduced by Cicero,
"*Ipse autem homo natus est ad mundum contemplandum et imitan-
dum*" (*de Nat. Deor.* II. 14. 37). All interpretations resting on later
ideas of the "world," as meaning simply the material universe, or
worldly pleasures, or worldly wisdom, have to be rejected as inconsistent with lexical usage. By some writers, however, the word, with
a variation in the vowels, has been taken as itself meaning "wisdom,"
but though this signification is found in a cognate word in Arabic, it is
unknown in Hebrew.

12. *for a man to rejoice, and to do good*] There is no instance in O. T.

good in his life. And also that every man should eat and 13
drink, and enjoy the good of all his labour, it *is* the gift of
God. I know that, whatsoever God doeth, it shall be for 14
ever: nothing can be put to it, nor any thing taken from it :
and God doeth *it*, that *men* should fear before him. That 15
which hath been, *is* now; and *that* which *is* to be hath
already been; and God requireth that which is past.

language of the phrase "do good" being used, like the Greek εὖ πράττειν,
in the sense of "prospering," or "enjoying one's self," and in ch.
vii. 20 it can only have its full ethical meaning, such as it has in Ps.
xxxiv. 14, xxxvii. 3; Isai. xxxviii. 3. On the whole, therefore, we are
led to assign that meaning to it here. Over and above the life of
honest labour and simple joys which had been recognised as good
before, the seeker has learnt that "honesty is the best policy," that
"doing good" (the term is more comprehensive in its range than our
"beneficence") is in some sense the best way of getting good. It is
not the highest ethical view of the end of life, but it was an advance on
his previous conclusion.

13. *And also that every man*] The addition of this clause confirms
the interpretation just given of the "doing good" of the preceding verse.
Had that meant simply enjoyment, this clause would have been an idle
repetition. As it is, "doing good" takes its place, as it did with the
nobler Epicureans, among the elements of happiness. So Epicurus
himself taught that "it is not possible to live happily without also living
wisely, and nobly, and justly" (Diog. Laert. x. 1, § 140).

14. *I know that, whatsoever God doeth*] We ask once again whether
we are brought face to face with the thought of an iron destiny immutably
fixing even the seeming accidents of life, and excluding man's volition
from any share in them, or whether the writer speaks of an order which
men may, in the exercise of their freedom, transgress. And the answer, as
before, is that the **Debater**, while he recognises man's freedom, has come
to see a purpose and an order even in those accidents. So Epicurus
himself taught that it was better to hold even the popular belief as to the
Gods than to be in bondage to the dogma of a destiny (Diog. Laert. x.
1, § 134). The Eternal Law fulfils itself, "whether men will hear or
whether they will forbear." They cannot add to it or take from it, but
they retain the power of obeying or resisting it. It partakes so far of
the character which was afterwards ascribed to a special revelation
(Rev. xxii. 18, 19).

God doeth it, that men should fear before him], There is a profound
psychological truth in the thought thus expressed. Men may dream that
they can propitiate or change an arbitrary will, but no reverential awe,
no fear of God, is so deep as that which rises from the contemplation of
a Righteousness that does not change. So, in like manner, the unchange-
ableness of the Divine Will is made a ground of confidence and hope in
the midst of perturbations (Mal. iii. 6).

15. *God requireth that which is past*] Better, **seeks after that**

16   And moreover I saw under the sun the place of judgment,
that wickedness *was* there; and the place of righteousness,
17 *that* iniquity *was* there.   I said in mine heart, God shall
judge the righteous and the wicked: for *there is* a time there
for every purpose and for every work.

which is put to flight. The old thought of the uniformity of sequence
in nature and in history which had before seemed oppressive in its
monotony, has been balanced by the thought of God's perfection and
the beauty of His order, and by the "fear" which grows out of it. It is
followed up by a new aspect of the same truth. The past is thought
of as vanishing, "put to flight," receding into the dim distance. It might
seem to be passing into the abyss of oblivion, but God **recalls** it (this
is obviously the meaning of "require" as used by the translators of
the A. V. in its strict etymological sense), brings back the same order,
or an analogous order of events, and so history repeats itself. The
strange rendering adopted by the Targum and some modern interpreters, "*God seeks the persecuted,*" *i.e.* visits and protects them,
though tenable as a translation, introduces an idea quite foreign to
the train of thought.

16. *I saw under the sun the place of judgment*] The Hebrew gives
slightly different forms of the same noun, so as to gain the emphasis,
without the monotony, of iteration, where the A.V. has the needless
variation of "wickedness" and "iniquity." Either word will do, but
it should be the same in both clauses. We enter on another phase of
the seeker's thoughts. The moral disorder of the world, its oppressive
rulers, its unjust judges, its religious hypocrisies, oppress him even more
than the failure of his own schemes of happiness. In part the feeling implies a step out of selfishness, sympathy with the sufferers, the perception of what ought to be, as contrasted with what is, and therefore an
upward step in the seeker's progress. In the "place of judgment" we
may see the tribunal where justice is administered: in that of "righteousness" the councils, secular, or, it may be, ecclesiastical, in which men
ought to have been witnesses for the divine law of Righteousness and
were self-seeking and ambitious.

17. *God shall judge the righteous and the wicked*] The words "I
said in my heart" introduce this as the first thought that rises unbidden
at the sight of the wrong-doing in the world. It was, as it were, an
immediate intuitive judgment, as distinguished from those which are
introduced by "I returned," or "I considered" (chap. iv. 1, 4, 7, 15).
In the emphatic "there is a time *there*," we may, perhaps, trace, as in
the grand abruptness of Medea's blessing on her children,

Εὐδαιμονοῖτον· ἀλλ' ἐκεῖ· τὰ δ' ἐνθάδε
Πάτηρ ἀφείλετ'.

"All good be with you!—but it must be *there;*
Here it is stolen from you by your sire."
EURIP. *Med.* 1065.

or in Plato, ἡ ἐκεῖσε πορεία, (= "the journey *thither*" *Phaed.* p. 107 *d*),

I said in my heart concerning the estate of the sons of 18
men, that God might manifest them, and that *they* might
see that they themselves are beasts. For that which befalleth 19
the sons of men befalleth beasts; even one thing befalleth
them: as the one dieth, so dieth the other; yea, they have

and in the "*that* world" of Luke xx. 35, a passing belief in a judgment
after death as redressing the wrongs of earth, soon to be, for a time, at
least, traversed and overclouded by the sceptical thoughts with which
the writer had come in contact. It is, however, possible that "there"
may refer to the unfathomed depths of the divine Judgment which
works, through long delay, at its appointed time, and in this case the
thought finds a parallel in the complaint and confession of Ps. lxxiii.
17—28. The one immediate conviction is, however, balanced in the
conflict of thought through which the **Debater** is passing, by another
which seems incompatible with it.

18. *I said in mine heart*] The word "estate" expresses fairly the
meaning of the Hebrew noun, which may be rendered "word,"
"matter," or "subject." In the next clause for "that God might
manifest them," we may better read, **that God might separate, sift, or
try them**, *i.e.* in modern phrase, He leaves the disorders of the world
unredressed, as part of man's probation. This comes into the heart of
the seeker as a partial explanation of the disorders noted in verse 16.

that they might see that they themselves are beasts] The pronoun in
the original has, as in the English version, the strong emphasis of
iteration, that **they are beasts, they by themselves.** The thought
implied is that without a higher faith of some kind—whether in the
Divine Righteousness or in Immortality, is not yet defined—Man
stands, as having only an animal life, on the same level as other
animals. In the words of an old English poet :

> "Unless above himself he can
> Erect himself, how poor a thing is man !"

19. *that which befalleth the sons of men*] More accurately, **chance
are the sons of men; chance is the beast; one chance is to both of
them.** The thought is emphasized by the threefold iteration of the depressing word. As so often throughout the book, we have an echo,
almost a verbal translation, of a Greek saying. So Solon had said to
Crœsus in a discourse which breathes the very spirit of Ecclesiastes
(Herod. i. 32), πᾶν ἐστι ἄνθρωπος συμφορή ("man is altogether a
chance").

as the one dieth, so dieth the other] The words are not without a
partial parallel in the more devotional literature of Israel. The writer
of Ps. xlix. had given utterance to the thought "man that is in honour
...is like the beasts that perish." With him, however, this was affirmed
only of those that "trust in their wealth," the triumphant, self-indulgent evildoers, and it was balanced by the belief that "God would
redeem" his soul "from the power of the grave." Here the same
thought is generalised in the tones of a half cynical despair, all the

all one breath; so that a man hath no preeminence above a
20 beast: for all *is* vanity.   All go unto one place; all are of
21 the dust, and all turn to dust again.   Who knoweth the

more striking if we assume that the belief in immortality, as afterwards
developed in the creed of Pharisaism, was at the time gaining a more
definite form among the writer's countrymen. It may be traceable either
to the reaction against the germs of Pharisaism which was afterwards
represented by the Sadducees, or, as seems more probable from the
general tone and character of the book, to the influence of the Greek
thought, such as was embodied in the teaching of Epicurus and Pyrrho,
with which the writer had come in contact.

yea, they have all one breath]   The word is the same as the "spirit"
of verse 23, and seems deliberately chosen with reference to the record
of Gen. ii. 7.   The writer asks, What after all was that "breath
of life?"   Was there not a like "breath of life" in every beast of the
field?   It is significant that this is the only passage in the Old Testament in which the word is used definitely for the living principle of
brutes, though we find it in Gen. vi. 17, vii. 15, 22; Ps. civ. 30 for the
life which is common both to them and man.   Commonly, as in Job
xii. 10, xxxii. 8, it is contrasted with the "soul" which represents their
lower life.

a man hath no preeminence above a beast]   This then was the conclusion to which the thinker was led by the materialism which he had
imbibed from his Greek or Sadducean teachers.   Put aside the belief in
the prolongation of existence after death, that what has been begun here
may be completed, and what has gone wrong here may be set right,
and man is but a more highly organised animal, the "cunningest of
Nature's clocks" (to use Huxley's phrase), and the high words which
men speak as to his greatness are found hollow.   They too are
"vanity."   He differs from the brutes around him only, or chiefly,
in having, what they have not, the burden of unsatisfied desires, the
longing after an eternity which after all is denied him.

20.   *All go unto one place*]   The "place" thus spoken of is not the
Sheol of the Hebrews or the *Hades* of the Greeks, which implied, however vaguely, some notion of a shadowy disembodied existence, for the
souls of men as distinct from those of brutes, but simply the earth as at
once the mother, the nourisher, and the sepulchre of every form of life.
So Lucretius, as a disciple of Epicurus, speaks (*De Rer. Nat.* v. 259) of
earth as being

"Omniparens eadem rerum commune sepulcrum."

"The mother and the sepulchre of all."

all are of the dust]   There is an obviously deliberate reference to the
narrative of the Creation in Gen. ii. 7.   To those who did not see
below the surface, it seemed to affirm, as it did to the Sadducee, the
denial of a life to come.   "Dust thou art and unto dust shalt thou
return" was the sentence passed, they might say, as on the brute
creation, so on man also (Gen. iii. 19).

spirit of man that goeth upward, and the spirit of the beast
that goeth downward to the earth? Wherefore I perceive 22
that *there is* nothing better, than that a man should rejoice
in his own works; for that *is* his portion: for who shall
bring him to see what shall be after him?

21. *Who knoweth the spirit of man that goeth upward*] The words
imply a strictly sceptical rather than a negative answer. They do not
actually deny, still less do they affirm, as some have thought, that the
spirit of man does ascend to a higher life, while that of the brute
returns to dust. This would indeed be inconsistent with the whole
context, and the *consensus* of the LXX., the Vulgate, the Targum, and
the Syriac versions, all of which give "Who knoweth whether the
spirit of man goeth upward?" is practically decisive. It is not till
nearly the close of the book, with all its many wanderings of thought,
that the seeker rests in that measure of the hope of immortality which
we find in ch. xii. 7. Here we have the accents, almost the very
formula, of Pyrrhonism (Diog. Laert. IX. 11, §. 73), as borrowed from
Euripides :

> τίς δ' οἶδεν εἰ τὸ ζῆν μὲν ἐστι κατθανεῖν,
> τὸ κατθανεῖν δὲ ζῆν νομίζεται βροτοῖς.

"Who knoweth if true life be found in death,
　　While mortals think of what is death as life?"

Once more Lucretius echoes the phase of thought through which the
Debater was passing :

> "Ignoratur enim quae sit natura animai,
> Nata sit an contra nascentibus insinuetur,
> Et simul intereat nobiscum morte dirempta,
> An tenebras Orci visat vastasque lacunas."

"We know not what the nature of the soul,
　Or born, or entering into men at birth,
　Or whether with our frame it perisheth,
　Or treads the gloom and regions vast of death."

De Rer. Nat. I. 113—116.

So far, however, as scepticism is a step above denial, we may note this
as an advance. There is at least the conception of a spirit that ascends
to a life higher than its own, as a possible solution of the great enigma
presented by the disorders of the world.

22. *Wherefore I perceive*] The lesson of a tranquil regulated Epicureanism with its blending of healthy labour and calm enjoyment, is
enforced as the conclusion from our ignorance of what comes after
death, as before it flowed from the experience of life (ch. ii. 24). Who
knows whether we shall even have the power to take cognizance of
what passes on earth after we are gone, or what our own state will be,
if we continue to exist at all? The feeling was not unknown even to

4   So I returned, and considered all the oppressions that *are*
done under the sun: and behold, the tears of such as were
oppressed, and they had no comforter; and on the side
of their oppressors *there was* power; but they had no
2 comforter.   Wherefore I praise the dead which are already
3 dead more than the living which are yet alive.   Yea, better
is he than both they, which hath not yet been, who hath not
seen the evil work that is done under the sun.

men of a higher faith than the **Debater** (Ps. xxx. 9, lxxxviii. 10—12,
Isai. xxxviii. 18).

CHAPTER IV.

1. *So I returned, and considered*]   The thought that follows is the
same in substance as that of chap. iii. 16, but, in the speaker's wanderings
of thought he passes once again, after the manner of the ἐποχή, or
"suspense" of Pyrrho, he looks at the same facts, the "oppressions"
and disorders of the world as from another stand-point, and that stand-
point is the negation of immortality, or, at least, the impossibility
of being sure of it.   It may be noted that the tone is that of a
deeper compassion than before.   He sees the tears of the oppressed
and sighs at their hopelessness: "Oh, the pity of it! the pity
of it !"   We can see in this new element of despair, that which was the
beginning of a better life.   The man was passing, to use modern terms,
from egoism to altruism, thinking more of the misery of others than of
his own enjoyment.

they had no comforter]   The iteration rings like a knell of doom.
The words have sometimes been taken as if they meant "they had no
advocate, none to plead their cause," but there is no sufficient reason for
abandoning the more natural meaning.   It was the bitterest drop in
their cup, that men met with no sympathy, no visits of consolation
such as Job's friends paid him.   They found none to pity or to comfort
them.   So the absence of comforters is the crown of sorrow in Ps. lxix.
20; Lam. i. 2; Jer. xvi. 7, as its presence was one of the consolations of
the bereaved household of Bethany (John xi. 19).   It may be noted,
that, as far as it goes, this picture of the social state in which the
Debater found himself is in favour of a later date than that of Solomon.
The picture of that king's reign was, like that of the days of "good
Queen Bess " in our own history, one of almost proverbial prosperity;
the people "eating, drinking and making merry " (1 Kings iv. 20),
and his administration, as far as his own subjects were concerned, one
of "judgment and justice " (1 Kings x. 9).   It was probably equally
true of the Persian kings and of the Ptolemies that their rule was cruel
and oppressive.   The picture which Justin gives of the state of Egypt
under Ptolemy Philopator (XXIX. 1) and Ptolemy Epiphanes exactly
corresponds with that drawn by Koheleth.

3. *Yea, better is he than both they*]   As the utterance of a personal

Again, I considered all travail, and every right work, that 4
for this a man is envied of his neighbour. This *is* also

feeling of despair we have a parallel in the words of Job (iii. 11—16).
As expressing a more generalised view of life we have multiform
echoes of the thought in the Greek writers, of whose influence, direct
or indirect, the book presents so many traces. Thus we have in
Theognis :

> Πάντων μὲν μὴ φῦναι ἐπιχθονίοισιν ἄριστον,
> μηδ' ἐσιδεῖν αὐγὰς ὀξέος ἠελίου·
> φύντα δ' ὅπως ὤκιστα πύλας 'Αΐδαο περῆσαι,
> καὶ κεῖσθαι πολλὴν γῆν ἐπαμησάμενον.

"Best lot for men is never to be born,
Nor ever see the bright rays of the morn :
Next best, when born, to haste with quickest tread
Where Hades' gates are open for the dead,
And rest with much earth gathered for our bed."

425—428.

Or in Sophocles :

> μὴ φῦναι τὸν ἄπαντα νικᾷ λόγον· τὸ δ', ἐπεὶ φανῇ,
> βῆναι κεῖθεν ὅθεν περ ἥκει,
> πολὺ δεύτερον, ὡς τάχιστα.

"Never to be at all
Excels all fame ;
Quickly, next best, to pass
From whence we came."

Oed. Col. 1225.

More remote but of yet deeper significance is the fact that the same
feeling lies at the root of Buddhism and its search after *Nirvana* (annihilation or unconsciousness) as the one refuge from the burden of
existence. Terrible as the depression thus indicated is, it is one step
higher than the hatred of life which appeared in chs. i. 14, ii. 17, 18.
That was simply the weariness of a selfish satiety ; this, like the feeling
of Çakya Mouni when he saw the miseries of old age and disease and
death, and of the Greek Chorus just quoted, rose from the contemplation of the sorrows of humanity at large. It was better not to be than
to see the evil work that was done under the sun. In marked contrast
with this dark view of life we have the words : "Good were it for that
man not to have been born" in Matt. xxvi. 24, as marking out an
altogether exceptional instance of guilt and therefore of misery.

4. *I considered all travail, and every right work*] The "right work,"
as in ch. ii. 21, is that which is **dexterous** and successful, without
any marked reference to its moral character. Men exult in such work
at the time, but they find it has the drawback of drawing on them the
envy and ill-will of their less successful neighbours, and this therefore
is also **vanity and feeding on wind.**

5 vanity and vexation of spirit. The fool foldeth his hands
6 together, and eateth his own flesh. Better *is* a handful
with quietness, than both the hands full *with* travail and
vexation of spirit.
7
8 Then I returned, and I saw vanity under the sun. There

5. *The fool foldeth his hands together*] Simple as the words seem
they have received very different interpretations : (1) The fool (the
word is the same as in ch. ii. 14—16, and is that, the prominence of
which in both Proverbs and Ecclesiastes serve as a connecting link
between the two Books), the man without aim or insight, leading a
half brutish life, "folds his hands" in the attitude of indolence (Prov.
vi. 10, xxiv. 33), and yet even he, with his limited desires, attains to
the fruition of those desires, "eats his meat" and rejoices more than
the wise and far-sighted who finds his dexterous and successful work
empty and unsatisfying. (So Ginsburg.) For this sense of the words
"eateth his flesh," we have the usage of Exod. xvi. 8, xxi. 28; Isai.
xxii. 13; Ezek. xxxix. 17. So taken, this thought coheres with the context, and expresses the sense of contrast between the failure of aspiring
activity and skill to attain the happiness they aim at, and the fact that
those who do not even work for enjoyment get as full a share of it—
perhaps, even a fuller—as those who do. (2) The last clause has been
interpreted, as in the A.V., as meaning literally that the slothful man
"consumes his own flesh," *i.e.* reduces himself literally to the poverty
and starvation which culminates in horrors such as this, as in Isai.
ix. 20; Jer. xix. 9, or, figuratively, pines away under the corroding
canker of envy and discontent. For the latter meaning, however,
we have no authority in the language of the Old Testament, and so
taken, the passage becomes only a warning, after the manner of the
Proverbs, against the sin of sloth, and as such, is not in harmony with
the dominant despondency of this stage of the writer's experience.
The view which sees in verse 5, the writer's condemnation of sloth, and
in verse 6 the answer of the slothful, seems out of keeping with the
context.

6. *Better is a handful with quietness*] The preposition is in both
clauses an interpolation, and we should read "**a handful of repose,...
two handfuls of travail and feeding on wind.**" In form the saying presents a parallel to Prov. xv. 17, "Better is a dinner of herbs where love
is, than a stalled ox and hatred therewith;" but the thought is obviously
of a less ethical character. The feeling expressed in verses 5 and 6
(the latter confirming the interpretation just given of the former) is such
as we may think of as rising in the mind of an ambitious statesman or
artist striving after fame, as he looks on the *dolce far niente* of a *lazzarone*
at Naples, half-naked, basking in the sun, and revelling in the enjoyment of his water-melon. The one would at such a time, almost change
places with the other, but that something after all forbids. The words
have almost a verbal parallelism in our common English proverb "a
bird in the hand is worth two in the bush."

is one *alone*, and *there is* not a second; yea, he hath neither child nor brother: yet *is there* no end of all his labour; neither is his eye satisfied *with* riches; neither *saith he*, For whom do I labour, and bereave my soul of good? This *is* also vanity, yea, it *is* a sore travail. Two *are* better than 9 one; because they have a good reward for their labour.

8. *There is one alone, and there is not a second*] The gaze of the seeker now falls on another picture. That which strikes him as another example of the vanity of human efforts is the frequent loneliness of the worshipper of wealth. He is one. and he has no companion, no partner or friend, often none bound to him by ties of blood, child or brother, yet he labours on, as though he meant to be the founder of a dynasty. "He heapeth up riches and knoweth not who shall gather them" Ps. xxxix. 6.

neither is his eye satisfied with riches] The words paint vividly the special characteristic of the insatiability of avarice,

"Crescit amor nummi quantum ipsa pecunia crescit."

"So grows our love of wealth as grows the wealth itself."

neither saith he, For whom do I labour] The words in italics " **saith he**" express the meaning of the original but deprive it of its dramatic boldness. The speaker imagines himself in the place of the miser and this is the question which in that case he would ask. The picture is, as it were, a *replica* of that already drawn in chap. ii. 18, 19.

9. *Two are better than one*] The strain of moralising which follows indicates at least the revived capacity for a better feeling. As the **Debater** had turned from the restless strivings of the seeker after wealth to the simple enjoyment of the labouring man or even the sensuous pleasure of the indolent, so now he turns from the isolation of the avaricious to the blessings of companionship. Here at least, in that which carries a man out of himself, there is a real good, a point scored as "gain." Here also, over and above his own experience the Seeker may have been helped by the current thought of his Greek teachers, the κοινά τὰ φίλων of the proverb, or the lines of Homer,

> Σύν τε δύ' ἐρχομένω, καί τε πρὸ ὃ τοῦ ἐνόησεν
> Ὅππως κέρδος ἔῃ· μοῦνος δ' εἴπερ τε νοήσῃ,
> Ἀλλά τε οἱ βράσσων τε νόυς λεπτὴ δέ τε μῆτις.

> "When two together go, each for the other
> Is first to think what best will help his brother;
> But one who walks alone, though wise in mind,
> Of purpose slow and counsel weak we find."
> *Iliad*, X. 224—6.

So the Greek proverb ran as to friends

> χεὶρ χεῖρα νίπτει, δακτυλός τε δάκτυλον.

> "Hand cleanseth hand, and finger finger helps."

10 For if they fall, the one will lift up his fellow: but woe to
him *that is* alone when he falleth; for *he hath* not another
11 to help him up.   Again, if two lie together, then they have
12 heat: but how can one be warm *alone?* And if one prevail
against him, two shall withstand him; and a three-fold cord
is not quickly broken.

The "good reward" is more than the mere money result of partnership,
and implies the joy of

> "United thoughts and counsels, equal hope
> And hazard."

The literature of well-nigh all ages and races abound in expressions
of the same thought.   Aristotle dedicates two whole books (VIII.
IX.) of his Ethics to the subject of Friendship, and Cicero made
it the theme of one of his most finished essays.   Commonly, however, men rested it, as the writer does here, mainly on the basis of
utility.   "The wise man," says Seneca (*Epist.* IX. 8) from his higher
Stoic standpoint, "needs a friend, not as Epicurus taught, that
he may have one to sit by his bed when he is ill, or to help
him when he is poor or in prison, but that he may have one by
whose bed he may sit, whom he may rescue when he is attacked by
foes."   We may point also to Prov. xvii. 17, xxvii. 17, and the Jewish
proverb "a man without friends is like a left hand without the right"
(*Pirke Aboth*, f. 30. 2) as utterances of a like nature.   It is, however
to be noted, in connexion with the line of thought that has been
hitherto followed in these notes as to the date and authorship of the
book, that the preciousness of friendship as one of the joys of life
was specially characteristic of the school of Epicurus (Zeller, *Stoics and
Epicureans*, c. XX.).   It was with them the highest of human goods,
and the wise would value it as the chief element of security (Diog.
Laert. X. 1. 148).   The principle thus asserted finds, it may be added,
its highest sanction in the wisdom of Him who sent out His disciples
"two and two together" (Luke x. 1).

if they fall]   The special illustration appears to be drawn from the
experience of two travellers.   If one slip or stumble on a steep or rocky
path the other is at hand to raise him, while, if left to himself, he
might have perished.

11. *if two lie together*]   Here again the experience of travel comes
before us.   Sleeping on a cold and stormy night, under the same
coverlet, or in Eastern houses, with their unglazed windows and many
draughts, two friends kept each other warm, while one resting by
himself would have shivered in discomfort.   Commonly as in Exod.
xxii. 6, the mantle of the day served also as the blanket of the night.
So, of course, it would be with those who travelled according to the
rule of Matt. x. 10.

12. *if one prevail against him*]   Better, **If a man overpowers him**

Better *is* a poor and a wise child than an old and foolish 13
king, who will no more be admonished. For out of prison 14
he cometh to reign; whereas also *he that is* born in his

that is alone, yet two shall withstand. Another incident of travel is
brought before us. The robber may lie in ambush. Against one his
attack would be successful; the two friends defend each other and are
saved.

a threefold cord is not quickly broken] Perhaps no words in Ecclesiastes are better known than this as a proverbial expression for the
strength of unity. It differs from the previous illustration in suggesting
the thought of a friendship in which more than two persons are joined.
"Threefold" is chosen as an epithet, partly as carrying on the thought
from two to three, as in Prov. xxx. 15, 18, 21, from three to four, partly
because "three" was for the Israelite the typical number for completeness, probably also because the rope of three strands was the strongest
cord in use. The proverbial form has naturally led to manifold application of the maxim, and the devout imagination of the interpreters has
seen in it a reference to the doctrine of the Three Persons in the unity of
the Godhead, to the union of Faith, Hope and Charity in the Christian
life, and so on. These, it need scarcely be said, lie altogether outside
the range of the thoughts of the **Debater.**

13. *Better is a poor and a wise child*] Better, **young man.** The
words are general enough but the ingenuity of commentators has sought
for examples in history, which the writer, according to the varying
theories as to his date, may have had in his thoughts. Such, *e.g.* as
Abraham and Nimrod, Joseph and Pharaoh, David and Saul (all these
are named in the *Midrash Koheleth*, see *Introduction*, ch. VI.), Joash and
Amaziah, Cyrus and Astyages, the high priest Onias and his nephew
Joseph (circ. B.C. 246—221, see Joseph. *Ant.* XII. 4, and Note on next
verse), or Herod and his son Alexander. None of these identifications
are altogether satisfactory, and it is quite possible that the writer may
simply have uttered a general statement or may have had in view some
events of which we have no record. In Wisd. iv. 8, 9 we have a more
eloquent utterance of the same thought, "Honourable age is not that
which standeth in length of time or that is measured by number of
years, but wisdom is the grey hair unto men and unspotted life is old
age." The word for "child" is used of Joseph at the age of 17 (Gen.
xxxvii. 30, xlii. 20) and even of the companions of Rehoboam when
the latter was over 40 (1 Kings xii. 8).

14. *For out of prison he cometh to reign*] The pronouns are ambiguous in the Hebrew as in English, and the clauses have consequently
been taken in very different ways, as referring to one and the same
person, or to the two who had been named in the preceding verse (1)
"**For one cometh out of prison to reign, though he (the young successor) was born poor in his kingdom**" (that of the old king, or that which
was afterwards to be his own); or (2) "**For one cometh out of prison
to reign, while a king becomes a beggar in his kingdom.**" Here also

15 kingdom becometh poor. I considered all the living which walk under the sun, with the second child that shall stand
16 *up* in his stead. *There is* no end of all the people, *even* of all that have been before them: they also that come after shall not rejoice in him. Surely this also *is* vanity and vexation of spirit.

a reference has been found to the history of Onias under Ptolemy Euergetes. Josephus describes him (*Ant.* XII. 4) as "of a little soul and a great lover of money" while his nephew Joseph "young in age" was "of great reputation for gravity, wisdom and justice," and obtained from the king permission to farm the revenues of Cœlesyria, Phœnicia, Samaria and Judæa. It can scarcely be said however that the case thus narrated is parallel with what we find in the verse before us. There is no king old or young, coming out of prison, or reduced to poverty. On the whole, unless the words refer to some unrecorded incident, some vague reminiscence of Cyrus and Astyages seems more likely to have been before the writer's mind. According to one version of that history Cyrus had been brought up in poverty (Herod. I. 112), and was so strictly guarded that Harpagus had recourse to stratagem to convey a letter into his hands (Herod. I. 123).

15. *with the second child that shall stand up in his stead*] If we take the word "second" in its natural meaning, the clause may point either to the wise young ruler of the previous verse, as succeeding (*i.e.* coming *second* to) the old and foolish king, or possibly to *his* successor, and points in either case to what we have learnt to call the "worship of the rising Sun." All gather round him, and their name is legion. There is "no end of all the people."

16. *There is no end of all the people*] The words continue the picture of the crowds who follow the young king.

even of all that have been before them] The last words are not of time but position. The people are before their king, or rather, **he is before them all**, going in and out before them (1 Sam. xviii. 16; 2 Chron. i. 10), ruling and guiding. The reference of the words to the Messianic child of Isai. vii. 14, ix. 6, falls under the same category as the interpretation which finds the doctrine of the Trinity in the "threefold cord" of verse 12. It is true of both that they may be devout applications of the words, but are in no sense explanatory of their meaning.

they also that come after] This is added as the crowning stroke of the irony of history. The reign which begins so brightly shares the inevitable doom, and ends in darkness, and murmuring and failure. "*Il n'y a pas d'homme necessaire,*" and the popular hero of the hour finds himself slighted even in life, and is forgotten by the next generation. The glory of the most popular and successful king shares the common doom and is but as a **feeding upon wind**. Here again the statement is so wide in its generalization that it is not easy to fix on any historical

Keep thy foot when thou goest to the house of God, 5
and *be* more ready to hear, than to give the sacrifice of fools:
for they consider not that *they* do evil.　Be not rash with 2

identification.　David, Solomon himself, Jeroboam, Cyrus, Antiochus
the Great, Herod have been suggested by the ingenuity of commentators.

<h2 style="text-align:center">CHAPTER V.</h2>

1.　*Keep thy foot*] In the Heb., LXX. and Vulg. this verse forms
the conclusion to chap. iv.　The English version is obviously right,
however, in its division of the chapter.　The moralist reviews a new
region of experience.　"Vanity" has been found in all that belongs to
the outward secular life of men.　Is their higher life, that which we call
their religion, free from it?　Must not the **Debater**, from his standpoint,
rebuke the follies and sins even of the godly?　Here, as might be
expected, we have an intermingling of two elements of thought, the
traditional teaching which the thinker has learnt from psalmist **and**
prophet, and the maxims which have come to him from his Greek,
probably from his Epicurean, teachers.　Both, it will be seen, find
echoes in the precepts that follow.　The precepts are suggestive as
shewing the kind of religion which the **Debater** had seen in Palestine,
the germs of the formalism and casuistry which afterwards developed
into Pharisaism.　To "keep the foot" was to walk in the right way,
the way of reverence and obedience (Ps. cxix. 32, 101).　The outward
act of putting the shoes off the feet on entering the Temple (Exod. iii. 5;
Josh. v. 15), from the earliest times to the present, the custom of the
East, was the outward symbol of such a reverential awe.　We note,
as characteristic, the substitution of the "house of God" for the more
familiar "house of the Lord" (2 Sam. xii. 20; Isai. xxxiii. 1, and elsewhere).　Possibly the term may be used, as in Ps. lxxiv. 8, lxxxiii. 12, to
include synagogues as well as the Temple.　The precept implies that he
who gives it had seen the need of it.　Men went to the place where
they worshipped with little thought that it was indeed a Beth-el, or
"house of God."

and be more ready to hear] The words have been differently interpreted : (1) "**And to draw near to hear is better than to offer the
sacrifice...** ;" and (2) "**To hear** (=obey) **is nearer** (*i.e.* is the truer way
for thy foot to take) **than to offer the sacrifice...**"　The general spirit of
the maxim or precept is identical with that of 1 Sam. xv. 22; Ps. xl.
6—8, l. 8—14, li. 16, 17.　The "sacrifice of fools" as in Prov. xxi. 27
is that offered by the ungodly, and therefore an abomination.

for they consider not that they do evil] The A. V. is perhaps sufficiently
expressive of the meaning, but the following various renderings have
been suggested : (1) "**they know not, so that they do evil.**" *i.e.* their
ignorance leads them to sin ; (2) "**they** (those who obey, hear) **know not
to do evil**," *i.e.* their obedience keeps them from it.　Of these (1) seems
preferable.　Protests against a superstition that was not godliness, the

thy mouth, and let not thine heart be hasty to utter *any*
thing before God: for God *is* in heaven, and thou upon
3 earth: therefore let thy words be few.   For a dream cometh
through the multitude of business; and a fool's voice *is*

δεισιδαιμονία of the Greeks (Acts xvii. 22), were, it need scarcely be said,
part of the current teaching of Epicurus and his followers. So Lucretius;

> " Nec pietas ullast velatum sæpe videri
>   Vertier ad lapidem atque omnes accedere ad aras,
>   Nec procumbere humi prostratum et pandere palmas
>   Ante deûm delubra, nec aras sanguine multo
>   Spargere quadrupedum, nec votis nectere vota,
>   Sed mage pacata posse omnia mente tueri."

> " True worship is not found in veiled heads
>   Turned to a statue, nor in drawing near
>   To many an altar, nor in form laid low
>   Upon the ground, nor sprinkling it with blood
>   Of bulls and goats, nor piling vows on vows;
>   But rather in the power which all surveys
>   With mind at rest and calm.".
>   *De Rer. Nat.* v. 1198—1203.

2. *Be not rash with thy mouth*]   The rule follows the worshipper
from the threshold into the Temple-court and tells him how he is to act
there.   We are reminded of our Lord's warning against "vain repeti-
tions," after the manner of the heathen (Matt. vi. 7).   The second
clause, though parallel to the first, carries the thought further.   The
"heart" or mind of the worshipper also is to be calm and deliberate.
We are not to turn every hasty wish into a prayer, but to ask ourselves
whether it is one of the things for which we ought to pray.   Here also
the precept has its analogies in the counsels of the wise of heart outside
the covenant of Israel.   See especially Juven. *Sat.* x.

therefore let thy words be few]   The Son of Sirach gives the same rule
for our speech when in the presence of the "great men" of earth (Ecclus.
xxxii. 9), and *à fortiori* the reverence due to God should shew itself in
the same form as our reverence for them.   In a Talmudic precept we
find the rule in nearly the same words, "the words of a man should
always be few in the presence of God" (*Berachoth,* 61 a, quoted by
Ginsburg).   Comp. also Hooker *E. P.* 1. 2. § 3.

3. *For a dream cometh through the multitude of business*]   The one
psychological fact is meant to illustrate the other.   The mind that has
lost the power to re-collect itself, haunted and harassed by the cares of
many things, cannot enjoy the sweet and calm repose of a dreamless
slumber, and that fevered state with its hot thoughts and wild fancies
is but too faithful a picture of the worshipper who pours out a multitude of wishes in a "multitude of words."   His very prayers are those
of a dreamer.   It seems obvious, from the particle that connects this
with the preceding verse, that the maxim refers specially to these

known by multitude of words.   When thou vowest a vow 4
unto God, defer not to pay it; for *he hath* no pleasure in
fools: pay that which thou hast vowed.   Better *is it* that 5
thou shouldest not vow, than that thou shouldest vow and
not pay.   Suffer not thy mouth to cause thy flesh to sin; 6

utterances of the fool and not merely to the folly of his speech in
general.   The words "is known," as the italics shew, have nothing
answering to them in the Hebrew.   The same verb was meant to serve
for both the clauses.

4. *When thou vowest a vow unto God*]   The words are almost a
reproduction of Deut. xxiii. 22—24.   They point to a time when vows,
such as are here referred to, entered largely into men's personal religion.
Memorable instances of such vows are found in the lives of Jacob
(Gen. xxviii. 20), Jephthah (Judg. xi. 30), Saul (1 Sam. xiv. 24).   In
later Judaism they came into a fresh prominence, as seen especially in
the Corban of Mark vii. 11, the revival of the Nazarite vow (Acts
xviii. 18, xx. 23; Joseph. *Wars* II. 15, p. 1), and the oath or anathema
of Acts xxiii. 21; and one of the treatises of the Mishna (*Nedarim*) was
devoted to an exhaustive casuistic treatment of the whole subject.   In
Matt. v. 23 we find the recognised rule of the Pharisees, "Thou shalt
perform unto the Lord thine oaths," as the conclusion of the whole
matter.   This the **Debater** also affirmed, but he, in his deeper wisdom,
went further, and bade men to consider well what kind of vows they
made.

for he hath no pleasure in fools]   The construction of the sentence in
the Hebrew is ambiguous, and may give either (1) that suggested by the
interpolated words in the A. V., or (2) **"there is no pleasure in fools,"**
i.e. **they please neither God nor man**, or (3) **"there is no fixed purpose
in fools,"** *i.e.* they are unstable in their vows as in everything else.   Of
these interpretations (2) has most to commend it.   In Prov. xx. 25, "It
is a snare...after vows to make inquiry," we have a striking parallel.

5. *Better is it that thou shouldest not vow*]   The point which the Teacher
seeks to press is obviously the optional character of vows.   They form
no part of the essentials of religion, they are to be deprecated rather than
otherwise; but to make them, and then delay or evade their fulfilment,
is to tamper with veracity and play fast and loose with conscience, and
so is fatally injurious.   The casuistry condemned by our Lord (Matt.
v. 33, xxiii. 16—22) shews how fertile was the ingenuity of Scribes in
devising expedients of this nature.

6. *Suffer not thy mouth to cause thy flesh to sin*]   The "mouth"
may refer either to the thoughtless utterance of the rash vow, such as
that of Jephthah (Judg. xi. 30) or Saul (1 Sam. xiv. 24), or to the
appetite which leads the man who has made a vow, say of the Nazarite
type, to indulge in the drink or food which he had bound himself to
renounce.   The former meaning seems more in harmony with the context.   The latter clause is translated by many Commentators *to bring
punishment* (the expiation for sin) *upon thy flesh*, but the A.V. is

neither say thou before the angel, that it *was* an error :
wherefore should God be angry at thy voice, and destroy
7 the work of thine hands? For in the multitude of dreams

probably correct. The "flesh" stands as in Gen. vi. 3; Ps. lxxviii. 39,
and in New Testament language (Rom. vii. 18, 25), for the corrupt
sensuous element in man's nature. The context forbids the extension of
the precept to sins of speech in general, as in the wider teaching of
James iii. 1—12.

neither say thou before the angel] The words have been taken by
most Jewish and some Christian interpreters as referring to the "angel"
in the strict sense of the term, who was believed in Rabbinic traditions
to preside over the Temple or the altar, and who, it is assumed, would
punish the evasion of the vow on the frivolous excuse that it had been
spoken inconsiderately. 1 Cor. xi. 13 and 1 Tim. v. 21 are referred to
as illustrations of the same thought. This interpretation, however,
seems scarcely in harmony with the generally Hellenised tone of the
book, and in Hagg. i. 13 and Mal. ii. 7 we have distinct evidence that
the term had come to be applied to prophets and priests, as in 2 Cor.
viii. 23 and Rev. i. 20 it is used of ministers in the Christian Church,
and this, it is obvious, gives a tenable, and, on the whole, a preferable
meaning. The man comes to the priest with an offering less in value
than he had vowed, or postpones the fulfilment of his vow indefinitely,
and using the technical language of Num. xv. 25, explains that the vow
had been made in ignorance, and therefore that he was not bound to
fulfil it to the letter. Other commentators again (Grätz) look on the
word as describing a subordinate officer of the Temple.

wherefore should God be angry at thy voice] The question is in form
like those of Ezra iv. 22, vii. 23, and is rhetorically more emphatic than
a direct assertion. The words are a more distinct assertion of a Divine
Government seen in earthly rewards and punishments than the book
has as yet presented. The vow made, as was common, to secure safety
or prosperity, could have no other result than loss and, it might be, ruin,
if it were vitiated from the first by a rashness which took refuge in
dishonesty.

7. *For in the multitude of dreams*] The order of the words in the
A. V. is not that of the Hebrew, which gives *For in the multitude of
dreams and vanities and many words*, but is adopted by many commentators as representing a more correct text. The introduction of the word
"vanities" (the "divers" of the A. V. has, as the italics shew, nothing
answering to it in the Hebrew,) indicates the purpose of the writer in
thus noting the weak points of popular religionism. They also, the
dreams which seemed to them as messages from heaven, the "many
words" of long and resounding prayers, took their place in the induction
which was to prove that "all is vanity." So Theophrastus (*Charact.*
XVI.) describes the superstitious man (δεισιδαίμων) as agitated when he
sees a vision and straightway going off to consult a soothsayer. In contrast with the garrulous rashness and the inconsiderate vows and the
unwise reliance on dreams which Judaism was learning from heathenism

and many words *there are* also *divers* vanities: but fear thou God.

If thou seest the oppression of the poor, and violent 8 perverting of judgment and justice in a province, marvel not at the matter: for *he that is* higher than the highest regardeth; and *there be* higher than they.

(Matt. vi. 7) Koheleth falls back on the "fear of God," the temper of reverential and silent awe, which was "the beginning of wisdom" (Prov. i. 7; Job xxviii. 28). It is significant that here again the teaching of Koheleth has a parallel in that of the Epicurean poet who traces the "religions" of mankind (in his sense of the word) in no small measure to the influence of dreams.

> "Quippe etenim jam tum divum mortalia sæcla
> Egregias animo facies vigilante videbant,
> Et magis in somnis mirando corporis auctu."

> "Even then the race of mortal men would see
> With waking soul the mighty forms of Gods,
> And in their dreams with shapes of wondrous size."
> LUCRET. *De Rer. Nat.* v. 1169—71.

8. *If thou seest the oppression of the poor*] From the follies of the religious life we pass to the disorders of the political. As in ch. iv. 16, the thinker looks on those disorders of the world, "the poor man's wrong, the proud man's contumely," and teaches others how he has learnt to think of them. The words "wonder not" tells us with scarcely the shadow of a doubt who had been his teachers. In that counsel we have a distinct echo from one of the floating maxims of Greek proverbial wisdom, from the Μηδὲν θαυμάζειν ("wonder at nothing") of Pythagoras, and Cebes (*Tabula*, p. 232), which has become more widely known through the *Nil admirari* of Horace (*Epist.* 1. 6. 1). Why men were not to wonder at the prevalence of oppression is explained afterwards. The word for "province" may be noted as one distinctly belonging to later Hebrew, found chiefly in the books of the Persian period, Ezra, Nehemiah, Esther and Daniel; once only in those of earlier date, 1 Kings xx. 14—17.

for he that is higher than the highest] The first impression made by the verse is that the **Debater** tells men not to wonder or be dismayed at the prevalence of wrong, on the ground that God is higher than the highest of the tyrants of the earth and will in the end punish their wrong-doing. So understood, the first and the last "higher" both refer to "God," or, as some take it, the last only, the first referring to the king as distinct from satraps or other officers, and the train of thought is supposed to be "Wonder not with the wonder of despair, at the seeming triumph of evil. The Supreme Judge (ch. iii. 17) will one day set all things right." The last "higher" is however plural in the Hebrew, and if it be understood of God, it must be by a somewhat unusual construction connecting it with the plural form (*Elohim*) of the

9 Moreover the profit of the earth *is* for all : the king *him-*
10 *self* is served by the field.   He that loveth silver shall not

name of God.   We have, it may be noted, another example of a like
construction in the use of the plural form for Creator in ch. xii. 1, and
for "the Holy" in Prov. ix. 10, xxx. 3.   Over and above the grammatical
difficulties, however (which, as has been shewn, are not insuperable), it
may be said that this thought is hardly in keeping with the tone of the
Debater's mind at this stage of his progress.   Belief in the righteous
government of God can hardly remove, though it may perhaps silence,
the wonder which men feel at the prevalence of evil.   It seems better
accordingly to fall back upon another interpretation.   The observer
looks upon the state of the Persian or Syrian or Egyptian Monarchy
and sees a system of Satraps and Governors which works like that of
the Pachas in modern Asiatic Turkey.   There is one **higher than
the high one,** the king who is despotic over the satraps : there are
others (the court favourites, king's friends, eunuchs, chamberlains)
who are higher or, at least, of more power, than both together, each
jealously watching the others, and bent on self-aggrandisement.   Who
can wonder that the result should be injustice and oppression?   The
system of government was rotten from the highest to the lowest,
suspicion and distrust pervading its whole administration.   Comp.
Aristotle's description of Asiatic monarchies as suppressing all public
spirit and mutual confidence (*Pol.* v. 11).   It may be suggested, lastly,
that the enigmatic form of the maxim may have been deliberately
chosen, so that men might read either the higher or the lower interpretation into it, according to their capacities.   It was a "word to
the wise" after the measure of their wisdom.   The grave irony of
such an ambiguous utterance was quite after the Teacher's method.
See notes on ch. xi. 1, 2.

   9. *Moreover the profit of the earth is for all*]   The verse is difficult
and has been very variously interpreted.   The most satisfactory renderings follow : **But the profit of a land every way is a king for the
field under tillage,** or, as some take the words, **a king devoted to the
field.**   In either case the main sense is the same.   The writer contrasts the
misery of the Oriental government of his time with the condition of
Judah under the model kings who gave themselves chiefly to the development of the resources of the country by agriculture, such *e.g.* as
Uzziah who "loved husbandry" (2 Chron. xxvi. 10).   This gives, it is
obvious, a much better sense than the rendering that "the king is
served by the field" or "is subject to the field," *i.e.* dependent on it.
Assuming the Alexandrian origin of the book, we may perhaps see in
the maxim a gentle hint to the Ptolemy of the time being to improve
his agricultural administration and to foster the growing export-trade in
corn.

   10. *He that loveth silver*]   The sequence of thought led the
Debater from the evils of the love of money as seen in mis-government
to those which are seen in the life of the individual man.   The conspicuous fact was the insatiableness of that passion for money ;

be satisfied *with* silver; nor he that loveth abundance *with* increase: this *is* also vanity. When goods increase, they ₁₁ are increased that eat them: and what good *is there* to the owners thereof, saving the beholding *of them* with their eyes? The sleep of a labouring *man is* sweet, whether he ₁₂

> "Semper avarus eget; hunc nulla pecunia replet."
>
> "The miser still is poor, no money fills his purse."
>
> JUVEN. Sat. XIV. 139.

The second clause may be taken either as in the A. V. as a maxim **He who clings to wealth** (the word implies the luxury that accompanies wealth as in Ps. xxxvii. 16; 1 Chron. xxix. 16; Isai. lx. 5), **there is no fruit thereof**, or as a question, **Who clings to wealth? There is no fruit thereof**, *i.e.* no real *revenue* or *return* for the labour of acquiring it. In this the Teacher found another illustration of his text that "all is vanity."

11. *When goods increase, they are increased that eat them*] The fact is one which has met the gaze of the moralists of all countries. A large household, numerous retainers, these are but so many elements of trouble. In the dialogue of Crœsus and Solon (Herod. I. 32), yet more closely in that of Pheraulas and Sacian (quoted by Ginsburg) in Xenophon (*Cyrop.* VIII. 3, pp. 35—44), we have distinct parallels. The latter presents so striking a resemblance as to be worth quoting, "Do you think, Sacian, that I live with the more pleasure the more I possess.... By having this abundance, I gain merely this, that I have to guard more, to distribute more to others, and to have the trouble of taking care of more; for a great many domestics now demand of me their food, their drink, and their clothes...Whosoever, therefore, is greatly pleased with the possession of riches will, be assured, feel much annoyed at the expenditure of them."

saving the beholding of them with their eyes] So Horace paints the miser:

> "Congestis undique saccis
> Indormis inhians, et tanquam parcere sacris
> Cogeris, aut pictis tanquam gaudere tabellis."

> "Sleepless thou gazest on thy heaped-up bags,
> And yet art forced to hold thy hand from them,
> As though they were too sacred to be touched,
> Or were but painted pictures for thine eyes."
>
> Sat. I. 1. 66.

12. *The sleep of a labouring man is sweet*] We may probably, as suggested in the "Ideal Biography" of the *Introduction* ch. III., see in this reflection the reminiscence of a state with which the writer had once been familiar, and after which, now that it had passed away, he yearned regretfully. Again we get on the track of the maxims of Epicurean teachers. So Horace;

eat little or much : but the abundance of the rich will not suffer him to sleep.

13 There is a sore evil *which* I have seen under the sun, *namely*, riches kept for the owners thereof to their hurt.
14 But those riches perish by evil travail : and he begetteth a
15 son, and *there is* nothing in his hand. As he came forth of his mother's womb, naked shall he return to go as he

> "Somnus agrestium
> Lenis virorum non humiles domos
> Fastidit umbrosamque ripam,
> Non Zephyris agitata Tempe."

> "Gentle slumber scorneth not
> The ploughman's poor and lowly cot,
> Nor yet the bank with sheltering shade,
> Nor Tempe with its breezy glade."

Od. III. I. 21—24.

See the passage from Virgil, *Georg.* IV., already quoted in the note on ch. ii. 24, and

> "Gives not the hawthorn-bush a sweeter shade
> To shepherds looking on their silly sheep,
> Than doth a rich embroider'd canopy
> To kings that fear their subjects' treachery?
> O, yes, it doth; a thousand-fold it doth.
> And to conclude, the shepherd's homely curds,
> His cold thin drink out of his leather bottle,
> His wonted sleep under a fresh tree's shade,
> All which secure and sweetly he enjoys,
> Is far beyond a prince's delicates,
> His viands sparkling in a golden cup,
> His body couched in a curious bed,
> When care, mistrust, and treason wait on him."

SHAKESPEARE, *Henry VI.* Act ii. Sc. 5.

13. *riches kept for the owners thereof*] Yet another aspect of the evils attendant on riches is brought before us, as in ch. ii. 18, 19. Not only do they fail to give any satisfying joy, but the man who reckoned on founding a family and leaving his heaped-up treasures to his son gains nothing but anxieties and cares, loses his wealth by some unforeseen chance, and leaves his son a pauper. By some commentators the possessive pronoun in "*his* hand" (verse 14) is referred to the father. The crowning sorrow for him is that he begets a son and then dies himself in poverty. The upshot of the two constructions is, of course, practically the same.

15. *As he came forth of his mother's womb*] The words so closely resemble those of Job i. 21 that it is natural to infer that the writer had that history in his mind as an example of a sudden reverse of fortune.

came, and shall take nothing of his labour, which he may carry away in his hand.   And this also *is* a sore evil, *that* in 16 all points as he came, so shall he go : and what profit hath he that hath laboured for the wind ?   All his days also 17 he eateth in darkness, and *he hath* much sorrow and wrath with his sickness.

Behold *that* which I have seen : *it is* good and comely 18 *for one* to eat and to drink, and to enjoy the good of all his labour that he taketh under the sun all the days of his life, which God giveth him : for it *is* his portion.   Every man 19 also to whom God hath given riches and wealth, and hath given him power to eat thereof, and to take his portion, and to rejoice in his labour ; this *is* the gift of God.   For 20

In both, earth, as the mother of all living, is thought of as the womb out of which each man comes (Ps. cxxxix. 15) and to which he must return at last, carrying none of his earthly possessions with him.   Comp. a striking parallel in Ecclus. xl. 1.

16.   *what profit hath he that hath laboured for the wind?*]   The ever-recurring question (ch. i. 3, ii. 22, iii. 9) rises once again, "What profit?"   In "labouring for the wind" we have a phrase almost identical with the **"feeding on wind"** or, as some render it, the "striving after the wind" which is the key-note of the whole book.   As in Prov. xi. 29; Isai. xxvi. 18; Job xvi. 3 the "wind" is the emblem of emptiness and nothingness.

17.   *he eateth in darkness*]   The words are so natural a figure of a cheerless life with no "sweetness and light" in it (comp. Mic. vii. 8), that there is something almost ludicrous in the prosaic literalism which interprets them, either (1) of the miser as eating in the dark to save candlelight, or (2) working all day and waiting till nightfall before he sits down to a meal.

much sorrow and wrath with his sickness]   Better, **and sickness and wrath.**   The Hebrew gives a conjunction and not a preposition.   The words have been variously taken, (1) "*is much disturbed and hath grief and vexation,*" (2) "*grieveth himself much, and oh ! for his sorrow and hatred,*" but the general meaning remains the same.   Koheleth teaches, as St Paul does, that "they that will be (*i.e.* set their hearts on being) rich, pierce themselves through with many sorrows" (1 Tim. vi. 6).

18.   *Behold that which I have seen*]   The thinker returns to the maxim of a calm regulated Epicureanism, as before in chs. ii. 24, iii. 22.   If a man has little, let him be content with that little.   If he has much, let him enjoy it without excess, and without seeking more.   In the combination of "good" and "comely" we have perhaps an endeavour to reproduce the familiar Greek combination of the ἀγαθὸν and the καλόν.

19.   *this is the gift of God*]   The words indicate a return to the sense of dependence on the Divine bounty. which we have seen in

he shall not much remember the days of his life; because
God answereth *him* in the joy of his heart.

6   There is an evil which I have seen under the sun, and it

chs. ii. 24, iii. 13. Life itself, and the outward goods of life, few or
many, and the power to enjoy these, all are alike God's gifts.

20. *he shall not much remember the days of his life*] This follows
the order of the Hebrew and gives a satisfying meaning: The man who
has learnt the secret of enjoyment is not anxious about the days of his
life, does not brood even over its transitoriness, but takes each day
tranquilly, as it comes, as God's gift to him. By some commentators,
however, the sentence is construed so as to give just the opposite sense,
"*He remembereth* (or *should remember*) *that the days of his life are not
many*," *i.e.* never loses sight of the shortness of human life. It is difficult to see how the translators of the A. V. could have been led to their
marginal reading "*Though he give not much, yet he remembereth the
days of his life.*"

because God answereth him in the joy of his heart] The verb has been very
variously rendered, (1) "*God occupies him with the joy...*," or (2) "*God
makes him sing with the joy...*," or (3) "*God causeth him to work for
the enjoyment...*," or (4) "*God makes all answer (i.e. correspond with)
his wishes*," or (5) "*God himself corresponds to his joy*," *i.e.* is felt to
approve it as harmonizing, in its calm evenness, with His own blessedness. The last is, perhaps, that which has most to commend it. So
taken, the words find a parallel in the teaching of Epicurus, "The
Blessed and the Immortal neither knows trouble of its own nor causeth it
to others. Wherefore it is not influenced either by wrath or favour,"
(Diog. Laert. X. 1. 139). The tranquillity of the wise man mirrors,
the Teacher implies, the tranquillity of God. So Lucretius;

> "Omnis enim per se divum natura necessest,
> Immortali ævo summâ cum pace fruatur,
> Semota ab nostris rebus sejunctaque longe;
> Nam privata dolore omni, privata periclis,
> Ipsa suis pollens opibus, nil indiga nostri,
> Nec bene promeritis capitur neque tangitur ira."

> "The nature of the Gods must need enjoy
> Life everlasting in supreme repose,
> Far from our poor concerns and separate:
> For from all pain exempt, exempt from risks,
> Rich in its own wealth, needing nought of ours,
> 'Tis neither soothed by gifts nor stirred by wrath."
> *De Rer. Nat.* II. 646—651.

CHAPTER VI.

1. *There is an evil which I have seen under the sun*] The picture is
substantially the same as that of ch. iv. 7, 8. The repetition is charac-

is common among men : a man to whom God hath given 2
riches, wealth, and honour, so that he wanteth nothing for
his soul of all that he desireth, yet God giveth him not
power to eat thereof, but a stranger eateth it : this *is* vanity,
and it *is* an evil disease.　If a man beget an hundred *chil-* 3
dren, and live many years, so that the days of his years be
many, and his soul be not filled with good, and also *that* he
have no burial; I say, *that* an untimely birth *is* better than

teristic, consciously or unconsciously, of the pessimism from which the
writer has not yet emancipated himself.　He broods over the same
thought, chews, as it were, the "cud of bitter fancies" only, "*semper
eandem canens cantilenam.*"　Here the picture is that of a man who
has all outward goods in abundance, but he just lacks that capacity for
enjoyment which is (as in ch. v. 20) the "gift of God," and he dies
childless and a stranger becomes the heir.　We are reminded of the
aged patriarch's exclamation, "I go childless, and the steward of my
house is this Eliezer of Damascus" (Gen. xv. 2).

3. *If a man beget an hundred children*]　A case is put, the very
opposite of that described in the preceding verse.　Instead of being
childless the rich man may have children, and children's children ; may
live out all his days.　What then?　Unless his "soul be filled with
good," unless there is the capacity for enjoyment, life is not worth
living.　Still, as before, "it were good never to have been born."
We may probably trace an allusive reference to Artaxerxes Mnemon,
who is reported to have had 115 children, and who died of grief at the
age of 94, at the suicide of one of his sons, and the murder of another,
both caused by a third son, Ochus, who succeeded him (Justin, x. 1).

and also that he have no burial]　The sequence of thought seems
at first strange.　Why should this be, from the writer's standpoint, as
the climax of sorrow?　Why should he who had noted so keenly the
vanities of life put seemingly so high a value on that which comes when
life is over and done with?　Some writers have felt this so strongly, that
they have suggested the interpretation, "*even if there be no grave
waiting for him*," *i.e.* even if he were to live for ever.　The natural
meaning is, however, tenable enough, and we have once more an echo
of Greek teaching.　Solon had taught that we are not to call any man
happy before his death, and by implication, in his story of the sons of
Tellus, had made the prospect of posthumous honour an element of
happiness (Herod. 1. 30).　So, in like manner, it was the direst of
woes for a man to know that he "should be buried with the burial of
an ass" (Jer. xxii. 19), or, in Homeric phrase, that his body should be
"cast out to dogs and vultures."　How could any man, however rich and
powerful, be sure that that fate might not be in store for him?　On
the assumption of the late date of the book, there may be a reference
to the death of Artaxerxes Ochus, who was murdered by the eunuch
Bagoas, and his body thrown to the cats.　Possibly, Koheleth himself
may have had some reason for an anxious doubt, whether the honours

4 he. For he cometh in with vanity, and departeth in dark-
5 ness, and his name shall be covered with darkness.   Moreover he hath not seen the sun, nor known *any thing:* this
6 hath more rest than the other.   Yea, though he live a
thousand years twice *told*, yet hath he seen no good : do
not all go to one place?
7   All the labour of man *is* for his mouth, and yet the appe-

of sepulture would be his. If, as seems likely, he was a stranger in a
strange land, alone and with no child to succeed him, perhaps with a
name cast out as evil or heretical, there was small chance of his being
laid to rest in the sepulchre of his fathers.   See the "Ideal Biography,"
Introduction, ch. III.

an untimely birth is better than he] The thought of ch. iv. 3 is
reproduced, but in a somewhat less generalized form.   There, never to
have been born, is asserted, after the manner of the Greek maxims
quoted in the notes, to be better than existence of any kind.   Here the
assertion is limited to the comparison with the joyless pursuit of wealth.
The "untimely birth" was the natural emblem of all abortive enterprise (Job iii. 16; Ps. lviii. 8).

4. *he cometh in with vanity*] The pronoun in the English Version
refers the clause to the man who has heaped up riches, and had a long
life with no real enjoyment.   Probably, however, the words describe, in
harmony with the thought of the preceding verse, the portion of the
still-born child.   It comes and goes, and is forgotten, and never sees
the sun, and tastes not the misery of life.   The last clause of verse 5,
there is rest to this rather than to that ("rest" idealised, as in Job
iii. 13, as in itself all but the supreme good that man can strive after),
seems to make this construction certain.   Possibly, however, the description of verse 4 is made to apply in part to both terms of the
comparison, so that it may be seen, on which side, both having so
much in common, the balance of advantage lies.   On "seeing the
sun" as an equivalent for living, see chs. vii. 11, xi. 7 ; Job iii. 16 ;
Ps. xlix. 20.

6. *Yea, though he live a thousand years twice told*] The weariness of life carries the thinker yet further.   Carry it to the furthest
point conceivable, and still the result is the same.   The longer it is,
the fuller of misery and woe.   The thought finds, as before, a parallel in
the speech of Solon to Crœsus (Herod. I. 32).   The man goes to the
same place,—to the dark, dreary world of Sheol, perhaps even to a more
entire annihilation than was implied in the Hebrew thought of that
unseen world,—as the abortive birth, with nothing but an accumulated
experience of wretchedness.   Depression could go no further.   See the
poem of Omar Khayyam in the *Appendix*.

7. *All the labour of man is for his mouth*] *i.e.* for self-preservation
and enjoyment.   That is assumed to be the universal aim, and yet even
that is not satisfied.   The "appetite," literally *soul* (not the higher,

tite is not filled.   For what hath the wise more than the 8
fool? what hath the poor, that knoweth to walk before the
living?   Better *is* the sight of the eyes than the wandering 9
of the desire: this *is* also vanity and vexation of spirit.
That which hath been is named already, and *it is* known 10

but the sensuous, element in man's nature), still craves for more.
Desire is progressive, and insatiable.

8. *For what hath the wise more than the fool?*] The question so
far is easy.   In this matter, the gifts of intellect make no difference.
The wise, no less than the fool, is subject to the pressure of bodily
necessities, and has to labour for them.   The second clause is somewhat less clear.   Of the many interpretations that have been given,
two have most to commend them, (1) supplying the subject of comparison from the first clause, **what advantage hath the poor that
knows to walk before the living** (*i.e. that has learnt the art to
live*) **over the fool** (*who is the mere slave of appetite*)? *what does
wisdom and self-control and freedom from the snares of wealth
really profit him?* and (2), treating the sentence as elliptical, **What
advantage hath the poor over him who knows how to walk before
the living** (*i.e.* the man of high birth or station, *who lives in public,
with the eyes of men on him*)?   The latter explanation has the merit
of giving a more balanced symmetry to the two clauses.   The question,
with its implied answer, seems at first at variance with the praise of
the lot of the labouring poor in ch. v. 12, "Don't trust," the writer
seems to say in his half-cynical, half-ironical mood, "even to poverty,
as a condition of happiness.   The poor man is as open to cares and
anxieties as the man of culture and refinement.   After all, poor and
rich stand on nearly the same level."

9. *Better is the sight of the eyes than the wandering of the desire*]
Literally, **than the wandering of the soul.**   The truth is substantially
that embodied in the fable of "the dog and his shadow" and in
proverbs like "a bird in the hand is worth two in the bush."   To
enjoy what we actually see, *i.e.* present opportunities, however limited,
is better than the cravings of a limitless desire, "wandering" at will
through all the region of possibilities.   In that wandering, there is
once more the **feeding upon wind.**   Perhaps, however, that sentence is
passed with an intentional ambiguity, characteristic of the writer (see
note on verse 9), upon the actual present enjoyment, as well as on the
unsatisfied desire, or upon the bare fact that the former with its lower
aims is better than the latter with its higher ones.

10. *That which hath been is named already*] ·The maxim is enigmatic.   As viewed by many commentators, it asserts that man is the
creature of a destiny, which he cannot resist.   Long ago, in the far
eternity, his name has been writtten, and what he will be.   He cannot
plead against the Power that is mightier than himself, *i.e.* against God.
There is nothing left but submission.   So taken, the words have a
parallel in all utterances in the Bible, or out of it, that assert, or seem

that it *is* man : neither may he contend with him that *is*
11 mightier than he.   Seeing there be many things that in-
12 crease vanity, what *is* man the better?   For who knoweth
what *is* good for man in *this* life, all the days of his vain

to assert, an absolutely predestinating fatalism (Isai. xlv. 9; Acts xv. 18;
Rom. ix. 20).   In such a fatalism, reconciled in some way or other
with man's freedom and responsibility, both the Stoics and Pharisees
believed, and so far there would be nothing strange in finding a like
maxim in a book which contains so many mingled and heterogeneous
elements, both Greek and Jewish, of oscillating thought.   There are,
however, what seem sufficient reasons for rejecting this interpretation.
The word for "already," which occurs only in this book (chs. i. 10,
ii. 12, iii. 15), is never used of the eternity of the Divine decrees, but,
as the passages referred to shew, of that which belongs essentially to
human history; that for "mightier," found in the O. T. only here and
in Ezr. iv. 20; Dan. ii. 40, 42, iv. 3, vii. 7, is not used, in any of
these passages, of God.   The sequence of thought leads the writer
to dwell on the shortness of man's life, rather than on its subjection to
a destiny.   The following explanation gives that sequence more clearly,
What he is, long ago his name was called.   In the last words
we find a reference to Gen. ii. 7, where the name of *Adam* (= man)
is connected with *Adamah* (= the ground), as *homo* was, by older philo-
logists, derived *ex humo*.   The very name of man bore witness to his
frailty.   This being so, he cannot take his stand in the cause, which
one "mightier" than himself pleads against him.   Death is that mightier
one, and will assert his power.   So taken, the thought is continuous
and harmonious throughout.

11.   *there be many things that increase vanity*]   The Hebrew noun,
as so often throughout the book, may stand either for *things* or *words*.
In the former case, the maxim points to the pressure of affairs, what
we call "business," the cares about many things, which make men feel
the hollowness of life.   In the latter, it probably refers to the speculative discussions on the chief good, destiny, and the like, which were
rife in the schools both of Jews and Greeks, and finds a parallel in
ch. xii. 12, and in Milton's description of like debates, as to

> "Fixed fate, free will, fore-knowledge absolute;
>   Vain wisdom all, and false philosophy."

The latter fits in best with the explanation which refers the previous
verse to the Divine decrees, the former with that which has been adopted
here.

what is man the better]   Literally, **what profit** (the word is another
form of that which occurs so frequently), what outcome, is there for
man ?

12.   *who knoweth what is good for man*]   We have once more the
distinctive formula of Pyrrhonism.   "Who knows ?" was the sceptic's
question, then as at all times.   See note on ch. iii. 21.   After all
discussions on the supreme good, some pointing to pleasure, and some

life which he spendeth as a shadow? for who can tell a
man what shall be after him under the sun?

A *good* name *is* better than precious ointment; and the **7**

to virtue, and some to apathy, who can give a definite and decisive
answer? Life remained after all vain, and not worth living. See again
the poem of Omar Khayyam in the *Appendix*.

which he spendeth as a shadow] The thought was so natural as to
be all but universal. It had been uttered by Job (viii. 9), and by
David (1 Chron. xxix. 15). It was uttered also by Sophocles :

ὁρῶ γὰρ ἡμᾶς οὐδὲν ὄντας ἄλλο, πλὴν
εἴδωλ᾽, ὅσοιπερ ζῶμεν, ἢ κούφην σκιάν.

"In this I see that we, all we that live,
Are but vain shadows, unsubstantial dreams."

Aias, **127**.

for who can tell a man] Man's ignorance of the future, of what may
become of children or estate, is, as before in chs. ii. 18, 19; iv. 7,
another element in the "vanity" of human life. Granted that it is
long and prosperous to the end, still the man is vexed or harassed with
the thought that his work may be all undone, his treasures wasted, his
plans frustrated.

CHAPTER VII.

1. *A good name is better than precious ointment*] The sequence of
thought is interrupted, and the writer, instead of carrying on the induction which is to prove that all is vanity, moralizes on the other results of
his experience. He has learnt to take a relative estimate of what men
count good or evil, truer than that which commonly prevails among
them. It lies almost in the nature of the case, that these moralizings
should take a somewhat discontinuous form, like that, *e.g.* of the *Pensées*
of Pascal or the *Meditations* of Marcus Aurelius, the entries, let us
say, which the thinker entered, day by day, in his tablets or on his *codex*.
They are marked, however, by a sufficient unity of tone. The same
pensive cast of thought is found in all, and it raises the thinker out of
a mere self-seeking, self-indulgent Epicureanism into a wider and nobler
sympathy. He rises as on the "stepping-stones" of his "dead self" to
higher things. Nor are the maxims indeed without a certain unity of
form, and the three words "it is better" in verses 1, 5, 8 serve as a
connecting link. The words and the maxims that follow in verses 2—5
have naturally been a stumblingblock to those who saw in Koheleth
nothing but the advocate of a sensual voluptuousness, and with the
desperate courage of men maintaining a theory, they argue (I take
Grätz as the representative of a school) that these are not the thoughts
of the **Debater** himself, but of some imaginary opponent of the ascetic
Essene type, against whom he afterwards enters his protest. The view
is, it is believed, just as untenable as that of the interpreters of the

2 day of death than the day of one's birth. *It is* better to

opposite school, who see in the oft-repeated precepts counselling moderate enjoyment nothing but the utterances of an ideal Epicurean, set
up for the purpose of being knocked down.

In the maxim which opens the series there is an alliterative emphasis, which is fairly represented by the German translation (Knobel)
"Besser gut Gerücht als güte Gerüche. The good name *(shem)* is
better than good ointment *(shemen)*, echoing in this respect the
words of Song Sol. i. 3, "A good name is better than good nard,"
is perhaps the nearest English approximation in this respect. The
maxim itself indicates a craving for something higher than the perfumed oil, which was the crowning luxury of Eastern life (Ps. xlv. 8;
Amos vi. 6; Luke vii. 37; Matt. xxvi. 7), even the praise and admiration of our fellow-men. To live in their memories, our name
as a sweet odour that fills the house, is better than the most refined
enjoyment. The student of the Gospel history will recall the contrast
between the rich man who fared sumptuously every day (Luke xvi.
19), whose very name is forgotten, and who is remembered only as a
type of evil, and the woman whose lavish gift of the ointment of
spikenard is told through the whole world as a memorial of her (Mark
xiv. 9), and who is identified by John, xii. 3, with Mary of Bethany.

and the day of death than the day of one's birth] The two parts of
the thought hang closely together. If the "good name" has been
earned in life, death removes the chance of failure and of shame. In
the language of Solon (Herod. I. 32) only he who crowns a prosperous
life by a peaceful death can be called truly happy. The thought
presents, however, a strange contrast to the craving for life which
was so strong an element, as in Hezekiah's elegy (Isai. xxxviii.
9—20), of Hebrew feeling, and is, like similar thoughts in ch. vi. 3, 4,
essentially ethnic in its character. So Herodotus (v. 4) relates that
the Trausi, a Thracian tribe, met on the birth of a child and bewailed
the woes and sorrows which were its inevitable portion, while they
buried their dead with joy and gladness, as believing that they were set
free from evils and had entered on happiness, or at least on the
unbroken rest of the eternal sleep. So Euripides, apparently with
reference to this practice, of which he may well have heard at the court
of Archelaus, writes in his *Cresphontes*,

> ἐδεῖ γὰρ ἡμᾶς σύλλογον ποιουμένους
> τὸν φύντα θρηνεῖν, εἰς ὅσ' ἔρχεται κακά·
> τὸν δ' αὖ θανόντα καὶ πόνων πεπαυμένον
> χαίροντας εὐφημοῦντας ἐκπέμπειν δόμων.

"It were well done, comparing things aright,
To wail the new-born child for all the ills
On which he enters; and for him who dies
And so has rest from labour, to rejoice
And with glad words to bear him from his home."

Strabo, who quotes the lines (xi. c. 12, p. 144), attributes the practice to

go to the house of mourning, than to go to the house of feasting: for that *is* the end of all men; and the living will lay *it* to his heart.   Sorrow *is* better than laughter: for by 3 the sadness of the countenance the heart is made better. The heart of the wise *is* in the house of mourning; but the 4

Asiatic nations, possibly to those who had come under the influence of that Buddhist teaching as to the vanity and misery of life of which even the partial pessimism of Koheleth may be as a far-off echo.

2. *It is better to go to the house of mourning, than to go to the house of feasting*]   The customs of Jewish mourning must be borne in mind to appreciate the full force of the maxim.   The lamentation lasting for seven (Ecclus. xxii. 10) or even for thirty, days, as in the case of Aaron (Num. xx. 29), and Moses (Deut. xxiv. 8), the loud wailing of the hired mourners (Jer. xxii. 18; Matt. ix. 23; Mark v. 38), the visits of consolation (John xi. 31), the sad meals of the bread and wine of affliction (Jer. xvi. 7; Hos. ix. 4; Job iv. 17),—the sight of these things checked the pride of life and called out sympathy, and reminded the visitor of the nearness of his own end,

> "Sunt lachrymæ rerum et mentem mortalia tangunt."

> "We needs must weep the chance and change of life,
> And mortal sorrows touch a mortal's heart."
>
> VIRG. *Æn.* I. 462.

The words manifestly record a personal experience, and lead us to think of the writer as having learnt to "visit the fatherless and widows in their affliction" (Jas. i. 27), and having found that there was some "profit" at least in this.

3. *Sorrow is better than laughter*]   The thought is essentially the same as that of the preceding verse, but is somewhat more generalized. We are reminded of the Greek axiom, παθεῖν, μαθεῖν ("Pain is gain"), of the teaching of Æschylus.

> Ζῆνα............
> τὸν φρονεῖν βροτοὺς ὁδώ-
> σαντα, τὸν πάθει μάθος
> θέντα κυρίως ἔχειν.

> "Yea, Zeus, who leadeth men in wisdom's way
> And fixeth fast the law
> That pain is gain."
>
> *Agam.* 170.

There is a moral improvement rising out of sorrow which is nót gained from enjoyment however blameless.   The "Penseroso" is after all a character of nobler stamp than the "Allegro."

4. *The heart of the wise*]   This follows as the natural sequel.   Like goes to like.   The impulse of the fool takes him to that which promises enjoyment; that of the wise leads him to that which has the promise of a higher wisdom and therefore of a more lasting gain.

5 heart of fools *is* in the house of mirth. *It is* better to hear
the rebuke of the wise, than for a man to hear the song of
6 fools.   For as the crackling of thorns under a pot, so *is* the
laughter of the fool : this also *is* vanity.

7   Surely oppression maketh a wise *man* mad ; and a gift

5. *It is better to hear the rebuke of the wise*] The word for " rebuke "
is characteristic of the sapiential books of the Old Testament (Prov.
xiii. 1, xvii. 10).   Here also the teacher finds the moral that " pain is
gain."   The " rebuke " is not pleasant, but it acts with a power to heal.
The " song of fools " points to the type of lyric poetry of which we
have examples in Anacreon, perhaps to the more wanton and impure
poems which entered so largely into Greek life, and are preserved in
such abundance in the *Anthologia Græca.*   The comic drinking songs
of a people represent at all times the lowest form of its animal life, and
with these also, either in his own country or in Greek-speaking lands,
the writer of the book had become acquainted.   Amos vi. 5 indicates
the existence of a like form of revelry in the older life of Israel.   Such
songs left a taint behind them and the man was permanently the worse
for it.   In Eph. v. 4 we may probably trace a reference to the same
form of literature.

6. *As the crackling of thorns under a pot*] As in verse 1 the epigrammatic proverb is pointed by a play of alliterative assonance (*sirim*
=thorns, *sir*=pot).   " As crackling nettles under kettles," " As
crackling stubble makes the pot bubble" are the nearest English equi-
valents.   The image is drawn from the Eastern use of hay, stubble,
and thorns for fuel (Matt. vi. 30; Ps. cxviii. 12).   A fire of such material,
burnt up more quickly than the charcoal embers (Jer. xxvi. 22;
John xviii. 18), which were also in common use, but then it also died out
quickly and left nothing but cold dead ashes.   So it would be with the
mirth which was merely frivolous or foul.   That also would take its
place in the catalogue of vanities.

7. *Surely oppression maketh a wise man mad*] Literally, **For oppression**... The sequence of thought is obscure and the English rendering is
an attempt to evade the difficulty by making what follows the beginning
of a new section.   One commentator (Delitzsch) cuts the knot by
supposing the first half of the verse to have been lost, and supplies
it conjecturally from Prov. xxxvii. 16 or xvi. 8, " Better is a little with
righteousness than great revenues without right," after which the
conjunction " for " comes in natural order.   Taking the text as it
stands we may yet trace a latent connexion.   The ' song ' and ' laughter '
of fools, *i. e.* of evil-doers, like those of Prov. i. 10—18; Wisd. ii. 1—20,
leads to selfish luxury, and therefore to all forms of unjust gain.   The
mirth of fools, *i. e.* of the godless, is vanity, *for* it issues in oppression and
in bribery.   It is a question whether the " wise man " who is thus mad-
dened by oppression is the oppressor or the oppressed.   The balance
seems to turn in favour of the former.   The oppressive exercise of
power is so demoralising that even the wise man, skilled in state-craft,

destroyeth the heart.   Better *is* the end of a thing than the 8
beginning thereof: *and* the patient in spirit *is* better than
the proud in spirit.   Be not hasty in thy spirit to be angry: 9
for anger resteth in the bosom of fools.   Say not thou, 10
What is *the cause* that the former days were better than

loses his wisdom.   There comes upon him, as the history of crime so
often shews, something like a mania of tyrannous cruelty.   And the
same effect follows on the practice of corruption.   It is true of the
giver as well as the receiver of a bribe, that he loses his "heart," *i.e.*
his power of moral discernment.

8.   *Better is the end of a thing than the beginning thereof*]   As in
ch. vi. 11, the noun translated "thing" may mean "word" and
this gives a preferable meaning.   It cannot be said of everything, good
and bad alike, that its "end is better than its beginning" (comp. Prov.
v. 3, 4, xvi. 25, xxiii. 32), and those who so interpret the maxim are
obliged to limit its meaning to good things, or to assume that the end
must be a good one.   Some (as Ginsburg) give to the "word" the sense
of "reproof," but this limitation is scarcely needed.   It may be said of
well-nigh every form of speech, for silence is better than speech, and
"in the multitude of words there wanteth not sin."   It is obvious that
this furnishes a closer parallel to the second clause.   The "patient in
spirit" is the man who knows how to check and control his speech,
and to listen to reproof.   The "proud" (literally, the **lofty** or **exalted**)
is one who has not learnt to curb his tongue, and to wait for the end
that is better than the beginning.   So interpreted the whole maxim
finds a parallel in James iii. 1—18, in the precepts of a thousand sages
of all times and countries.

9.   *Be not hasty in thy spirit to be angry*]   From sins of speech
in general, the teacher passes on to that which is the source from
which they most often flow.   Anger, alike from the Stoic and Epicurean stand-point (and the writer, as we have seen, had points of
contact with each of them), was the note of unwisdom.   If it be·right
at all, it is when it is calm and deliberate, an indignation against
moral evil.   The hasty anger of wounded self-love is, as in the teaching
of the Sermon on the Mount (Matt. v. 22), destructive of the tran·
quillity of true wisdom, and, transient and impulsive as it seems at first,
may harden "in the bosom of the fool" into a settled antipathy or
malignant scorn.

10.   *What is the cause that the former days were better than these*]
It would be a mistake to treat this as describing merely the
temper of one who is a "*laudator temporis acti, se puero.*"   That
is, as the poet noted (Hor. *Epist. ad Pis.* 173), but the infirmity of
age.   What is condemned as unwise, as we should call it in modern
phrase, unphilosophical, is the temper so common in the decay and
decadence of national life (and pointing therefore to the age in which
the **Debater** lived) which looks back upon the past as an age of heroes
or an age of faith, idealizing the distant time with a barren admiration,

these? for thou dost not inquire wisely concerning this.
11 Wisdom *is* good with an inheritance: and *by it there is*
12 profit to them that see the sun.   For wisdom *is* a defence,
and money *is* a defence: but the excellency of knowledge

apathetic and discontented with the present, desponding as to the
future. Such complaints are in fact (and this is the link which connects
this maxim with the preceding) but another form of the spirit which
is hasty to be angry, as with individual men that thwart its wishes,
so with the drift and tendency of the times in which it lives. The
wise man will rather accept that tendency and make the best of it.
Below the surface there lies perhaps the suggestion of a previous
question, Were the times really better? Had not each age had its
own special evils, its own special gains? Illustrations crowd upon
one's memory. Greeks looking back to the age of those who fought
at Marathon; Romans under the Empire recalling the vanished greatness of the Republic; Frenchmen mourning over the *ancien régime*,
or Englishmen over the good old days of the Tudors, are all examples
of the same unwisdom.

11. *Wisdom is good with an inheritance*] The words fall on our
ears with something like a ring of cynicism, as though the teacher said
with a sneer, "wisdom is all very well if you have property to fall back
upon." If that sense were however admissible at all, it could only
be by emphasizing the word "inheritance," as contrasted with the
treasure which a man heaps up for himself. The inherited estate, be
it great or small, does not interfere with wisdom as money-making
does. The ἀρχαιόπλουτοι ("rich with ancestral wealth") are, as Aristotle taught, of a nobler stamp than those who make their fortunes
(*Rhet.* II. 9. 9). Comp. Aesch. *Agam.* 1043. Even so taken, however,
the tone is entirely out of harmony with the immediate context, and
a far more satisfactory meaning is obtained by taking the preposition
as a particle of comparison (it is often so used, as in ch. ii. 17;
Ps. lxxiii. 5, cxx. 4 (probably); Job ix. 20); and so we get
"Wisdom is good **as** an inheritance."

and by it there is profit to them that see the sun] Better, **And it
is profitable for them that see the sun.** It stands instead of both
inherited and acquired wealth. In the use of the term "those that
see the sun" as an equivalent we note again an echo of Greek poetic
feeling. The very phrase ὁρᾶν φάος ἠελίοιο ("to see the light of the
sun") is essentially Homeric. Here, as in chap. xii. 7, it seems
chosen as half conveying the thought that there is after all a bright
side of life.

12. *For wisdom is a defence, and money is a defence*] Better, **as
a shadow**, or, **as a shelter**, in both clauses. The Hebrew, as the
italics shew, has no "and." "Shadow" as in Ps. xvii. 8, xci. 1,
stands for shelter and protection. This, the writer says, not without
a touch of his wonted irony in coupling the two things together,
to those who looked to wealth as their only means of safety (Prov.
xiii. 8), is found not less effectually in wisdom.

is, that wisdom giveth life to them that have it. Consider ₁₃
the work of God : for who can make *that* straight, which he
hath made crooked?   In the day of prosperity be joyful, ₁₄
but in the day of adversity consider: God also hath set
the one over against the other, to the end that man should
find nothing after him.

but the excellency of knowledge] Better, **the profit**, thus keeping
up what we may call the catch-word of the book. Wisdom, the
Debater says, does more than give shelter, as money, in its way,
does. It quickens those who have it to a new and higher life. The
use of the word ζωοποιήσει ("shall quicken"), by the LXX. connects
the maxim with the higher teaching of John v. 21, vi. 63; 2 Cor. iii. 6.
The Spirit which alone gives the wisdom that "cometh from above"
does the work which is here ascribed to wisdom as an abstract quality.
It is clearly out of harmony with the whole train of thought to see in
the "life" which wisdom gives only that of the body which is preserved by the prudence that avoids dangers. It is as much beside the
point to interpret it of the "life" of the resurrection.

13. *who can make that straight, which he hath made crooked*] The
sequence of thought is as follows. To "consider the work of God"
intelligently is one application of the wisdom which has been praised
in verses 11, 12. In so considering, the mind of the **Debater** goes
back to verse 10, and he bids men accept the outward facts of life
as they come. If they are "crooked," *i.e.* crossing and thwarting
our inclinations, we cannot alter them. It is idle, to take up a
Christian phrase that expresses the same thought, to seek to "change
our cross." We cannot alter the events of life, and our wisdom is
not merely to accept them as inevitable, but to adapt ourselves to
them. It is a striking example of Rabbinic literalism that the Chaldee
Targum refers the words to the impossibility of removing bodily
deformities, such as those of the blind, the hunchback, and the lame.
The word and the thought are clearly the same as in ch. i. 15.

14. *In the day of prosperity be joyful*] Literally, **In the day of good,
be in good**, *i.e.* use it as it should be used. True wisdom, the teacher
urges, is found in a man's enjoying whatever good actually comes
to him. The warning is against the temper which "taking thought for
the morrow," is

"over exquisite
To cast the fashion of uncertain evils."

And on the other hand he adds **In the day of evil, look well**, *i.e.*
consider why it comes, and what may be gained from it.

God also hath set the one over against the other] The words
assert what we should call the doctrine of averages in the distribution
of outward good and evil. **God has made one like** (or parallel with)
the other, balances this against that and this **in order that man may
find nothing at all after him.** The last words may mean either

15 All *things* have I seen in the days of my vanity: there is

(1) that man may have nothing more to learn or discover in his own hereafter; or (2) that man may fail to forecast what shall come to pass on earth after he has left it, as in ch. vi. 12, and may look to the future calmly, free from the idle dreams of pessimism or optimism. The last meaning seems most in harmony with the dominant tone of the book, and has parallels in the teaching of moralists who have given counsel based on like *data*.

In the noble hymn of Cleanthes to Zeus (18) we have the Stoic view in language presenting a striking parallel to that of verses 13, 14.

> ἀλλὰ σὺ καὶ τὰ περισσὰ ἐπίστασαι ἄρτια θεῖναι,
> καὶ κοσμεῖν τὰ ἄκοσμα, καὶ οὐ φίλα, σοὶ φίλα ἐστιν·
> ὧδε γὰρ εἰς ἓν ἅπαντα συνήρμοσας ἐσθλὰ κακοῖσιν,
> ὥσθ' ἕνα γίγνεσθαι πάντων λόγον αἰὲν ἐόντα.

> " Thou alone knowest how to change the odd
> To even, and to make the crooked straight,
> And things discordant find accord in Thee.
> Thus in one whole Thou blendest ill with good,
> So that one law works on for evermore."

The Epicurean poet writes:

> " Prudens futuri temporis exitum
> Caliginosa nocte premit Deus,
> Ridetque, si mortalis ultra
> Fas trepidat. Quod adest, memento
> Componere aequus; cetera fluminis
> Ritu feruntur, nunc medio alveo
> Cum pace delabentis Etruscum
> In mare, nunc lapides adesos,
> Stirpesque raptas et pecus et domos
> Volventis unâ."

> "God in His wisdom hides from sight,
> Veiled in impenetrable night,
> The future chance and change,
> And smiles when mortals' anxious fears,
> Forecasting ills of coming years,
> Beyond their limit range.

> "Use then the present well, and deem
> All else drifts onward, like a stream
> Whose waters seaward flow,
> Now gliding in its tranquil course,
> Now rushing on with headlong force
> O'er rocks that lie below."

Od. III. 29. 29—38.

a just *man* that perisheth in his righteousness, and there
is a wicked *man* that prolongeth *his life* in his wickedness.
Be not righteous over much ; neither make thyself over 16
wise : why shouldest thou destroy thyself? Be not over 17
much wicked, neither be thou foolish : why shouldest thou

15. *there is a just man that perisheth in his righteousness*] The
writer looks back on what he calls "the days of his vanity," his fleeting
and profitless life, and notes, as before in ch. ii. 14, 16, the disorders
and anomalies of the world. The righteous are "of all men most
miserable;" (1 Cor. xv. 19) the ungodly "prosper in the world " and
"come in no peril of death, but are lusty and strong," Ps. lxxiii. 4
(P. B. version).   Here indeed those disorders present themselves
in their most aggravated form.   It is not only, as in ch. iii. 19, that
there is one event to the righteous and the wicked, but that there is an
apparent inversion of the right apportionment of good and evil.   The
thought is the same as that of Ps. lxxiii., and the **Debater** has not as yet
entered, as the Psalmist did, into the sanctuary of God, and so learnt to
"understand the end of these men" (Ps. lxxiii. 17).   The same problem
in the moral order of the Universe furnishes a theme for the discussions
of the Book of Job.

16. *Be not righteous over much*] Here again we have a distinct
reproduction of one of the current maxims of Greek thought, Μηδὲν
ἀγὰν (*Ne quid nimis*—Nothing in excess) of Theognis 402. and of Chilon
(Diog. Laert. 1. 1, § 41).   Even in that which is in itself good, virtue
lies, as Aristotle had taught (*Eth. Nicom.* 11. 6. 7), in a mean between
opposite extremes.   Popular language has embodied the thought in the
proverb, *Summum jus, summa injuria*.   Even in the other sense of
"righteousness," as meaning personal integrity, personal religion, there
might be, as in the ideal of the Pharisees and Essenes and Stoics, the
"vaulting ambition" that o'erleaps itself."   And " what was true of
righteousness was true also of speculative philosophy.   The wisdom
that will not be content to rest in ignorance of the unknowable is
indeed unwisdom, and "fools rush in where angels fear to tread."

why shouldest thou destroy thyself?] The primary meaning of the verb
in the form used here is that of "being amazed, stunned, astonished,"
and may have been chosen to express the besotted and bedazed spiritual
pride which St Paul paints by the participle "puffed up" (τυφωθείς) in
1 Tim. iii. 5, and which was but too commonly the accompaniment of
fancied excellence in knowledge or in conduct.

17. *Be not over much wicked*] There seems something like a paradox
in the counsel.   Surely, we think, the teacher is carrying his doctrine
of the mean too far when he gives a precept, which, by forbidding
excess, seems to sanction a moderate amount of wickedness.   Various
attempts have been made to tone down the precept by taking "wicked"
as = not subject to rule, or = engaged in worldly affairs (the "mammon of
unrighteousness") that so often lead to wickedness.   The difficulty
vanishes, however, if we will but admit that the writer might have

18 die before thy time? *It is* good that thou shouldest take
hold of this; yea, also from this withdraw not thine hand:
for he that feareth God shall come forth of them all.
19 Wisdom strengtheneth the wise more than ten mighty *men*

learnt the art of a playful irony from his Greek teachers. He has uttered
the precept, "Be not righteous over-much." That most men would
receive as a true application of the doctrine of "Nothing in excess," or,
in the phrase we owe to Talleyrand, "*Surtout, point de zêle.*" He
mentally sees, as it were, the complacent smile of those who were in no
danger of that fault and who think that the precept gives them just the
license they want, and he meets the feeling it expresses by another
maxim. "Yes, my friends," he seems to say, "but there is another
'over-much,' against which you need a warning, and its results are
even more fatal than those of the other." In avoiding one extreme men
might fall easily into the other.

why shouldest thou die before thy time?] Literally, **Not in thy time.**
The form of the warning is singularly appropriate. The vices thought
of and the end to which they lead are clearly those of the sensual
license described in Prov. vii. Death is the issue here, as the loss of
spiritual discernment was of the Pharisaic or the over-philosophizing
temper described in the preceding verse. In both precepts we may
trace Koheleth's personal experience. Ch. ii. traces the history of
one who in his life experiments had been both "over much wise," and,
it must be feared, "over much wicked."

18. *It is good*] The sentence is somewhat enigmatic, and its meaning
depends on the reference given to the two pronouns. Commonly, the
first "this" is referred to the "righteousness and wisdom" of verse 16,
the second "this" to the "wickedness and folly" of verse 17, and the
Teacher is supposed to recommend a wide experience of life, the tasting of "the fruit of the tree of knowledge of good and evil," which, as in
ch. i. 17, shall embrace both, and bring with it a corresponding largeness of heart. This gives, of course, a perfectly intelligible meaning, though
it is not that of a high-toned morality, and belongs to the earlier rather
than the later stage of the **Debater's** progress. The close parallelism
of ch. xi. 6 suggests however another and preferable interpretation.
The first and the second "this" and "that" of that verse are both indefinite, used alike of such work and opportunities as God gives. So
taken, the precept now before us runs much in the same line of thought,
"Lay hold on this—do not let that slip—do what thy hand findeth to
do. Only be sure that it is done in the right spirit, for "he that feareth
God," he, and he alone, "comes forth of all things well," *i.e.* does
his duty and leaves the result to God. This temper, in exact harmony
with the practical good sense of moderation, is contrasted with the
falsehood of extremes condemned in the two previous verses.

19. *Wisdom strengtheneth the wise*] The fact that the **Debater** had
not forgotten that "the fear of the Lord is the beginning of wisdom"
(Prov. i. 7; Ps. cxi. 10; Job xxviii. 21) serves as the connecting link

which are in the city. For *there is* not a just man upon 20
earth, that doeth good, and sinneth not. Also take no 21
heed unto all words that are spoken; lest thou hear thy

between this and the pieceding verse. The "ten mighty men" stand
as a vague number, *certus pro incerto* (comp. Gen. xxxi. 7; Num. xiv.
22), and it is a fantastic line of interpretation to connect them with
any definite political organization, Assyrian viceroys, Persian vice-
satraps, Roman decurions, or the like. It is, however, an interesting
coincidence, pointed out by Mr Tyler, that a city was defined by the
Mishna (*Megila* 1. 3) to be a town in which there were ten *Batlanim*, or
men of leisure, to constitute a synagogue. A striking parallel is found in
Ecclus. xxxvii. 14, "A man's mind is wont to tell him more than seven
men that sit upon a tower." What is meant is generally that the
wisdom that fears God is better than mere force, that moral strength is
in the long run mightier than material. Wise statesmen may do more
than generals.

20. *For there is not a just man upon earth*] The sequence of thought
is again obscure. We fail at first to see how the fact of man's sinfulness
is the ground of the maxim that wisdom is a better defence than material
strength. The following train of associations may perhaps supply the
missing link. There had been a time when the presence of *ten* righteous
men would have preserved a guilty city from destruction (Gen. xviii. 32).
But no such men were found, and the city therefore perished. And
experience shews that no such men—altogether faultless—will be found
anywhere. No one therefore can on that ground claim exemption
from chastisement. What remains for the wise man but to fall
back on the wisdom which consists in the "fear of God" (verse
13), the reverential awe which will at least keep him from pre-
sumptuous sins. Substantially the thought is that of a later teaching,
that "in many things we offend all" (James iii. 2), and therefore that
a man is justified by faith (the New Testament equivalent for "the
fear of the Lord" as the foundation of a righteous life), and not by
works, though not without them. Here again we may compare the
Stoic teaching, "Wise men are rare. Here and there legends tell
of one good man, or it may be two, as of strange præter-natural being
rarer than the Phœnix....All are evil and on a level with each other, so
that this differs not from that, but all are alike insane" (Alex. Aphrod.
de Fato 28).

21. *Also take no heed unto all words that are spoken*] The train of
thought leads on to another rule of conduct. The fact that all men
sin is shewn by the words with which men talk of the faults and
weaknesses of their neighbours. To such words, the idle gossip of
rumour, the comments on words or acts, no wise man will give heed.
For him, in St Paul's language, it will be "a very small thing to be
judged of man's judgment" (1 Cor. iv. 3). An idle curiosity to know
what other people say of us will for the most part bring with it the
mortification of finding that they blame rather than praise. No man is
a hero to his valet, and if he is anxious to know his servant's estimate

22 servant curse thee: for oftentimes also thine own heart knoweth that thou thyself likewise hast cursed others.

23   All this have I proved by wisdom: I said, I will be wise; 24 but it *was* far from me. That which is far off, and exceed- 25 ing deep, who can find it out? I applied mine heart to know, and to search, and to seek out wisdom, and the

of him, he may discover, however wise and good he strives to be, that it may find utterance in a curse and not a blessing. So, in political life, men have been known (*e.g.* Pompeius in the case of Sertorius) to burn the papers of their fallen foes. So in literary life some of the wise of heart have laid it down as a rule not to read reviews of their own writings. The same feeling finds an epigrammatic expression in the proud motto of a Scotch family:

"They say: What say they? Let them say!"

22. *For oftentimes also thine own heart*] The rule of the previous verse is backed by an appeal to a man's own conscience, *"mutato nomine de te fabula narratur."* "Thou too art not free from the habit of censorious censure, of hard and bitter speeches; even, it may be, of 'cursing,' where blessing would have been better."

23. *I said, I will be wise; but it was far from me*] The words express at once the high aim of the seeker and his sense of in- completeness. Wisdom in its fulness was for him, as for Job (chap. xxviii.) far above out of his reach. He had to give up the attempt to solve the problems of the Universe, and to confine himself to rules of conduct, content if he could find guidance there.

24. *That which is far off and exceeding deep*] The English of the latter clause scarcely expresses the Hebrew more emphatic iteration **and deep deep.** By some interpreters a like iteration is supplied in the first clause, **far off is that which is far,** but there does not seem adequate ground for thus altering the text. Rather are the first words to be taken of substantial being, **far off from us is that which is** (the τὰ ὄντα of Greek thought, the sum total of things past and present). So in another and later Jewish book impregnated, like this, with Greek thought, wisdom is described as a τῶν ὄντων γνῶσις ἀψευδής ("a true knowledge of the things that are" Wisd. vii. 17). Comp. Job. xi. 7, 8; Rom. xi. 33, for like language as to the Divine Counsels.

25. *I applied mine heart to know*] The present text and punc- tuation give, as in the marginal reading of the A. V., **I and my heart.** The expression has no exact parallel in O. T. language, but harmonizes with the common mode of speech, familiar enough in the poetry of all times and countries, furnishing a title ("My Soul and I") to a poem of Whittier's, in which a man addresses his heart or soul (comp. Luke xii. 19), as something distinguishable from himself. So in ch. i. 13 we have "I gave my heart." Here the thought implied seems to be that of an intense retrospective consciousness of the experience, or experiment, of life which the seeker is about to narrate.

reason *of things*, and to know the wickedness of folly, even
of foolishness *and* madness : and I find more bitter than 26
death the woman, whose heart *is* snares and nets, *and* her

The words indicate another return to the results of that experience
and the lessons it had taught him. He turned to ask the *"reason,"*
better perhaps, the *plan* or *rationale*, of the prevalence of madness
and folly. We note, as before in ch. ii. 12, the Stoic manner of
dealing with the follies of men as a kind of mental aberration.

26. *And I find more bitter than death*] The result is a strange
one in its contrast to the dominant tendency of Hebrew thought;
especially we may add to that thought as represented by the Son of
David with whom the **Debater** identifies himself. We think of the
praises of the Shulamite in the Song of Solomon; of the language of
Prov. v. 13; and (though that is probably of later date) of the acrostic
panegyric on the virtuous woman in Prov. xxxi. 10—31; and we find
here nothing like an echo of them, but rather a tone of scorn, cul-
minating in verse 28 in that which reminds us of the misogyny of
the later maxim-makers of Greece, or of the Eastern king who never
heard of any great calamity or crime without asking, Who is *she?*
Such a change might, it is true, be explained as the result of the
satiety into which the historical Solomon might have fallen as the
penalty of his sensuality; and has its parallel in the cynical scorn of
Catullus for the Lesbia whom he had once loved so tenderly (see
Introduction, ch. iii.) and in that of a thousand others. Doubtless the
words speak of such a personal experience on the part of the **Debater**.
He had found no wickedness like that of the "strange woman," such
as she is painted in Prov. ii. 16—19, vii. 1—27. But we can scarcely
fail to trace the influence of the Greek thought with which, as we have
seen, the writer had come into contact. Of this the following may
serve as samples out of a somewhat large collection.

> Μεστὸν κακῶν πέφυκε φορτίον γυνή.

"A woman is a burden full of ills."

> Ὅπου γυναῖκες εἰσι, πάντ' ἐκεῖ κακά.

"Where women are, all evils there are found."

> Θηρῶν ἁπάντων ἀγριωτέρα γυνή.

"Woman is fiercer than all beasts of prey."

> *Poet. Graec. Gnomici*, Ed. Tauchnitz, p. 182.

It might, perhaps, be pleaded in reference to this verse that the
writer speaks of one class of women only, probably that represented
in the pictures of Prov. ii. or vii. and that the "*corruptio optimi est
pessima,*" but the next verse makes the condemnation yet more sweeping.
The suggestion that the writer allegorizes, and means by "the woman"
here the abstract ideal of sensuality is quite untenable.

In the imagery of "snares" and "nets" and "bands" some critics

hands *as* bands : whoso pleaseth God shall escape from her;
27 but the sinner shall be taken by her.   Behold, this have I
found, saith the Preacher, *counting* one by one, to find out
28 the account: which yet my soul seeketh, but I find not:
one man among a thousand have I found; but a woman

(Tyler) have traced a reminiscence of the history of Samson and
Delilah (Judg. xvi.).   Such a reference to Hebrew history is however
not at all after the writer's manner, and it is far more natural to see
in it the result of his own personal experience (see *Introduction*, ch. III.).
The Son of Sirach follows, it may be noted, in the same track of thought,
though with a somewhat less sweeping condemnation (Ecclus. xxv.
15—26, xxvi. 6—12).

whoso pleaseth God]   The marginal reading, **whoso is good before
God** should be noted as closer to the Hebrew.

27.   *saith the Preacher*]   The passage is remarkable as being the
solitary instance in the book in which the name *Koheleth*, feminine in
form, yet elsewhere treated as masculine, is joined with the feminine
form of the verb.   It is possible, however, that this may be only an
error of transcription, the transfer of a single letter from the end of
one word to the beginning of another, restoring the verse to the more
common construction, as found, *e. g.* in chap. xii. 8, where, as here,
adopting this reading, the article is prefixed to the word Koheleth, elsewhere treated as a proper name.

counting one by one]   The words remind us, on the one hand, of
Diogenes the Cynic, with his lantern, looking for an honest man at
Athens, and answering, when asked where such men might be found,
that good *men* were to be found nowhere, and good *boys* only in
Sparta (Diog. Laert. VI. 2. 27); and on the other, of Jeremiah's search
to see "if there were any in Jerusalem that sought after God" (Jer.
v. 1—5).   The words, as it were, drag their slow length along, as
if expressing the toil and weariness of the search.   And after all he
had failed to find.

28. *one man among a thousand have I found*]   We have, in the absence
of an adjective, to supply the thought "a man such as he ought to be,
truthful and righteous."   The form in which the rare exceptional discovery
is given is as an echo from Job ix. 3, xxxiii. 23.   It represents we cannot doubt the capacity of the writer for a warm and earnest friendship.
It shews that he had found one such friend.   But what the seeker found
among men, he sought in vain among women.   Corruption there was,
from his point of view, absolutely without exception.   The interesting
parallelism of Heine's language has been noticed in the *Introduction*,
ch. III.   The words may be received as recording the writer's personal
experience of the corrupt social state under the government of Persian
or Egyptian kings.   One commentator (Hitzig) has even ventured to
identify the "woman more bitter than death" with a historical character,
Agathoclea, the mistress of Ptolemy Philopator.   Justin (xxx. 1)
describes the King's life "*Meretricis illecebris capitur...noctes in stupris,
dies in conviviis consumit.*"

among all those have I not found. Lo, this only have I 29
found, that God hath made man upright; but they have
sought out many inventions.

Here also we have an echo of the darker side of Greek thought.
The **Debater** catches the tone of the woman-hater Euripides.

> ἀλλ' ὡς τὸ μῶρον ἀνδράσιν μὲν οὐκ ἔνι,
> γυναιξὶ δ' ἐμπέφυκεν.

> "But folly does not find its home with men,
>   But roots in women's hearts."

EURIP. Hippol. 920.

So a later Rabbinic proverb gives a like judgment : "woe to the age
whose leader is a woman" (Dukes, *Rabbin. Blumenl.* No. 32).

29. *They have sought out many inventions*] The Hebrew word
implies an ingenuity exercised mainly for evil but takes within its range,
as in 2 Chron. xxvi. 15, the varied acts of life which are in themselves
neither good nor evil. This inventive faculty, non-moral at the best,
often absolutely immoral, was what struck the thinker as characterising
mankind at large.

In this thought again we have an unmistakable echo of the language
of Greek thinkers. Of this the most memorable example is, perhaps,
the well-known chorus in the *Antigone* 332—5

> πολλὰ τὰ δεινὰ κοὐδὲν ἀνθρώπου δεινότερον πέλει.
> *　　*　　*　　*　　*　　*

> σοφόν τι τὸ μηχανόεν τέχνας ὑπὲρ ἐλπίδ' ἔχων,
> ποτὲ μὲν κακόν, ἀλλοτ' ἐπ' ἐσθλὸν ἕρπει.

> "Many the things that strange and wondrous are,
>   None stranger and more wonderful than man.
> *　　*　　*　　*　　*　　*

>   And lo, with all this skill,
>   Wise and inventive still
>   Beyond hope's dream,
>   He now to good inclines
>   And now to ill."

Looking to the relation in which the poem of Lucretius stands to the
system of Epicurus it is probable that the history of human inventions
in the *De Rerum Natura*, v. 1281—1435 had its fore-runner in some of
the Greek writings with which the author of *Ecclesiastes* appears to have
been acquainted. The student will find another parallel in the narrative
of the progress of mankind in the *Prometheus Bound* of Æschylus
(450—514). Both these passages are somewhat too long to quote.

8   Who *is* as the wise *man?* and who knoweth the interpretation of a thing? a man's wisdom maketh his face to shine,
2 and the boldness of his face shall be changed. I *counsel thee* to keep the king's commandment, and *that* in regard of

CHAPTER VIII.

1. *Who is as the wise man?*] The question comes in abruptly as from a teacher who calls the attention of his scholars to things that are φωνήεντα συνέτοισιν ("significant to those who understand") and remind us of the "He that hath ears to hear let him hear" in our Lord's teaching (Matt. xi. 15, xiii. 9; Mark iv. 9). Something there was in what he is about to add, to be read between the lines. It required a a man to "know the interpretation" (the noun is Chaldaean and is found, with a slight variation, as the prominent word in Dan. iv. v. vii.) of the "thing" or better, "of the **word.**" We find the probable explanation of this suggestive question in the fact that the writer veils a protest against despotism in the garb of the maxims of servility.

a man's wisdom maketh his face to shine] Literally, **illuminates his face.** The word paints with a wonderful vividness the almost transfiguring effect of the "sweetness and light" of a serene wisdom, or of the joy that brightens a man's countenance when he utters his *Eureka* over the solution of a long-pondered problem.

the boldness of his face shall be changed] Literally, **the strength of face,** *i.e.* its **sternness.** The words have been very variously translated, (1) as in the LXX. "his shameless face shall be hated," (2) as by Ewald "the brightness of his countenance shall be doubled." There is no ground, however, for rejecting the Authorised Version. The "boldness of the face" is, as in the "fierce countenance" of Deut. xxviii. 50; Dan. viii. 23, the "impudent face" of Prov. vii. 13, the coarse ferocity of ignorance, and this is transformed by culture. The maxim is like that of the familiar lines of Ovid,

> "Adde quod ingenuas didicisse fideliter artes,
>   Emollit mores nec sinit esse feros."

> "To learn in truth the nobler arts of life,
>   Makes manners gentle, rescues them from strife."

> *Epp. ex Ponto* II. 9. 47.

2. *I counsel thee to keep the king's commandment*] The words in Italics "*counsel thee*," have nothing answering to them in the Hebrew, and the grammar of the sentence does not allow us to translate with the Vulgate, "I keep the king's commandment." The pronoun on the other hand is emphatic and it introduces a series of precepts. We have therefore to supply a verb, *I, for my part, say*, which is practically equivalent to the English Version. The reference to the king is not without its bearing on the political surroundings of the writer and therefore on the date of the book. It is a natural inference from it that

the oath of God. Be not hasty to go out of his sight: 3
stand not in an evil thing; for he doeth whatsoever pleaseth

the writer, whether living in Palestine or elsewhere, was actually under
a kingly government and not under that of a Satrap or Governor under
the Persian King, and that the book must therefore have been written
after the Persian rule had become a thing of the past. On this view
Ptolemy Philopator has been suggested by one writer (Hitzig); Herod
the Great by another (Grätz). See *Introduction*, ch. II. The interpretation
which explains the word as referring to the Divine King must be rejected
as allegorising and unreal. The whole tone of the passage, it may be
added, is against the Solomonic authorship of the book. The writer
speaks as an observer studying the life of courts from without, not as a
king asserting his own prerogative. Even on the assumption that Prov.
xxv. 2—6 came from the lips of Solomon, they are pitched in a very
different key from that which we find here.

and that in regard of the oath of God] It is not without significance
as bearing on the question of the date and authorship of the book,
that Josephus relates (*Ant.* XII. 1) that Ptolemy Soter, the Son of
Lagus, carried into Egypt a large number of captives from Judæa and
Samaria, and settled them at Alexandria, and knowing their scrupulous
reverence for oaths, bound them by a solemn covenant to obey him and
his successors. Such an oath the **Debater** ·bids men observe, as St
Paul bade Christians obey the Emperor, "not only for wrath but also for
conscience' sake" (Rom. xiii. 5). Submission was the part of a wise
man seeking for tranquillity, however bad the government might be.
Of such covenants between a people and their king we have an example
in 1 Chron. xxix. 24.

3. *Be not hasty to go out of his sight*] The phrase is explained by
Gen. iv. 16; Hos. xi. 2 as implying flight or desertion. Such a flight
the Teacher looks on as an act of impatient unwisdom. It is better to
bear the yoke, than to seek an unattainable independence. So those
who have grown grey in politics warn younger and more impetuous
men against the folly of a premature resignation of their office.

stand not in an evil thing] The Hebrew noun (as so often elsewhere) may mean either "word" or "thing:" the verb may mean
"standing" either in the attitude (1) of persistence, or (2) protest, or
(3) of hesitation, or (4) of obedient compliance. Hence we get as
possible renderings, (1) "Persist not in an evil thing;" *i.e.* in conspiracies against the king's life or power. (2) Protest not against an
evil (*i.e.* angry) word. (3) Stand not, hesitate not, at an evil thing, *i.e.*
comply with the king's commands however unrighteous. (4) Obey not
in an evil thing, *i.e.* obey, but let the higher law of conscience limit thy
obedience. Of these (1) seems most in harmony with the context, and
with O. T. usage as in Ps. I. 1. Perhaps, however, after the manner
of an enigmatic oracle, not without a touch of irony, requiring the
discernment of a wise interpreter, there is an intentional ambiguity,
allowing the reader if he likes, to adopt (3) or (4) and so acting as a
test of character.

4 him.   Where the word of a king *is*, *there is* power : and who
5 may say unto him, What doest thou?   Whoso keepeth the
commandment shall feel no evil thing : and a wise *man*'s
heart discerneth *both* time and judgment.

he doeth whatsoever pleaseth him]   The words paint a sovereignty such
as Greek poets loved to hold up for men's abhorence,

ἀλλ' ἡ τυραννὶς πολλά τ' ἄλλ' εὐδαιμονεῖ,
κἄξεστιν αὐτῇ δρᾶν λέγειν δ' ἃ βούλεται.

"The tyrant's might in much besides excels,
And it may do and say whate'er it wills."
SOPH. *Antig.* 507.

Here also we have an echo of the prudential counsel of Epicurus, who
deliberately preferred a despotic to a democratic government (Sen.
Ep. XXIX. 10), and laid it down as a rule, that the wise man should at
every opportune season court the favour of the monarch (καὶ μόναρχον
ἐν καιρῷ θεραπεύσει), Diog. Laert. X. 1, § 121.

4.   *Where the word of a king is, there is power*]   Better, **Forasmuch
as the word of a king is power**, or rather **authority**.   The latter
word in the Hebrew text is used in Chaldee as meaning a ruler, or
potentate.   In the last clause, "Who may say unto him, What doest
thou?" we have an echo of Job xxxiv. 13, where the question is asked
in reference to the sovereignty of God.   The covert protest of the writer
shews itself in thus transferring, as with a grave irony, what belonged
to the Divine King to the earthly ruler who claimed a like authority.
The despot stands, or thinks he stands, as much above the questionings
and complaints of his subjects, as the Supreme Ruler of the Universe
does those of men in general.

5.   *Whoso keepeth the commandment shall feel no evil thing*]   The
words are once again ambiguous.   If the "commandment" is that of
the king, obedience enjoins unhesitating servile as in the interpretation (3) of verse 3.   If, according to the all but invariable use of the word
in the O. T., we take it as the "commandment" of God, the meaning is
in harmony with the interpretation (4) of the previous precept, and
parallel with the French motto, "*Fais ton devoir, avienne que pourra*"
("Do thy duty, come what may").   Here again, it seems natural to assume an intentional ambiguity.   A like doubt hangs over the words "shall
feel (literally **know**) no evil thing" which may mean either "shall be
anxious about no moral evil," or more probably "shall suffer no physical
evil as the penalty of moral."   Can we not imagine the writer here
also with a grave irony, uttering his Delphic oracles, and leaving men
to choose their interpretation, according as their character was servile
or noble, moved by "the fear of the Lord," or only by the fear of men?

a wise man's heart discerneth both time and judgment]   The "heart"
as, for the most part, elsewhere in the Old Testament, includes the
intellectual as well as the moral element in man's nature.   In the
word "time" we have, as in ch. iii. 1, the καιρός or "season" on
which Greek sages laid so great a stress.   What is meant is that the

Because to every purpose there is time and judgment, 6 therefore the misery of man *is* great upon him. For he 7 knoweth not that which shall be: for who can tell him when it shall be? *There is* no man that hath power over 8 the spirit to retain the spirit; neither *hath he* power in the

wise man, understanding the true meaning of the previous maxim, will not be impatient under oppression, but will bide his time, and wait in patience for the working of the Divine Law of retribution. This meaning is, however, as before, partially veiled, and the sentence might seem to imply that he should let his action depend on opportunities and be a time-server in the bad sense.

6. *Because to every purpose there is time and judgment, therefore*] The English conjunctions misrepresent the sequence of thought, and we should read "**For** to every purpose there is time and judgment, **for** the misery (or, better, *the wickedness*) of man..." The wise man waits for the time of judgment, for he knows that such a time must come, and that the evil of the man (*i.e.* of the tyrant) is great upon him, weighs on him as a burden under which he must at last sink. This seems the most natural and legitimate interpretation, but the sentence is obscure, and has been very differently interpreted. (1) The evil of man (of the oppressor) is heavy upon him (the oppressed). (2) Though there is a time and a judgment, yet the misery of man is great, because (as in the next verse) he knows not when it is to come.

7. *For he knoweth not that which shall be*] The subject of the sentence is apparently the wicked and tyrannous ruler. He goes on with infatuated blindness to the doom that lies before him. The same thought appears in the mediæval proverb, "*Quem Deus vult perdere prius dementat,*" or, in our modern condemnation of the rulers or the parties, who "learn nothing, and forget nothing." The temper condemned is that (1) of the cynical egoism, which says, "*Apres moi, le deluge,*" (2) of those who act, because judgment is delayed, as if it would never come.

8. *There is no man that hath power over the spirit*] The word for "spirit," may mean either "the wind" or the "spirit," the "breath of life" in man, and each sense has been adopted by many commentators. Taking the former, which seems preferable, the latter involving a repetition of the same thought in the two clauses of the verse, we have a parallel in Prov. xxx. 4, perhaps also in John iii. 8. Man is powerless to control the course of the wind, so also is he powerless (the words, though general in form, point especially to the tyrannous oppressor,) to control the drift of things, that is bearing him on to his inevitable doom. The worst despotism is, as Talleyrand said of Russia, "tempered by assassination."

neither hath he power in the day of death] Better, **over the day of death.** The analogy of the previous clause, as to man's impotence to control or direct the wind, suggests that which is its counterpart. When "the day of death" comes, whether by the hand of the assassin,

day of death : and *there is* no discharge in *that* war ; neither
9 shall wickedness deliver those that are given to it.   All
this have I seen, and applied my heart unto every work
that is done under the sun : *there is* a time wherein one
10 man ruleth over another to his own hurt.   And so I saw

or by disease and decay, man (in this case again the generalized
thought applies especially to the oppressor) has no power, by any
exercise of will, to avert the end.   The word for "power" in the
second clause is, as in Dan. iii. 3, the concrete of the abstract form
in the first, **There is no ruler in the day of death.**

there is no discharge in that war]   The word for "discharge" occurs
elsewhere only in Ps. lxxviii. 49, where it is rendered "sending,"
and as the marginal reading ("no casting of weapons") shews has been
variously interpreted.   That reading suggests the meaning that "in
that war (against death), there is no weapon that will avail."   The
victorious leader of armies must at last succumb to a conqueror mightier
than himself.   The text of the English version is probably, however,
correct as a whole, and the interpolated "*thát*," though not wanted, is
perhaps excusable.   The reference is to the law (Deut. xx. 5—8) which
allowed a furlough, or release from military duty, in certain cases, and
which the writer contrasts with the inexorable sternness which summons
men to their battle with the king of terrors, and that a battle with a
foregone and inevitable conclusion.   Here the strict rigour of Persian
rule under Darius and Xerxes, which permitted no exemption from
service in time of war, was the true parallel (Herod. IV. 84, VII. 38).

neither shall wickedness deliver those that are given to it]   Better,
neither shall wickedness deliver its lord.   The last word is the same
as Baal, in the sense of a "lord" or "possessor," and is joined with
words expressing qualities to denote that they are possessed in the
highest degree.   Thus "a lord of tongue" is a "babbler" (ch. x. 11),
"lord of hair" is "a hairy man" (2 Kings i. 8), and so on.   Here,
therefore, it means those who are specially conspicuous for their
wickedness.   The thought is as before, that a time comes at last, when
all the schemes and plans of the oppressor fail to avert his punishment,
as surely as all efforts to prolong life fail at last to avert death.

9.   *All this have I seen*]   The formula which had been used before
(chs. v. 18, vii. 23) to enforce the results of the **Debater's** experience
of life in general, is now employed to emphasize the wide range of the
political induction on which the conclusions of the previous verses
rested.

there is a time wherein one man ruleth over another to his own hurt]
The Hebrew is, as in so many other instances, ambiguous.   The English
reflexive pronoun, in which our Version follows the Vulgate, misrepre-
sents the purport of the sentence.   What is described is, as before, the
misrule of the tyrant-king who rules over others (the indefinite "another"
standing for the plural) to **their** hurt.   The wide induction had not
been uniform in its results.   The law of Nemesis was traversed by

the wicked buried, who had come and gone from the place
of the holy, and they were forgotten in the city where they
had so done: this *is* also vanity.

the law of apparent impunity. We have the "two voices" once
again, and the writer passes, like Abelard in his *Sic et Non*, from
affirmation to denial. The English version seems to have originated
in the wish to make this verse also repeat the affirmation of the
preceding. The immediate context that follows shews however that
this is not now the writer's thought, and that he is troubled by the
apparent exceptions to it.

10. *And so I saw the wicked buried*] The English version is
scarcely intelligible, and as far as it is so, goes altogether astray.
We must therefore begin with a new translation, **And so I have seen
the wicked buried and they went their way** (*i.e.* died a natural death
and were carried to the grave); **but from the holy place they de-
parted** (*i.e.* were treated with shame and contumely, in some way
counted unholy and put under a ban), **and were forgotten in the
city, even such as acted rightly.**

The verse will require, however, some explanation in details. In
the burial of the wicked we have a parallel to the pregnant significance of the word in the parable of, Dives and Lazarus, where
"the rich man died and was buried" (Luke xvi. 22). This, from the
Jewish standpoint, was the fit close of a prosperous and honoured
life (comp. 2 Chron. xvi. 14, xxvi. 23, xxviii. 27; Jer. xxii. 18,
19). It implied a public and stately ceremonial. The words "they
are gone" are not, as some have thought, equivalent to "they have
entered into rest" (Isai. lvii. 2), but, as in ch. i. 4, are given as
the way in which men speak respectfully of the dead as "gone"
or "gathered to their fathers." So the Latins said *Abiit ad plures.*
So we speak, half-pityingly, of the dead, "Ah, he's gone!"

The "holy place" may possibly mean the consecrated ground
(I do not use the word in its modern technical sense) of sepulture,
but there is no evidence that the term was ever so used among the
Jews, and it is more natural to take it, as explained by the use of
the same term in Matt. xxiv. 15, as referring to the Temple. The
writer has in his mind those whose names had been cast out as evil,
who had been, as it were, excommunicated, "put out of the synagogue"
(as in John ix. 22, xii. 42), compelled to leave the Temple they had
loved and worshipped in, departing with slow and sorrowing tread
(comp. Ps. xxxviii. 6; Job xxx. 28). And soon their place knows
them no more. A generation rises up that knows them not, and they
are forgotten in the very city where they had once been honoured.
The reflection was, perhaps, the result of a personal experience. The
Debater himself may have been so treated. The hypocrites whom he
condemned (ch. v. 1—7) may have passed their sentence upon him as
heretical, as some did afterwards upon his writings (see *Introduction*,
ch. III.). If he was suspected of being in any way a follower of
Epicurus, that would seem to them a sufficient ground for their

12—2

11   Because sentence *against* an evil work is not executed
speedily, therefore the heart of the sons of men is fully set
12 in them to do evil.   Though a sinner do evil an hundred

anathemas. Epicureanism was, as it were, to the later Rabbis the
deadliest of all heresies, and when they wanted to brand the believers in Christ with the last stigma of opprobrium, they called them
not Christians, or even Nazarenes, but Epicureans. Something of
this feeling may be traced, as has been shewn in the *Introduction*, ch. v., even in the *Wisdom of Solomon*. The main thought, so far as
it refers only to the perishableness of human fame, has been common
to the observers of the mutability of human things in all ages, and the
Debater had himself dwelt on it (chaps. i. 11, vi. 4). It finds, perhaps,
its most striking echo in a book which has much in common with
one aspect of Ecclesiastes, the *De Imitatione Christi* of à Kempis
(B. i. 3).   In substituting "such as acted rightly" for "where they
had so done," I follow the use of the word which the A. V. translates
as "so" (*ken*); in 2 Kings vii. 9 ("we do not *well*"); Num. xxvii. 7
("speak *right*"); Exod. x. 29 ("thou hast spoken *well*"); Josh. ii. 4;
Prov. xv. 7; Isai. xvi. 6; Jer. viii. 6, xxiii. 10, and other passages.
   I have given what seems to me (following wholly, or in part,' on the
lines of Ginsburg, Delitzsch, Knobel, and Bullock); the true meaning
of this somewhat difficult verse, and it does not seem expedient, in a
work of this nature, to enter at length into a discussion of the ten
or twelve conflicting and complicated interpretations which seem to
me, on various grounds, untenable. The chief points at issue are
(1) whether the "departing from the place of the holy" belongs to
"the wicked" of the first clause, or to those who are referred to in
the second; (2) whether it describes that which was looked on as
honourable or dishonourable, a stately funeral procession from temple
or synagogue, or a penal and disgraceful expulsion; and (3) whether
the latter are those who "act *so*," *i.e.* as the wicked, or, as above,
those who act rightly; and out of the varying combinations of the
answers to these questions and of the various meanings attached to
the phrases themselves, we get an almost indefinite number of theories
as to the writer's meaning.
   this is also vanity] The recurrence of the *refrain* of the book at
this point is interesting. It is precisely the survey of the moral anomalies of the world that originates and sustains the feeling so expressed.
   11. *Because sentence against an evil work*] The word for "sentence" is only found here and in Esth. i. 20, where it is translated
"decree" and is probably of Persian origin. Its primary meaning
seems to be "a thing sent" and so the king's missive or edict. The
point of the reflection is that the anomaly noted in the previous verse
was not only evil in itself, but the cause of further evil by leading
men to think they could go on transgressing with impunity.
   is fully set in them to do evil] Literally, **their heart is full in
them**.

times, and his *days* be prolonged, yet surely I know that it shall be well with them that fear God, which fear before him: but it shall not be well with the wicked, neither shall 13 he prolong *his* days, *which are* as a shadow; because he feareth not before God.

12. *Though a sinner do evil an hundred times*] The definite number is used, of course, as in Prov. xvii. 10; or the "hundred years" of Isaiah lxv. 20; or the "seventy times seven" of Matt. xviii. 22, for the indefinite. There is no adequate reason for inserting "years" instead of "times." By some grammarians it is maintained that the conjunctions should be read "*Because* a sinner..." and "*although* I know," but the Authorised Version is supported by high authority.

yet surely I know that it shall be well with them that fear God] The adverb "surely" has nothing answering to it in the Hebrew, and seems an attempt to represent the emphasis of the Hebrew pronoun. Better, perhaps, **I for my part.** We may compare the manner in which Æschylus utters a like truth on the moral government of the world:

δίχα δ' ἄλλων μονόφρων εἰμί. τὸ γὰρ δυσσεβὲς ἔργον
μετὰ μὲν πλείονα τίκτει, σφετέρᾳ δ' εἰκότα γέννᾳ.

"But I, apart from all,
　Hold this my creed alone:
For impious act it is that offspring breeds,
　Like to their parent stock."

Agam. 757, 8.

There is an obviously intentional contrast between what the thinker has *seen* (verse 9), and what he now says he *knows* as by an intuitive conviction. His faith is gaining strength, and he believes, though, it may be, with no sharply defined notion as to time and manner, that the righteousness of God, which seems to be thwarted by the anomalies of the world, will in the long run assert itself. There is at least an inward peace with those who fear God, which no tyrant or oppressor can interfere with. The seeming tautology of the last clause is best explained by supposing that the term "God-fearers" had become (as in Mal. iii. 16) the distinctive name of a religious class, such as the *Chasidim* (the "Assideans" of 1 Macc. ii. 42, vii. 13; 2 Macc. xiv. 6), or "devout ones" were in the time of the Maccabees. The **Debater**, with the keen scent for the weaknesses of a hypocritical formalism, which we have seen in ch. v. 1—7, says with emphatic iteration, as it were, "when I say 'God-fearing' I mean those that do fear God in reality as well as name." So in French men talk of *la vérité vraie*, or we might speak of "a liberal indeed liberal," "religious people who *are* religious," and so on.

13. *neither shall he prolong his days, which are as a shadow*] The words seem at first in direct contradiction to the admission of the previous verse. But it is of the nature of the method of the book to teach by

14   There is a vanity which is done upon the earth; that
there be just *men*, unto whom it happeneth according to
the work of the wicked; again, there be wicked *men*, to
whom it happeneth according to the work of the righteous:
15   I said that this also *is* vanity.   Then I commended mirth,
because a man hath no better *thing* under the sun, than to
eat, and to drink, and to be merry: for that shall abide with
him of his labour the days of his life, which God giveth
him under the sun.
16   When I applied mine heart to know wisdom, and to see

paradoxes, and to let the actual contradictions of the world reflect
themselves in his teaching.   What is meant is that the wicked does
not gain by a prolonged life; that, as Isaiah had taught of old, "the
sinner though he die a hundred years old, is as one accursed" (Isai.
lxv. 20).   His life is still a shadow and "he disquieteth himself
in vain" (Ps. xxxix. 6).   So the writer of the *Wisdom of Solomon*
(iv. 8) writes, probably not without a reference to this very passage,
that "honourable age is not that which standeth in length of time,
nor that is measured by the number of the years."   In the "days which
are as a shadow," so far as they refer to the shortness of human life in
general, we find, as before in ch. vi. 12, echoes of Greek thought.

It is noticeable that in Wisd. ii. 5, in accordance with what one may
call the polemic tendency of the writer, the thought and the phrase are
put into the mouth of the "ungodly, who reasoned not aright."   The
universal fact, however, has become a universal thought and finds
echoes everywhere (Ps. cii. 11, cxliv. 4).

14. *There is a vanity*]   There is something almost painful in the
iteration of the ever-recurring thought that after all there are disorders
in the world.   A modern writer, we feel, would have pruned, con-
densed, and avoided such a repetition of himself.   We are dealing,
however, with "Thoughts" like Pascal's *Pensées*, rather than with a
treatise, jotted down, it may be, day by day, as has been said before,
on his tablets or his papyrus, and there is, as has been said before,
something significant in the fact that, wherever the thinker turns, the
same anomalies stare him in the face.

15. *Then I commended mirth*]   As before in chs. ii. 14, iii. 12, 22,
v. 18, the Epicurean element of thought mingles with the higher fear of
God, to which the seeker had just risen.   There, at least, in regulated
enjoyment, free from vices, and not without the fear of God which
keeps men from them, there was something tangible, and it was better
to make the best of that than to pine, with unsatisfied desires, after the
impossible ideal of a perfectly righteous government in which there are
no anomalies.   For "of his labour" read **in his labour.**

16. *When I applied mine heart to know wisdom*]   The opening
formula has met us before in ch. i. 13.   The parenthetical clause
expresses, with a familiar imagery, the sleepless meditation that had

the business that is done upon the earth : (for also *there is that* neither day nor night seeth sleep with his eyes :) then ₁₇ I beheld all the work of God, that a man cannot find out the work that is done under the sun : because though a man labour to seek *it* out, yet he shall not find *it;* yea further, though a wise *man* think to know *it*, yet shall he not be able to find *it*.

For all this I considered in my heart even to declare all **9** this, that the righteous, and the wise, and their works, *are*

sought in vain the solution of the problem which the order and disorder of the world presented. So Cicero (*ad Fam.* VII. 30) says "*Fuit mirificâ vigilantiâ qui toto suo consulatu somnum non vidit.*"

17. *then I beheld all the work of God*]   The confession is like that which we have had before in chap. vii. 23, 24 : perhaps, also, we may add, like that of a very different writer dealing with a very different question, "How unsearchable are His judgments, and His ways past finding out" (Rom. xi. 33). The English reader may be reminded of Bishop Butler's Sermon (XV.) on the "Ignorance of Man," of which these verses supply the text. What is noticeable here is that the ignorance (we may use a modern term and say the Agnosticism) is not atheistic. That which the seeker contemplates he recognises as the work of God. Before that work, the wise man bows in reverence with the confession that it lies beyond him. The Finite cannot grasp the Infinite. We may compare Hooker's noble words "Dangerous it were for the feeble brain of man to wade far into the doings of the Most High; whom although to know be life, and joy to make mention of His name; yet our soundest knowledge is to know that we know Him not as indeed He is, neither can know Him, and our safest eloquence concerning Him is our silence, when we confess without confession that His glory is inexplicable, His greatness above our capacity and reach. He is above, and we upon earth; therefore it behoveth our words to be wary and few" (*Eccl. Pol.* I. 2, § 3).

CHAPTER IX.

For all this I considered in my heart]   More literally, **For to all this I gave my heart to dig through,** *i.e.* to explain and penetrate to the secret of the great enigma of life.

that the righteous, and the wise, and their works, are in the hand of God]   The words hover, as it were, between the thought of Destiny and Providence, the latter, perhaps, slightly predominating. The wise and good need not despair, though they remain in ignorance of the working of the Divine Will. It is enough for them to know that they are in Its power, under Its care, and that It is in its essence as righteous as It is almighty.

in the hand of God: no man knoweth either love or hatred
2 *by* all *that is* before them.   All *things come* alike to all:

no man knoweth either love or hatred]   The words have been differently interpreted according as the "love" and "hatred" are referred
to God or man.   In the former case, the thought would be, that as
things are, no man knows by the outward events of his life whether he
is the object of God's favour or displeasure, in the latter that no man
knows who, as he passes through life, will be the objects of his love or
hate.   Both interpretations are tenable, but the former seems more in
harmony with what follows.   The latter has the interest of finding a
parallel in the thought of Sophocles as to the mutability of human
life :

> φθίνει μὲν ἰσχὺς γῆς, φθίνει δὲ σώματος,
> θνῄσκει δὲ πίστις, βλαστάνει δ' ἀπιστία,
> καὶ πνεῦμα ταὐτὸν οὔ ποτ' οὔτ' ἐν ἀνδράσιν
> φίλοις βέβηκεν, οὔτε πρὸς πόλιν πόλει.
> τοῖς μὲν γὰρ ἤδη, τοῖς δ' ἐν ὑστέρῳ χρόνῳ
> τὰ τερπνὰ πικρὰ γίγνεται καὖθις φίλα.

"Earth's strength doth wither, withers strength of limb,
And trust dies out, and mistrust grows apace,
And the same spirit lasts not among them
Who once were friends, nor joineth state with state.
To these at once, to those in after years,
Sweet things grow bitter, then turn sweet again."

Œd. Col. 610—615.

by all that is before them]   Better, **all is before them**, *i. e.* as in
what follows: all chances and changes of life coming from love or
wrath, are possible in the future.

2. *All things come alike to all*]   As before, the seeker sees no order
or purpose in the chances and changes of life.   Earthquakes, pestilences,
tempests make no discrimination between good and evil.   As with the
melancholy emphasis of iteration, the various forms of contrasted characters are grouped together.   "The righteous and the wicked" point
to men's conduct relative to their neighbours, the "good and pure"
(the first word is probably added to shew that a moral and not merely
a ceremonial purity is meant) to what we call "self-regarding" actions,
the self-reverence of purity in act and thought.   "Sacrifice" is the
outward expression of man's relation to God.   "The good" and "the
sinner" are wider in their range and express the totality of character.
The last group is not without difficulty. .As commonly interpreted, "he
that sweareth" is the man who swears falsely or rashly, as in Zech. v. 3,
he " that feareth an oath " is either the man who looks on its obligation with a solemn awe, or one whose communication is Yea, yea,
Nay, nay, and who shrinks in reverential awe from any formal use of
the Divine Name.   On this view, the words probably point to the
tendency of thought which was developed in the teaching of the
Essenes, who placed every oath on the same level as perjury (Jos.

there is one event to the righteous, and to the wicked; to the good and to the clean, and to the unclean; to him that sacrificeth, and to him that sacrificeth not: as *is* the good, so *is* the sinner; *and* he that sweareth, as he that feareth an oath.   This *is* an evil among all *things* that are done under 3 the sun, that *there is* one event unto all: yea, also the heart of the sons of men is full *of* evil, and madness *is* in their heart while they live, and after that *they go* to the dead. For to him that is joined to all the living there is hope: for 4

Wars, ii. 8, § 6), and was in part sanctioned in the Sermon on the Mount (Matt. v. 33—37). It may be noted, however, that in all the other groups, the good side is placed first, and I do not feel quite sure that it is not so in this case also. The man "that sweareth" may be he who does what most religious Jews held to be their duty, truthfully and well (comp Deut. vi. 13; Isai. lxv. 16; Ps. lxiii. 11), he who "fears the oath," may be the man whose "coward conscience" makes him shrink from the oath either of compurgation on the part of an accused person (comp. Aristot. *Rhet.* I. 27), or of testimony. The former was in frequent use in Jewish as in Greek trials. Comp. Exod. xxii. 10, 11; 1 Kings viii. 31; 2 Chron. vi. 22; Num. v. 19—22. It may be added that this view agrees better with the language about "the oath of God" in ch. v. 2.

3. *This is an evil among all things*]   The pessimism of the thinker returns once more upon him, and he falls into the strain which we have heard before in chs. ii. 14—16, iii. 19, v. 15, vi. 12. The great leveller comes and sweeps away all distinctions, and there is no assured hope of immortality. Life is "evil" even while it lasts, and death is the same for all, when the curtain drops on the great drama.

madness is in their heart while they live]   The "madness" is that of chs. i. 17, ii. 12. All man's life, in its vain strivings, its fond hopes, its wild desires, seems to the pessimist but as the "*delirantium somnia.*" The English version seems to imply that the writer laid stress on the fact that the evildoers did not continue in existence to bear the penalty they deserved, but rested in the grave like others;

"After life's fitful fever they sleep well,"

but it is rather the Epicurean thought of death as the common lot, and the sigh with which it is uttered is, as it were, the unconscious protest of the philosophising Hebrew against the outcome of his philosophy. In what he heard of as a "short life and merry" he finds an insanity that ends in nothingness.

4. *For to him that is joined to all the living there is hope*]   A different and preferable punctuation gives the rendering: **For who is specially chosen,** *i.e.* **who is excepted** from the common lot of death. **To all the living there is hope.** The passage has, however, received many conflicting interpretations, of which this seems, on the whole, the best. It was quite after the tone of Greek thought to find in the inextinguishable hope which survives in most men even to the end, even though

5 a living dog *is* better than a dead lion. For the living know that they shall die: but the dead know not any thing, nei-

the hope does not stretch beyond the horizon of the grave, their one consolation, that which made life at least liveable, even if not worth living. So Hope was found at the bottom of Pandora's treasure-chest of evils. So Sophocles:

ἃ γὰρ δὴ πολύπλαγκτος ἐλπὶς πολλοῖς μὲν ὄνασις ἀνδρῶν.

"For unto men comes many-wandering hope,
   Bringing vain joy."
                                        Antig. 613.

a living dog is better than a dead lion] The point of the proverb lies, of course, in the Eastern estimate of the dog as the vilest of all animals (1 Sam. xvii. 43; Ps. lxix. 6; 2 Kings viii. 13; Matt vii. 6, xv. 26; Rev. xxii. 15, *et al.*), while the lion, with both Jew and Greek, was, as the king of beasts (Prov. xxx. 30), the natural symbol of human sovereignty. A like proverb is found in Arabic.

The pessimist view of life, co-existing with the shrinking from death, finds a parallel in Euripides (*Hippol.* 190—197):

πᾶς δ' ὀδυνηρὸς βίος ἀνθρώπων,
κοὐκ ἔστι πόνων ἀνάπαυσις
ἀλλ' ὅ τι τοῦ ζῆν φίλτερον ἄλλο
σκότος ἀμπίσχων κρύπτει νεφέλαις·
δυσέρωτες δὴ φαινόμεθ' ὄντες
τοῦ δ'· ὅτι τοῦτο στίλβει κατὰ γᾶν.
δι' ἀπειροσύναν ἄλλου βιότου,
κοὐκ ἀπόδειξιν τῶν ὑπὸ γαίας.

"Yea, every life of man is full of grief,
   Nor is there any respite from his toils:
But whatsoe'er is dearer than our life,
   Darkness comes o'er it, covering all with clouds;
And yet of this we seem all madly fond,
   For this at least is bright upon the earth,
Through utter nescience of a life elsewhere,
   And the 'no-proof' of all beneath the earth."

5. *For the living know that they shall die*] The writer in one of the strange paradoxes of the mood of pessimism finds that though life is vanity, it is yet better than the death which he looks upon as its only outcome. There is a greatness in the very consciousness of the coming doom. Man, knowing he must perish and lamenting over his fate, is nobler than those that are already numbered with the dead. There is a pride even in the cry with which those who enter on the arena as doomed to death greet the sovereign Power that dooms them:

"Ave, Cæsar; morituri te salutamus."

"Hail to thee Cæsar, hail! on our way to our death-doom we
   greet thee."

ther have they any more a reward ; for the memory of them is forgotten.   Also their love, and their hatred, and their 6 envy, is now perished; neither have they any more a portion for ever in any *thing* that is done under the sun.

Go *thy way*, eat thy bread with joy, and drink thy wine 7

They were nobler then than when their bleeding and mangled carcases on the arena were all that was left of them.

neither have they any more a reward] The words exclude the thought (in the then phase of the **Debater's** feeling) of reward in a life after death, but the primary meaning of the word is that of "hire" and "wages" (Gen. xxx. 28 ; Exod. ii. 9), and the idea conveyed is that the dead no longer find, as on earth, that which rewards their labour.   There is no longer even death to look forward to as the wages of his life.

So we have in Shakespeare :

> "Thou thy worldly task hast done,
> Home art gone and ta'en thy wages."
> *Cymbeline*, Act iv., Sc. 2.

for the memory of them is forgotten] The Hebrew gives an assonance between "reward" (*sheker*) and "memory" (*zeker*), which it is hard to reproduce in English.   "Reward" and "record" suggest themselves as the nearest approximation.   For the thought see note on ch. i. 11. Even the immortality of living in the memory of others, which modern thinkers have substituted for the Christian hope, is denied to the vast majority of mankind.

6.   *Also their love, and their hatred, and their envy, is now perished*] The three passions are named as strongest and most vehement in their action.   Even these are all hushed in the calm of the grave.   There are no passions there, and the deadliest foes, rival statesmen and bitter controversialists, rest side by side together.   The thought of the state of the dead stands on nearly the same level as that of the elegy of Hezekiah (Isai. xxxviii. 9—20).

7.   *Go thy way, eat thy bread with joy*]   The· **Debater** falls back, as before, on the Epicurean rule of tranquil regulated enjoyment, as in chs. ii. 24, iii. 12, 22, v. 18.   Life was after all liveable, if a man would but set himself to look at its brighter side.   The specific mention of "wine" for the first time in this connexion does not imply anything more than the moderate use of it commended in Prov. xxxi. 67 ; Ps. civ. 15.   What is asserted, is that asceticism is not the right remedy for pessimism.   Experience indeed seems to shew that too often it does but intensify it.   Whatever else might be doubtful, if such a life were accepted as God's gift (chs. ii. 24, viii. 15), He approved of the deeds of the man who so lived.   The "other, and more cheerful, voice" utters a protest against the mere gloom of despair.   We have oscillations of thought, but not, as some have supposed, the maxims of a sensualist introduced only to be condemned.

with a merry heart; for God now accepteth thy works.
8 Let thy garments be always white; and let thy head lack no
9 ointment. Live joyfully with the wife whom thou lovest all
the days of the life of thy vanity, which he hath given thee
under the sun, all the days of thy vanity: for that *is* thy
portion in *this* life, and in thy labour which thou takest

8. *Let thy garments be always white*] In the symbolism of colours,
so universal that we may almost call it natural, white garments, cool
and refreshing in the heat of an Eastern climate, have always been
associated with the idea of purity and joy (2 Chron. v. 12; Esth. viii.
15). In the religious symbolism of Rev. iii. 4, 5, 18, vi. 11, the idea of
purity is, perhaps, predominant over that of joy. So in Roman life
the term "*albatus*" (clothed in white garments) was used of one who
took part in a festive banquet (Hor. *Sat.* II. 2. 61; Cic. *in Vatin.* c. 13).
A singular instance of literalism is recorded in the life of Sisinnius,
the Novatian bishop of Constantinople, who, as in obedience to this
precept, never wore any but white garments (Socr. *H. E.* VI. 21).
Chrysostom censures his ostentation.

let thy head lack no ointment] Here, again, illustrations from Hebrew,
Greek and Roman life crowd on us. We think of the "oil of gladness" of Ps. xlv. 7; the "oil of joy" of Isai. lxi. 3; of "the sweet
smell" of Isai. iii. 24; of "the costly wine and ointments" of Wisd.
ii. 7; of the "*perfusus liquidis odoribus*" of Hor. *Od.* I. 5; of the
"*Assyriaque nardo potamus uncti*" ("let us drink anointed with
Assyrian nard ") of Hor. *Od.* II. 11.

9. *Live joyfully with the wife whom thou lovest*] The absence
of the article from the Hebrew noun for "woman" has been wrongly
pressed by interpreters who see in the **Debater** the advocate of sensuality, as indicating indifference to the marriage union ("live joyfully
with *a* woman whom thou lovest, whether wife or not "), and is simply the
indefinite form natural to a general maxim. So we should say naturally
"live with *a* wife whom you love." The conclusion in which the writer
for the present rests is that while sensual indulgence in excess leads
to misery and shame, and brings men into contact with the most
hateful form of womanhood (chs. ii. 11, vii. 26), there is a calm
peacefulness in the life of a happy home, which, though it cannot
remove the sense of the "vanity" and transitoriness of life, at least
makes it endurable. If there is, as some have thought, an undertone
of irony, it is one which springs from a sympathy with the joy as
well as the sorrow of life, and not that of a morose cynicism, saying,
"enjoy...if you can."

all the days of thy vanity] The iteration emphasizes the wisdom of
making the most of the few days of life. The thought is essentially
the same as that expressed in the *Carpe diem* of Hor. *Od.* I. 11.

that is thy portion in this life] This, the calm regulated enjoyment
of the wiser Epicureans.

under the sun. Whatsoever thy hand findeth to do, do *it* 10
with thy might ; for *there is* no work, nor device, nor knowledge, nor wisdom, in the grave, whither thou goest.

I returned, and saw under the sun, that the race *is* not to 11
the swift, nor the battle to the strong, neither yet bread to

10. *Whatsoever thy hand findeth to do*] Here again men have
interpreted the maxim according to their characters ; some seeing in
"whatsoever thy hand findeth" simply opportunities for enjoyment;
others taking the precept as meaning practically, "do whatever thou
hast strength to do, let might be right with thee ;" others, as it seems,
more truly, finding in it a call to work as well as enjoyment; to work
as the condition of enjoyment (chs. i. 24, v. 12). It may be
questioned whether the word for "work" is ever used of mere activity
in sensual pleasure. For the phrase "whatsoever thy hand findeth"
see the marginal reading of 1 Sam. x. 7; Judg. ix. 33.

for there is no work, nor device] The words find a parallel, though
in a far higher region, and with a far nobler meaning, in those which
were spoken by the Son of Man, "I must work the works of Him
that sent me while it is day: the night cometh when no man can
work" (John ix. 4). From the standpoint of the **Debater** the region
behind the veil, if there be a region there, is seen as a shadow-world
in which all the energies that belong to a man as a "being of large discourse looking before and after" are hushed in the deep sleep of death.
The common saying, often in men's mouths as if it came from the
Bible, "There is no repentance in the grave," is probably an echo of
this passage. It is obvious, however, that the state of the dead which
is in the writer's thoughts approximates to a theory of annihilation
rather than to that of a state of torment in which repentance is impossible or unavailing. The "grave" stands as elsewhere (Job vii. 9; Ps.
vi. 5, *et al.*) for the Hebrew *Sheôl*, the Hades of the Greek, the unseen
world of the dead. It is noticeable that this is the only passage in
the book in which the word occurs.

11. *that the race is not to the swift*] The sequence of thought
is that while it is a man's wisdom to do the work which he finds ready
to his hand, he must not reckon on immediate and visible results. The
course of the world witnesses many apparent failures even where men
fulfil the apparent conditions of success. The wise and skilful often
gain neither "bread" nor "favour," and the injustice of fortune is
worse than that painted in the words of the Satirist, "*Probitas laudatur
et alget*" (Juven. I. 74). So a poet of our own time has sung,

> "Oh, if we draw a circle premature,
>   Heedless of far gain,
>   Greedy of quick return of profits, sure
>   Bad is our bargain."

> BROWNING. *A Grammarian's Funeral.*

The thought of "the race" seems to belong to a time when contests

the wise, nor yet riches to men of understanding, nor yet
favour to men of skill; but time and chance happeneth to
12 them all.   For man also knoweth not his time: as the
fishes that are taken in an evil net, and as the birds that
are caught in the snare; so *are* the sons of men snared in
an evil time, when it falleth suddenly upon them.

13   This wisdom have I seen also under the sun, and it

of this nature had become familiar to the dwellers in Palestine, *i.e.*
after they had come in contact with Greek habits, and is so far an
argument for the later date of the book. In 1 Macc. i. 14; 2 Macc.
iv. 9—14, games of this kind are said to have been introduced in
Jerusalem under Antiochus Epiphanes.   On the assumption of Alexandrian authorship we may think of the hippodrome of that city as
present to the writer's mind.

time and chance]   The first word is that which is so prominent in
ch. iii. 1—8; the second is found elsewhere only in 1 Kings v. 4,
where it is translated "occurrent," the latter word being used, as commonly in the English of the 16th and 17th centuries, as a substantive.
So in Shakespeare we have "So tell him, with the *occurrents* more and
less," in *Hamlet*, v. 2.

12.   *as the fishes that are taken in an evil net*]   The words paint
vividly the suddenness of calamities which defeat all men's purposes
and plans.   The imagery was a natural one in any country, and meets
us in Hos. vii.; Ezek. xii. 13, xxxii. 3; Prov. vii. 23; but it is interesting to note a parallel in the poetry of Greece.   So Æschylus:

> ἥτ᾽ ἐπὶ Τροίας πύργοις ἔβαλες
> στεγανὸν δίκτυον, ὡς μήτε μέγαν
> μήτ᾽ οὖν νεαρῶν τιν᾽ ὑπερτελέσαι
> μέγα δουλείας
> γάγγαμον, ἄτης παναλώτου.

> "Who upon the towers of Troïa
>   Castedst snare of closest meshes,
>   So that none, full-grown or youthful,
>   Could o'erleap the net of bondage,
>   Woe of universal capture."

Agam. 347—350.

We may compare the parallels, for the illustration drawn from the
"snare of the fowler," of Pss. xci. 3, cxxiv. 7; Prov. i. 17, vi. 5.

13.   *This wisdom have I seen also*]   The **Debater** points the
moral of his previous maxim by a special illustration and it can scarcely
be doubted that it was one which his first readers would recognise,
though the nature of his method led him to speak as in hints and dark
sayings, eschewing the historical element altogether, except so far
as men might be able to read between the lines.

seemed great unto me: *there was* a little city, and few men 14
within it; and there came a great king against it, and besieged it, and built great bulwarks against it: now there 15
was found in it a poor wise man, and he by his wisdom
delivered the city; yet no man remembered that *same* poor
man.   Then said I, Wisdom *is* better than strength: never- 16
theless the poor *man*'s wisdom *is* despised, and his words
are not heard.   The words of wise *men are* heard in quiet, 17

14.   *there was a little city*]   The city has been identified by one
commentator (Hitzig) with Dora, which was besieged unsuccessfully
by Antiochus the Great in B.C. 218 (Polyb. v. 66).   Josephus describes
it, in his narrative of its siege by Antiochus Sidetes (*Ant.* XIII. 7, § 2),
as " a city hard to be taken," but we know nothing of any special incidents corresponding to the allusion in this passage.   The term "*great
king*" fits in with the hypothesis, as also does the fact that the siege was
raised, but that is all.   The spiritualising interpretations which have found
favour with Jewish and Christian commentators, in which the history
represents something like the attack of Satan on the town of Mansoul
(as in Bunyan's *Holy War*), must be rejected as altogether arbitrary and
fantastic.
     and built great bulwarks against it]   The "bulwarks," as in the
Old Testament generally, are the out-works of the besiegers, the banks
or mounds from which missiles were thrown into the city (comp.
Deut. xx. 20; 2 Sam. xx. 15; 2 Chron. xxvi. 15).
     15.   *and he by his wisdom delivered the city*]   The history of the
siege of Abel-beth-Maachah in 2 Sam. xx. 14—20 presents a suggestive
parallel, but there the wisdom that delivered the city was that of a
woman.
     16.   *Wisdom is better than strength*]   The maxim of ch. vii. 19
is reproduced, but it is traversed by the fact that the wisdom must
often be content to remain unrecognised.   The power of the purse
too often prevails against the wisdom of the poor.   At the best,
often, in words already quoted (verse 11),

              "Probitas laudatur et alget."

              "Virtue is praised, and left out in the cold."

                              JUVENAL, *Sat.* I. 74.

The marginal reference in the A. V. to Mark vi. 2, 3 is not without
significance as indicating the highest illustration of the maxim, in the
question which asked "Is not this the carpenter's son?   Is he not
himself a carpenter?"   The chief butler's forgetfulness of Joseph (Gen.
xl. 23) supplies another obvious parallel.
     17.   *The words of wise men are heard in quiet*]   The thought is
like that of the "great cry and little wool" of the English proverb.
That which tells on men, in the long run, is the wisdom whose words
are wary, and calm, and few, not the declamation of the wind-bags

18 more than the cry of him that ruleth among fools. Wisdom
is better than weapons of war : but one sinner destroyeth
much good.

10   Dead flies cause the ointment of the apothecary to send
forth a stinking savour: *so doth* a little folly *him that is* in
reputation for wisdom *and* honour.

of popular oratory. Comp. the description of the highest type of
wisdom in Isai. xlii. 2; Matt. xii. 19. He that " ruleth among fools "
is not the foolish ruler, but the man who takes the highest place in
the company of fools, and graduates, as it were, as the Senior Wrangler
in that class-list. Such an one is as the "prating fool" of Prov.
x. 10.

18. *Wisdom is better than weapons of war*] The maxim presents
another illustration of the irony of history. The excellence of wisdom
is acknowledged. Counsel is more than the *materiel* of war; the statesman more than the general, and yet one man by his guilt or folly, by
the perversity which includes both (the Hebrew verb for "sinneth"
has this meaning, as in Prov. viii. 36), may mar what it has taken years
to bring to a good issue. The defeat of an army, the most terrible
catastrophe, may often be traced to the fact that " some one has
blundered," in carelessness or passion. It is probable enough that, as
in verse 14, the writer had some definite historical fact present to his
thoughts which we are unable to identify. The history of Achan, in
Josh. vii. 1—12, presents a sufficient illustration.

CHAPTER X.

1. *Dead flies cause the ointment of the apothecary*] The division of
the chapters obscures the connexion. The maxim now before us is but
the figurative expression of the fact stated, without a parable, in the
last verse of ch. ix. The "dead flies" are, in the Hebrew, "flies of
death," probably, *i.e.* poisonous, or stinging flies of the dung-fly, or
carrion-fly type. Such insects, finding their way into a vase of precious
ointment, would turn its fragrance into a fœtid odour. The work of
an "apothecary" or manufacturer of unguents was one held in honour
in Jerusalem, and the guilds to which they belonged had a special
street or bazaar. Few similitudes could describe more vividly the
tainting influence of folly, moral or intellectual. It is to the full as
expressive as " a little leaven leaveneth the whole lump" of 1 Cor. v. 6.
The experience of every day shews us how little sins mar the nobleness
of a great character; procrastination, talkativeness, indecision, over-
sensitiveness to praise or blame, undue levity or undue despondency,
want of self-control over appetites or passions, these turn the fragrance
of a good name (ch. vii. 1) into the "ill savour" which stinks in the
nostrils of mankind.

so doth a little folly] The completeness of the proverb in the English
is obtained by the insertion of the words "so doth." This is, however,

A wise *man*'s heart *is* at his right hand; but a fool's ₂

a somewhat over-bold manipulation of the text, and it remains to see whether we can get an adequate meaning without it. The true rendering seems to be as follows, **More prevailing** (this takes the place of " him that is in reputation," the primary meaning of the root being that of weight) **than wisdom and honour is a little folly.** This gives substantially the same meaning as the present English text, though in a different manner. The "little folly" outweighs the wisdom, and diminishes both its actual value and the estimate men form of it. Looking to the language of ch. vii. 1, the effect of a little folly on the reputation of the wise would seem to be the prominent thought. By some commentators the English meaning of the word is retained even with this construction " *More highly prized* (*i. e.* in the opinion of the unthinking) *is a little folly than wisdom and honour,*" but this destroys the parallelism with the first clause. The writer does not here speak of the undue honour paid to folly, but of its really destructive power even when matched against wisdom. The saying ascribed to the Chancellor Oxenstiern comes to one's mind, "*Quantulâ sapientiâ regatur mundus!*" One foolish prince, or favourite, or orator prevails against many wise. One element of folly in the character prevails over many excellencies.

2. *A wise man's heart is at his right hand*] The symbolism of the right or the left hand, the former pointing to effective, the latter to ineffective, action, is so natural that it is scarcely necessary to look for its origin in the special thoughts or customs of this or that nation. It is, however, noticeable, probably as another trace of the Greek influence which pervades the book, that this special symbolism is not found elsewhere in the Old Testament, in which to "be on the right hand" of a man is a synonym for protecting him (Ps. xvi. 8, cx. 5), while to "sit on the right hand," is to occupy the place of honour (Ps. cx. 1). In Greece, on the other hand, the figurative significance was widely recognised. The left was with augurs and diviners the unlucky quarter of the heavens. So the suitors of Penelope see an ill-boding omen :

> αὐτὰρ ὁ τοῖσιν ἀριστερὸς ἤλυθεν ὄρνις
> αἰετὸς ὑψιπέτης, ἔχε δὲ τρήρωνα πέλειαν.

"But to them came an omen on the left,
A lofty eagle, holding in its claws
A timid dove."

Od. xx. 242.

Or still more closely parallel, as indicating a mind warped and perverted by unwisdom, in Sophocles :

> οὔποτε γὰρ φρενόθεν γ' ἐπ' ἀριστερά,
> ποῖ Τελαμῶνος, ἔβας τόσσον.

"For never else, O son of Telamon,
Had'st thou from reason gone so far astray,
Treading the left-hand path."

Aias 184.

3 heart at his left.   Yea also, when he that is a fool walketh
by the way, his wisdom faileth *him*, and he saith to every
one *that* he *is* a fool.

4   If the spirit of the ruler rise up against thee, leave not
thy place ; for yielding pacifieth great offences.

5   There is an evil *which* I have seen under the sun, as an
6 error *which* proceedeth from the ruler : folly is set in great

Our own use of the word "sinister" is of course, a survival of the
same feeling. The highest application of the symbolism is found in
those that are set "on the right hand" and "on the left" in the
parable of Matt. xxv. 31—46.

3. *Yea also, when he that is a fool walketh by the way*] The general
drift of the proverb seems plain enough. "*Even when the fool is in
the way* (either literally, 'whenever and wherever he goes,' or figuratively, 'when he has been put in the right path of conduct'), *his
heart (i. e.* his intellect) *fails him, and he manifests his folly.*" The last
clause, however, admits of two constructions, each of which has the
support of high authorities, (1) *he saith to every one that he* (the fool
himself) *is a fool, i.e.* betrays his unwisdom in every word he utters ;
or (2) *he says to every man that he* (the man he meets) *is a fool, i.e.*
in his self-conceit he thinks that he alone is wise (comp. Rom. xii. 16).
On the whole the latter construction seems preferable. So it is no-
toriously the most significant symptom of insanity that the patient looks
on all others as insane. It may be noted that (1) finds a parallel in
Prov. xiii. 16, xviii. 2 ; (2) in Prov. xxvi. 16.

4. *If the spirit of the ruler rise up against thee*] To the picture of the
boastful self-assertion of the fool is appended as a contrast, that of the
self-effacement of the wise. The scene brought before us is that of a
statesman, or minister, whose advice runs counter to that of the ruler.
The "spirit," what we should call the "temper," of the latter "rises up"
against the former. What shall the adviser do? His natural impulse
is to "leave his place," *i.e.* either to cut short his interview, or, resign
his office. He won't be slighted, will not put up with contradiction.
That, however, is precisely what the wise of heart will not do. *Yielding,
i.e.* the temper of conciliation (the Hebrew noun is literally the *healing,*
or the *healthy, mood of mind*) *puts to rest,* or *puts a stop to, great offences.*
The history of all nations, our own included, presents manifold instances
of both modes of action, sometimes, as in the case of Chatham's behaviour
to George III., in the same statesman at different times, sometimes in
the attitude of rival statesmen towards the same sovereign. Interpreters
after their manner, seeing either the golden or the silver side of the
shields, have referred the last words either to the angry acts of the
ruler, or to the sins of rebellion in the minister. It can scarcely be
questioned, however, that the proverb includes both. The maxim has
its parallel in our English proverb, "Least said is soonest mended."

5. *as an error which proceedeth from the ruler*] The last word
serves as a link connecting this verse with the preceding. It might

dignity, and the rich sit in low place.　I have seen servants 7
upon horses, and princes walking as servants upon the earth.
　He that diggeth a pit shall fall into it ; and whoso break- 8

be wise at times to bow to the temper of a despotic ruler, but the
ruler was not always right.　What the **Debater** had seen was to
him a blot upon the government of him who allowed it.　There lies
below the surface the half-suppressed thought that this anomaly, stated
in the next verse, was as a blot in the government of the supreme
Ruler of the Universe.　Technically the word was used in the Mosaic
Law of the involuntary sins of ignorance (Lev. iv. 22, 27, v. 18).　The
unequal distribution of honours seemed to men as a blunder of Providence.

　　6.　*Folly is set in great dignity, and the rich sit in low place*]　For
"great dignity," literally **great heights.**　The "rich" here are those
who by birth and station are looked on as the natural rulers of
mankind.　Such men, like the ἀρχαιόπλουτοι (the "men of ancestral
wealth") of Greek political writers, (Aristot. *Rhet.* II. 9 ; Aesch. *Agam.*
1043) a wise ruler associates with himself as counsellors.　The tyrant,
on the other hand, like Louis XI. exalts the baseborn to the place
of honour, or like Edward II. or James I. of England, or Henry III.
of France, lavishes dignities on his minions.　So the writer may have
seen Agathoclea and her brother, all-powerful, as mistress and favourite,
in the court of Ptolemy Philopator (Justin XXX. 1).

　　7.　*I have seen servants upon horses*]　The general fact of the
previous verse is reproduced with more dramatic vividness.　To ride
upon horses was with the Parthians a special distinction of the nobly
born (Justin XLI. 3).　So Mordecai rides on horseback through the
city as one whom the king delighted to honour (Esth. v. 8, 9).　So
the *Hippeis* in the polity of Solon, and the *Equites* in that of Servius
Tullius, took their place as representing the element of aristocratic
wealth.　So Aristotle notes that the keeping a horse (ἱπποτροφία)
was the special distinction of the rich, and therefore that all cities
which aimed at military strength were essentially aristocratic (*Pol.*
IV. 23, VI. 7).　So in the earlier days of European intercourse with
Turkey, Europeans generally were only allowed to ride on asses
or mules, a special exception being made for the consuls of the great
powers (Maundrell, *Journey from Aleppo,* p. 492, Bohn's Edition).
Our own proverb "Set a beggar on horseback, and he will ride to
the devil" is a survival of the same feeling.　The reign of Ptolemy
Philopator and Epiphanes may have presented many illustrations of
what the writer notes.

　　8.　*He that diggeth a pit shall fall into it*]　It is scarcely a profitable
task to endeavour to trace a very close connexion between this and
the preceding verses.　The writer has got into what we may call the
gnomic, or proverb-making, state of mind, and, as in the Book of
Proverbs, his reflections come out with no very definite or logical
sequence.　All that we can say is that the context seems to indicate
that the maxims which follow, like those which have gone before,

9 eth a hedge, a serpent shall bite him.   Whoso removeth stones shall be hurt therewith ; *and* he that cleaveth wood shall be endangered thereby.

indicate a wide experience in the life of courts, and that the experience of a courtier rather than of a king, and accordingly find their chief application in the region of man's political life, and that their general drift is that all great enterprises, especially perhaps all enterprises that involve change, destruction, revolution, have each of them its special danger.   The first of the proverbs is verbally from Prov. xxvi. 27, and finds parallels in Ps. vii. 15, 16, ix. 15, x. 2, lvii. 6.   The thought is that of the Nemesis which comes on the evil doer.   He digs a pit that his enemy may fall into it, and he falls into it himself. Plots and conspiracies are as often fatal to the conspirators as to the intended victims.   The literature of all nations is full of like sayings, among which that of the engineer "hoist with his own petard" is perhaps the most familiar.

whoso breaketh a hedge, a serpent shall bite him] Better, **whoso breaketh down a fence** or **a stone wall**, as in Prov. xxiv. 31 ; Lam. iii. 9, and elsewhere.   Hedges, in the English sense of the word, are rare in the landscapes of Syria or Egypt.   The crannies of such structures were the natural haunts of serpents (Isai. xxxiv. 15 ; Amos v. 19), and the man who chose to do the work of destruction instead of being "a repairer of the breach" (Isai. lviii. 12), might find his retribution in being bitten by them.   The proverb, like many like sayings, is double-edged, and may have, as we consider the breaking down of the wall to be a good or evil work, a twofold meaning : (1) If you injure your neighbour's property, and act as an oppressor, there may come an instrument of retribution out of the circumstances of the act itself. (2) If you are too daring a reformer, removing the tottering wall of a decayed and corrupt institution, you may expect that the serpents in the crannies, those who have "vested interests" in the abuse, will bite the hand that disturbs them.   You need beforehand to "count the cost" of the work of reformation.

9. *Whoso removeth stones shall be hurt therewith*]   The words are referred by some commentators to an act like that of the previous verse, by others to hewing stone in the quarry.   In the former case, however, we get but a tame repetition, in the latter there is nothing in the act that deserves retribution.   We get a more natural meaning, if we think of the curse pronounced on him who "removes his neighbour's landmark" (Deut. xix. 14, xxvii. 17).   Such landmarks often consisted of cairns or heaps of stones, as in Gen. xxxi. 46—48, or a pillar, and the act of removing it would be one of wrongful aggression. For the stone to fall on a man so acting would be once more an instance of the Nemesis which is presented in these similitudes.

he that cleaveth wood shall be endangered thereby]   Better, "he that cleaveth **trees** or **logs**," as in Gen. i. 11, ii. 16, xxiii. 16; Isai. xl. 20, and elsewhere.   Here again the proverb seems to have a double edge. (1) On the one hand it might seem that an act of unjust aggression is

If the iron be blunt, and he do not whet the edge, then 10 must he put to more strength: but wisdom *is* profitable to direct,

Surely the serpent will bite without enchantment; and a 11

contemplated. The special sacredness of trees as standing above most other forms of property is recognised in Deut. xx. 19, 20, and the frequency of accidents in the process was provided for by the special legislation (Deut. xix. 5), which exempted from penalty one who in this way was the involuntary cause of his neighbour's death. The primary thought in the saying, so taken, is, as before, that retribution comes on the evil-doer out of the very deed of evil. Out of our "pleasant vices" the gods "make whips to scourge us." The attack on sacred and time-honoured institutions is not without peril. (2) On the other hand, eastern as well as western thought recognises in decayed trees the types of corrupt institutions that need to be reformed, and, as in the last proverb, the work of the reformer is not always a safe or easy one. Popular political rhetoric has made us familiar both with the appeal to "spare the tree" under the shadow of whose branches our fathers lived, and with that which bids men lop branch after branch from the "deadly Upas" of oppression and iniquity, especially of corrupt kingdoms (Isai. xiv. 15; Ezek. xxxiv. 3; Dan. ix. 10, 14; Matt. iii. 10; Luke xiii. 7, 9).

10. *If the iron be blunt*] The proverb seems obviously suggested by that of the preceding verse, but its meaning is far from clear. The axe (literally, **the iron**) is used to cut wood. What if it fail to cut (*i. e.* if, going below the imagery, the man has not the sharpness or strength to carry his plans promptly into effect), **if he** (the cutter down of trees) **has not sharpened its edge**, literally **its face** as in Ezek. xxi. 21, *i.e.* if he has entered on his plans without due preparation. In that case he must "put to more strength," must increase his force (*i. e.* the impact of his stroke). He will have to do by the iteration of main force what might have been effected by sagacity and finesse. So interpreted, the whole imagery is consistent. The man who enters on the perilous enterprise of reform or revolution has to face not only the danger that he may perish in the attempt, but the risk of failure through the disproportion of his resources to his ends. The meaning of the proverb would be clear to any one who united the character of an expert in felling timber with the experience of a political reformer. Briefly paraphrased, the maxim would run thus in colloquial English, "If you must cut down trees, take care that you sharpen your axe."

but wisdom is profitable to direct] Better, **But it is a gain to use wisdom with success,** *i.e.* It is better to sharpen the axe than to go on hammering with a blunt one, better to succeed by skill and tact than by mere brute strength.

11. *Surely the serpent will bite without enchantment*] Literally, **If the serpent will bite without enchantment,** *i.e.* in the absence of skill to charm it. It is hardly necessary to dwell at length on a topic so familiar as the serpent-charming of the East. It will be enough to say that

12 babbler is no better.   The words of a wise *man*'s mouth
are gracious; but the lips of a fool will swallow up himself.
13 The beginning of the words of his mouth *is* foolishness:

from time immemorial in Egypt, Syria, Persia, India, there have been
classes of persons who in some way or other have gained a power over
many kinds of snakes, drawing them from their retreats, handling
them with impunity, making them follow their footsteps like a tame
dog.   The power was really or ostensibly connected with certain mut-
tered words or peculiar intonations of the voice.   We find the earliest
traces of it in the magicians of Pharaoh's court (Exod. vii. 11).   So the
"deaf adder that cannot be charmed" becomes the type of those whom
no appeal to reason or conscience can restrain (Ps. lviii. 5; Jer. viii.
17; Ecclus. xii. 13).   The proverb obviously stands in the same relation
to the "breaking down of walls" in verse 8, as that of the "blunt axe"
did to the "cutting down trees" of verse 9.   "If a serpent meets you
as you go on with your work, if the adder's poison that is on the lips
of the traitor or the slanderer (Ps. cxl. 3; Rom. iii. 13) is about to do
its deadly work, are you sure that you have the power to charm?   If
not, you are not likely to escape being bitten."   The apodosis of the
sentence interprets the proverb.   "If a serpent will bite in the absence
of the charmer, **there is no profit in a babbler** (literally, **a lord** or
master of tongue, see note on ch. v. 10), who does not know the
secret of the intonation that charms it."   No floods of wind-bag eloquence will avail in the statesman or the orator if the skill that per-
suades is wanting.

   12.   *The words of a wise man's mouth*]   The mention of the
babbling eloquence of "the master of tongue" in the previous verse
is naturally followed by precepts fashioned after the type of those in
Prov. x. 8, 14, 32, xii. 13, xv. 2, xvii. 7 as to that which is of the essence
of true eloquence.   In "are gracious" (literally **are grace itself**) we find
a parallel to the "gracious words" (literally **words of grace**) of Luke
iv. 22.   They describe the quality in speech which wins favour, what
the Greeks called the ἠθικὴ πίστις (*moral suasion*), which conciliates the
good will of the hearers (Aristot. *Rhet.* I. 2, § 3).

   the lips of a fool will swallow up himself]   The English version
rightly preserves the vivid force of the original, instead of weakly para-
phrasing it by "destroy" or "consume."   Who has not heard orators
who, while they thought they were demolishing their opponents, were
simply demolishing themselves, swallowing up their own reputation
for honesty or consistency, greeted by the ironical cheers of their
opponents, while those of their own party listen in speechless dismay?
Our own familiar phrase, when we speak of an imprudent orator having
"to eat his own words," expresses another aspect of the same idea.

   13.   *The beginning of the words of his mouth is foolishness*]   The
words point, with a profound insight into human nature, to the progress
from bad to worse in one who has the gift of speech without discretion.
He begins with what is simply folly, unwise but harmless, but "*vires*

and the end of his talk *is* mischievous madness. A fool 14
also is full of words : a man cannot tell what shall be ; and
what shall be after him, who can tell him ? The labour of 15
the foolish wearieth every one of them, because he knoweth
not how to go to the city.

acquirit eundo" he is borne along on the swelling floods of his own
declamatory fluency, and ends in what is "mischievous madness."
He commits himself to statements and conclusions which, in his calmer
moments, he would have shrunk from. As has been said of such an
orator or preacher, without plan or forethought, he "goes forth, not
knowing whither he goeth."

14. *A fool also is full of words*] Literally, **multiplies words**.
The introduction of "a man" is not an idle pleonasm. The "man"
is not the "fool," but the fool forgets the limitations of human knowledge, as to what lies in the near future of his own life, or the more
distant future that follows on his death, and speaks as if it all lay before
him as an open scroll. The point of the maxim is like that with which
we have become familiar in the region of political prediction in the
words "Don't prophesy unless you know." Boasting of this kind, as
regards a man's own future, finds its reproof, as in the wisdom of all
ages, so especially in the teaching of Luke xii. 16—20; James iv.
13—16.

15. *The labour of the foolish wearieth every one of them*] The
word for "labour" as in chap. i. 3 ; Gen. xli. 52; Job iii. 3, as with
our word "travail," carries with it the connotation of trouble as well as
toil. He labours to no result, for he is destitute of common sense.
Not to know "the way to the city" is clearly a proverbial phrase for
the *crassa ignorantia* of the most patent facts of experience that lie
within all men's experience. If a man fails to see that, how will he
fare in the difficulties which lead him as into the "bye-ways" of life?
We are reminded of the saying, attributed, if I remember rightly, to
the Emperor Akbar that "None but a fool is lost on a straight road,"
or of Shakespeare's "The 'why' is plain as way to parish Church"
(*As You Like It*, II. 7).

he knoweth not how to go to the city] The words probably imply a
reminiscence of a childhood not far from Jerusalem as *the* city of which
the proverb spoke. Isaiah's description of the road to the restored
Jerusalem as being such that "the wayfaring men, though fools, shall
not err therein" (Isai. xxxv. 8) supplies an interesting parallel. The
ingenuity of interpreters has, however, read other meanings into the
simple words and "the city" has been taken (1) for the city's ways
and customs, its policy and intrigue which the "fool" does not understand, (2) for the city of God, the new Jerusalem, or some ideal city of
the wise, while (3) some, more eccentric than their fellows, have seen in
it a hit at the Essenes who, like the Rechabites (Jer. xxxv. 7), shunned
the life of cities and dwelt in the desert country by the Dead Sea.

16 Woe to thee, O land, when thy king *is* a child, and thy
17 princes eat in the morning.   Blessed *art* thou, O land,

Woe to thee, O land, when thy king is a child]   The gnomic temper
which we have seen in verse 7 still continues, and passes from the weaknesses of subjects and popular leaders to those of rulers. It is, of course,
probable that the writer had a specific instance in his thoughts, but as
the Hebrew word for "child" has a wide range including any age from
infancy (Ex. ii. 6; Judg. xiii. 5) to manhood (Gen. xxxiv. 19; 1 Kings iii.
7), it is not easy to fix the reference. In Isai. iii. 12 a like word appears
to be used of Ahaz. The old school of interpreters saw in it Solomon's
prophetic foresight of the folly of Rehoboam (1 Kings xii. 1—11). One
commentator (Hitzig) connects it, with some plausibility, with the reign
of Ptolemy Epiphanes who was but fifteen years of age on his father's
accession to the throne (Justin XXX. 2) and whose government, as
described by Justin ("*tribunatus, prefecturas et ducatus mulieres ordina-
bant*") resembled that painted by Isaiah (iii. 12), the queen mother
Agathoclea (see Note on ch. vii. 26) and her brother being the real
rulers. Grätz, adapting the words to his theory of the date of the book
takes the word child as=servant, and refers it to the ignoble origin of
Herod the Great.

thy princes eat in the morning]   The word "eat" is, of course,
equivalent to "feast" or "banquet," and the kind of life condemned is
the profligate luxury which begins the day with revels, instead of giving
the morning hours to "sitting in the gate" and doing justice and judgment.   Morning revelling was looked upon naturally as the extreme of
profligacy.   So St Peter repudiates the charge of drunkenness on the
ground that it was but "the third hour of the day" *i. e.* 9 A.M. (Acts
ii. 15). So Cicero (*Philipp.* II. 41) emphasizes the fact "*ab horâ tertiâ
bibebatur.*"   So Catullus (XLVII. 5)

"Vos convivia lauta sumtuose
De die facitis."

"Ye from daybreak onward make
Your sumptuous feasts and revelry."

So Juvenal (*Sat.* I. 49) "*Exsul ab octavâ Marius bibit*" ("In exile
Marius from the eighth hour drinks"). So Isaiah (v. 11) utters his woe
against those that "rise up early in the morning that they may follow
strong drink."

17.   *Blessed art thou, O land, when thy king is the son of nobles*]   The
epithet has been taken as instance of the Hebrew of expressing character by the phrase "the son of...," and hence as having a meaning
here like that of the Latin *generosus*. Probably, however, the maxim
reflects the thought of Greek political writers that they "are truly
noble who can point to ancestors distinguished for both excellence and
wealth" (Aristot. *Polit.* v. 17) that if there were any one family with
an hereditary character for excellence, it was just that it should be
recognised as kingly, and that the king should be chosen from it (*Ibid.*
III. 16). Such, the writer may have meant covertly to imply, ought a

when thy king *is* the son of nobles, and thy princes eat in
due season, for strength, and not for drunkenness.

By much slothfulness the building decayeth ; and through 18
idleness of the hands the house droppeth through.

A feast is made for laughter, and wine maketh merry: 19
but money answereth all *things.*

true descendant of the Ptolemies to have been instead of sinking into a
degenerate profligacy.

thy princes eat in due season] The word "season" reminds us of the
sense in which in chap. iii. 1—8 it is said that every thing, feasting
included, has its proper "time." In the case supposed the character
of the king is reflected in the princes that rule under him. The words
"for strength" may, perhaps, mean "**in** strength," *i.e.* with the self-
control of temperance, the ἐγκρατεία of Greek ethics, and not in the
drunkenness which accompanies the morning revels.

18. *By much slothfulness the building decayeth*] The maxim, though
generalised in form, and applicable to every form of the evil which it
condemns, may fairly be contemplated, in relation to its context, as
having a political bearing. There, *laissez-faire*, the policy of indolent
procrastination, may be as fatal to the good government and prosperity
of a state as the most reckless profligacy. The figure is singularly apt.
The fabric of a state, like that of the house (Amos ix. 11), needs from
time to time to be surveyed and repaired. "Time," as Bacon has said,
"alters all things" (houses of both kinds included) "for the worse." "The
timber framework of the house decays." The decay may be hidden
at first (this seems the point implied in the relation of the two parts of
the proverb) but the latent cause soon shews itself in a very patent
effect, "The house **lets in the rain**," there is the "continual dropping,"
the "drip, drip, drip," which, to the householder seeking comfort, is the
type of all extremest discomfort (Prov. xix. 13). Delitzsch quotes
a curious Arab proverb that "there are three things that make a house
intolerable, rain leaking through the roof, an ill-tempered wife, and the
cimex lectularius." So is it with the state. The timbers are the funda-
mental laws or principles by which its fabric is supported. Corruption
or discord (the "beginning of strife" which is "as when one letteth
out of water," Prov. xvii. 14) is the visible token that these are worm-
eaten and decayed through long neglect.

19. *money answereth all things*] The maxim as it stands in the
English Version, has a somewhat cynical ring, reminding us only too
closely of the counsel condemned by the Roman satirist,

> "O cives, cives, quærenda pecunia primum est;
>   Virtus post nummos."

> "Money, my townsmen, must be sought for first;
>   Virtue comes after guineas,"

or

20   Curse not the king, no not in thy thought; and curse

> "Isne tibi melius suadet, qui rem facias; rem,
> Si possis, recte; si non, quocunque modo rem?"

> "Does he give better counsel whom we hear,
> 'Make money, money; justly if you can,
> But if not, then in any way, make money?'"

HOR. *Epp.* I. I. 53, 65.

So Menander (quoted by Delitzsch) "Silver and gold—these are the Gods who profit most. If these are in thy house pray for what thou wilt and it shall be thine," and Horace:

> "Scilicet uxorem cum dote, fidemque, et amicos,
> Et genus, et formam, regina pecunia donat;
> Ac bene nummatum decorat Suadela Venusque."

> "Seek'st thou a dowried wife, or friends, or trust,
> Beauty or rank, Queen Money gives thee all;
> Put money in thy purse, and thou shalt lack
> Nor suasive power nor comeliness of form."

Epp. I. 6. 36—38.

The truer rendering of the Hebrew, however, gives not so much a maxim as the statement of a fact and is entirely in harmony with the preceding verses. **For revelry they** (*i.e.* "man," indefinitely) **prepare food** (literally, **bread**) **and wine that rejoices life, and money answereth all things,** *i.e.* meets all they want. The words obviously point to the conduct of the luxurious and slothful princes condemned in verses 16, 18. Regardless of their duty as rulers and of the sufferings of their people, they aim only at self-indulgence and they look to money, however gained, as the means of satisfying their desires. So, in our own times, Armenians or Fellaheen may die by thousands of famine or pestilence, but the palaces of the Sultan and the Khedive are as full of luxury and magnificence as ever. The State may be bankrupt and creditors unpaid, but they manage somehow to get what they want. The money which they squeeze out from a starving province is for them as the God they worship who grants all they wish.

20. *Curse not the king, no not in thy thought*] The words paint, as from a painful experience, the all-pervading espionage, which, as in the *delatores* of the Roman Empire, associates itself naturally with the police of a despotic government. The wise man must recognise that espionage as a fact and gives his counsel accordingly, but it is not the less clear that the counsel itself conveys, in its grave irony, a condemnation of the practice. It may be noted that the addition of "curse not the rich" makes the irony clearer, and takes the maxim out of the hands of those who would read in it the serious condemnation of all independence of thought and speech in face of the "right divine of kings to govern wrong." For the purposes of the teacher, in the maxims in which the irony of indignation veils itself in the garb of a servile prudence, the rich man and the king stand on the same level.

not the rich in thy bedchamber: for a bird of the air shall carry the voice, and that which hath wings shall tell the matter.

in thy bedchamber] This is, as in 2 Kings vi. 12, like the "closet" of Matt. vi. 6, proverbial for the extremest retirement.

a bird of the air shall carry the voice] The figure is so natural, answering to the "walls have ears" of the Rabbinic, German, English proverbs, that any more special reference scarcely need to be sought for, but it is interesting to note the close parallel presented by the familiar Greek proverb of "the cranes of Ibycos." For the reader who does not know the story it may be well to tell it. Ibycos was a lyric poet of Rhegium, circ. B.C. 540. He was murdered by robbers near Corinth and, as he died, called on a flock of cranes that chanced to fly over him, to avenge his death. His murderers went with their plunder to Corinth, and mingled with the crowd in the theatre. It chanced that the cranes appeared and hovered over the heads of the spectators, and one of the murderers betrayed himself by the terror-stricken cry "Behold the avengers of Ibycos!" (Suidas Ἴβυκος. Apollon. Sidon in the *Anthol. Graec.* B. VII. 745, ed. Tauchnitz). Suggestive parallels are also found in Greek comedy.

> οὐδεὶς οἶδεν τὸν θησαυρὸν τὸν ἐμὸν
> πλὴν εἴ τις ἄρ' ὄρνις.

"No one knows of my treasure, save, it may be, a bird."

ARISTOPH. *Birds*, 575.

> ἡ κορώνη μοὶ πάλαι
> ἄνω τι φράζει.

"Long since the raven tells me from on high."

ARISTOPH. *Birds*, 50.

Possibly, however, the words may refer to the employment of carrier pigeons in the police espionage of despots. Their use goes back to a remote antiquity and is at least as old as Anacreon's "Ode to a pigeon." The pigeon speaks:

> Ἐγὼ δ' Ἀνακρέοντι
> Διακονῶ τοσαῦτα,
> Καὶ νῦν ὁρᾶς ἐκείνου
> Ἐπιστολὰς κομίζω.

"Now I render service due
To Anacreon, Master true,
And I bear his billets-doux."

Frequently they were employed to keep up communication between generals, as in the case of Brutus and Hirtius at the battle of Mutina. "What availed it," says Pliny, in words that coincide almost verbally with the text (*Hist. Nat.* x. 37), "that nets were stretched across the river while the messenger was cleaving the air" ("*per cælum eunte nuntio*").

11   Cast thy bread upon the waters: for thou shalt find it

CHAPTER XI.

1. *Cast thy bread upon the waters*] The book, as it draws nearer to its close, becomes more and more enigmatic, and each single verse is as a parable and dark saying. It is not to be wondered at, in such a case, that interpreters should, after their nature, read their own thoughts between the lines and so "find what they have sought." This precept accordingly has been taken by some commentators (*e.g.* Grätz) as recommending an unrestrained licentiousness. By others it has been raised almost to the level of the counsel which bids us "do good, hoping for nothing again, even to the unthankful and the evil" (Matt. v. 44—46; Luke vi. 32—35). The latter is, it need hardly be said, infinitely more in accordance with the context and with the conclusion to which the writer is drawing near. Here again we find guidance in the parallelism of Greek thought. As Lowth pointed out (*De Sac. Poes. Heb.* x.) the words refer to the Greek proverbial phrase σπείρειν ἐπὶ πόντῳ ("to sow in the ocean") as indicating a thankless labour. So Theognis, v. 105,

> Δειλοὺς δ' εὖ ἔρδοντι ματαιοτάτη χάρις ἐστιν,
> Ἴσον γὰρ σπείρειν πόντον ἁλὸς πολιῆς.
> Οὔτε γὰρ ἂν πόντον σπείρων βαθὺ λήϊον ἀμῷς,
> Οὔτε κακοὺς εὖ δρῶν εὖ πάλιν ἀντιλάβοις.

> "Vain is thy bounty, giving to the base,
>   Like scattering seed upon the salt sea's plain;
> Sowing the sea, thou shalt no harvest reap,
>   Nor, giving to the vile, reward shalt gain."

Other parallels are found (1) in the Aramaic version of the proverbs of Sirach "Cast thy bread upon the water and the land, and at last thou shalt find it again" (Dukes, *Rabbin. Blumenl.* p. 73). (2) In an Arabic proverb, the moral of a long legend narrating how Mohammed the son of Hassan had been in the daily habit of throwing loaves into a river, how the life of an adopted son of the Caliph Mutewekjil, who had narrowly escaped drowning by clambering to a rock, was thus preserved, and how Mohammed saw in this a proof of the proverb he had learnt in his youth "Do good; cast thy bread upon the waters, and one day thou shalt be rewarded" (Diez, *Denkwürdigkeiten von Asien*, I. p. 106, quoted by Dukes, *ut supra*). (3) In a Turkish proverb, also quoted by Dukes from Diez, "Do good, cast thy bread upon the water. If the fish know it not, yet the Creator knows."

The writer holds himself aloof from the selfish prudence of the maxim of Theognis, and bids men not to be afraid "to cast their bread (the generic term stands for "corn," as in Gen. xli. 54; Isai. xxviii. 28) even upon the face of the thankless waters." Sooner or later they shall reap as they have sown. Comp. 2 Cor. ix. 6—10. It is not without interest to note that this interpretation is adopted by Voltaire in his *Précis de l'Ecclesiaste*,

after many days.　Give a portion to seven, and also to ²
eight; for thou knowest not what evil shall be upon the

> "Répandez vos bienfaits avec magnificence,
> Même aux moins vertueux ne les refusez pas."

Other interpretations may be briefly noted, but have not much to
commend them: (1) that the figure is drawn from agriculture, and that
the corn is to be sown in a well irrigated field, but this gives a meaning precisely the opposite of the true one; (2) that it is drawn from
commerce and commends a venturous spirit of enterprise like that of
exporting corn, which is certain to bring profit in the long run; but this
again, unless we make the venture one of benevolence, is foreign to the
spirit of the context; (3) that it speaks of throwing cakes of bread upon
the water, that float away and seem to be wasted; but this, though leading
to the same result as the interpretation here adopted, and having the
support of the Arab legend quoted above, lacks the point of the reference to the Greek proverb ; (4) last and· basest, the imagination of one
interpreter mentioned above that the precept sanctions a boundless
sensual indulgen̓ce.

2.　*Give a portion to seven, and also to eight*]　The precept is
clearly a pendant to verse 1 and has received the same variety of interpretations.　Following the same line of thought as before, we find in
it the counsel to give freely as opportunities present themselves.　The
combination of "to seven and also to eight," is, like that of "six and
seven" in Job v. 19, of "three and four" in Amos i. ii., like the
"seventy times seven" of Matt. xviii. 22, a Hebrew form of the definite
for the indefinite.　There is, in our acts of kindness, to be no grudging
narrowness.　In such things

> "Kind heaven disdains the lore
> Of nicely calculated less or more."

And the reason given fits in with the counsel, "Thou knowest not
what evil shall be on earth."　"Hard times may come, when thou shalt
have no means for giving;' therefore waste not the present opportunity.
Help those to whom thou givest to meet the hazards of the uncertain
future."　Here again men interpret according to their character, and so,
we have, as before, the licentious moralist finding a plea for unlimited
voluptuousness, while the prudential adviser sees in the precept, which
he renders "Divide the portion into seven, yea eight parts," a caution
like that which led Jacob to divide his caravan into two portions for
the sake of safety (Gen. xxxii. 7, 8).　Taken in this last sense the precept
stands on a level with the current saying of the Stock Exchange that it
isn't wise to "put all your eggs into one basket," with the "hedging" of
those who bet on more than one horse at the Derby and other races.
It may well be left to the student to decide which of these interpretations has most to commend it.

It may be admitted, however, as it is the enigmatic form of the
precept which has given rise to these discordant views as to its meaning,

3 earth.   If the clouds be full *of* rain, they empty *themselves* upon the earth : and if the tree fall toward the south, or toward the north, *in* the place where the tree falleth, there 4 it shall be.   He that observeth the wind shall not sow ; and 5 he that regardeth the clouds shall not reap.   As thou knowest not what *is* the way of the spirit, *nor* how the bones *do*

that the grave irony of the writer, which we have already traced in ch. x. 4, 20 may have led him to adopt that form because it served as a test of character, each scholar finding what he sought.   Here also it might be added "Who hath ears to hear, let him hear" (Matt. xiii. 9).

3. *If the clouds be full of rain*]   The thought is linked to that which precedes it by the mention of the "evil coming upon the earth." In regard to that evil, the sweeping calamities that lie beyond man's control, he is as powerless as he is when the black clouds gather and the winds rush wildly.   He knows only that the clouds will pour down their rain, that the tree will lie as the tempest has blown it down. Is he therefore to pause, and hesitate and stand still, indulging the temper

"over exquisite
To cast the fashion of uncertain evils"?

That question is answered in the next verse.   It may be noted, as an illustration of the way in which the after-thoughts of theology have worked their way into the interpretation of Scripture, that the latter clause has been expounded as meaning that the state in which men chance to be when death comes on them is unalterable, that there is "no repentance in the grave."   So far as it expresses the general truth that our efforts to alter the character of others for the better must cease when the man dies, that when the tree falls to south or north, towards the region of light or that of darkness, we, who are still on earth, cannot prune, or dig about, or dung it (Luke xiii. 8), the inference may be legitimate enough, but it is clear that it is not that thought which was prominent in the mind of the writer.

4. *He that observeth the wind shall not sow*]   This is, as has been said above, the answer to the question suggested in verse 3.   Our ignorance of the future is not to put a stop to action.   If we allowed that "taking thought for the morrow" (Matt. vi. 25) to hinder us from doing good, we should be as the husbandman who is always observing the clouds and lets the time of sowing pass by ; who when harvest comes, watches the wind as it blows round him, till "the harvest is past, and the summer ended" (Jer. viii. 20) and he can no longer reap. The very watching for opportunities may end in missing them.   There are times when it is our wisdom to "be instant *out* of season" (2 Tim. iv. 2).

5. *As thou knowest not what is the way of the spirit*]   The Hebrew word for "spirit" has also the meaning of "wind" as in the verse immediately preceding, and this has led many commentators (as with the corresponding Greek word in John iii. 8) to prefer that meaning,

grow in the womb of her that is with child : even so thou knowest not the works of God who maketh all.   In the 6 morning sow thy seed, and in the evening withhold not

here. Two different examples of man's ignorance of the processes of the common phenomena of nature are adduced on this view as analogous to his ignorance of the "work of God," of what we call the Divine Government of the Universe. It may be questioned however whether, both here and in John iii. 8, a more adequate meaning is not given by retaining the idea of "spirit" as the "breath of life" of Gen. ii. 7. The growth of the human embryo was for the early observers of nature an impenetrable mystery (Job x. 11; Ps. cxxxix. 13—17). It became yet more mysterious when men thought of life, with all its phenomena of sensation and consciousness entering into the material structure thus "fearfully and wonderfully made."   This sense of the word agrees it will be seen, with its use in chaps. iii. 21, xii. 7. The word "nor" has nothing answering to it in the Hebrew and the sentence should run thus, describing not two distinct phenomena but one complex fact, "**as thou knowest not the way of the spirit** (the breath of life) **how the framework of the body** (literally **the bones**, but the word is used commonly for the whole body as in Lam. iv. 7; Job vii. 15; Prov. xv. 30, xvi. 24 and elsewhere) **is in the womb of her that is with child.**

the works of God who maketh all] So in ch. vii. 13, we had " Consider the work of God." Here the addition of " who maketh all " indicates a higher stage of faith. That " never-failing Providence orders all things both in heaven and earth." The agnosticism of the **Debater** is, like that of Hooker (*Eccl. Pol.* I. 2. § 3), the utterance of a devout Theism, content to keep within the limits of the Knowable, but not placing the object of its adoration in the category of the Unknown and Unknowable.

6. *In the morning sow thy seed*] Once again the enigmatic form, as in verse 2, is the touchstone of interpreters. It has been held to mean (1) that men are to seek sensual pleasures not in the morning of their youth only, but in the eventide of age, not to be afraid of begetting children, in or out of wedlock, in any period of their life; or (2) that man is to work, as we say, early and late, doing his appointed task, regardless of the chances of life; or (3) with a more specific application of the same general principle, that he is to sow the seed of good and kindly deeds, and wait for the harvest, the prospect of which is hidden from him. Of these (3) seems every way the truest and most satisfying interpretation. In " withdraw not thy hand," and in the use of the two demonstrative pronouns (in the Hebrew, however, the same pronoun is repeated, **this or this**), we have a parallel to the thought and language of ch. vii. 18. The whole precept is a call to activity in good, not unlike that of Him who said "I must work the works of Him that sent me, while it is called to day: the night cometh, when no man can work" (John ix. 4); who taught men to labour in the vineyard, even though they were not called to begin

thine hand: for thou knowest not whether shall prosper, either this or that, or whether they both *shall be* alike good.

7 Truly the light *is* sweet, and a pleasant *thing it is* for the 8 eyes to behold the sun : but if a man live many years, *and*

their work till the eleventh hour when it was "toward evening, and the day far spent" (Matt. xx. 1—16).

thou knowest not whether shall prosper] The ignorance of men as to the results of their labour, still more the apparent or the actual failure of their earlier efforts, tempts them too often to despondency and indolence. The maxim, like that of verse 6, bids them take comfort from that very ignorance. The seed sown in the morning of life may bear its harvest at once, or not till the evening of age. The man may reap at one and the same time the fruits of his earlier and his later sowing, and may find that "both are alike good."

7. *Truly the light is sweet*] Better, **And the light is sweet.** The conjunction is simply the usual copulative particle. The word for "sweet" is that used of honey in Judg. xiv. 14; of the honeycomb in Prov. xxiv. 13. The pessimism of the thinker is passing away under the sunshine of the wiser plan of life in which he at last finds guidance. Life may after all, rightly ordered, be pleasant and comely, not without the "sweetness and light" on which the modern preachers of wisdom lay stress. A remarkable parallel to the form of the maxim (quoted by Ginsburg) is found in Euripides:

Μή μ' ἀπολέσῃς ἄωρον· ἡδὺ γὰρ τὸ φῶς
λεύσσειν, τὰ δ' ὑπὸ γῆν μὴ μ' ἰδεῖν ἀναγκάσῃς.

"Destroy me not before my youth is ripe:
For pleasant sure it is to see the sun;
Compel me not to see what lies below."

Iphig. in Aul. 1219.

So Theognis contemplating death:

κείσομαι ὥστε λίθος
ἄφθογγος, λείψω δ' ἐρατὸν φάος ἠελίοιο.

"Then shall I lie, as voiceless as a stone,
And see no more the loved light of the sun."

The use of the phrase "seeing the sun" for living, may be noted as essentially Hellenic in its tone. So we have again "seeing the light of the sun" for "living" in Eurip. *Hippol.* 4.

8. *But if a man live many years*...] Better, **For** *if a man*... The relation is one of connexion rather than contrast. In the calm, enjoyable because beneficent, life which the thinker now contemplates as within his reach, the remembrance of the darkness which lies beyond is to be a motive, not for a fretful pessimism, but for a deliberate effort to enjoy rightly. The figure of a corpse which was carried about in the banquets of the Egyptians was intended not to destroy or damp the joy, but to make it more lasting by making it more

rejoice in them all; yet let him remember the days of darkness; for they shall be many.   All that cometh *is* vanity.

controlled (Herod. II. 78). The teaching now is something more
than the "Let us eat and drink, for to-morrow we die" of the sensualist
(Wisd. ii. 1—6; 1 Cor. xv. 32). *"Respice finem; Memento mori,"*
these rules teach us to use life wisely and therefore well.

let him remember the days of darkness] These are clearly not the
days of sorrow or adversity (though the phrase as such might admit
that meaning), but those of the darkness which is contrasted with the
light of the sun, with the light of life, the land that lies behind the
veil, in the unseen world of Hades or of Sheol, the darkness of the
valley of the shadow of death. As the Greeks spoke of the dead as οἱ
πλείονες "the many," so does the writer speak of the days after death
as "many." The night will be long and dreary, therefore it is well to
make the most of the day. The teaching of the whole verse finds, as
might be expected, an echo in that of the Epicurean poet, when he
greets his friend on the return of spring, but the echo is in a lower key.

> Nunc decet aut viridi nitidum caput impedire myrto
>   Aut flore, terræ quem ferunt solutæ,
>   *   *   *   *   *   *   *
> Pallida Mors æquo pulsat pede pauperum tabernas
>   Regumque turres.   O beate Sexti,
> Vitæ summa brevis spem nos vetat inchoare longam,
>   Jam te premet nox, fabulæque Manes
> Et domus exilis Plutonia.

> "Now is it meet to crown bright brow
>   With wreaths of fresh green myrtle; now,
>   With flowers that owe their timely birth
>   To spring's soft influence o'er the earth.
>   *   *   *   *   *   *
>   With equal foot the pauper's cell
>   Death visits, and where emperors dwell,
>   Wherefore my Sextus, good and dear,
>   Life's little span forbids us here
>   To start, if we indeed are wise,
>   On some far-reaching enterprise:
>   Soon Night and fabled forms of dread,
>   Where Pluto lords it o'er the dead,
>   Shall meet thee in thy narrow bed."

HOR. *Od.* 1. 4.

All that cometh is vanity] There is a significance in the new form
of the burden of the **Debater's** song. The sentence of "vanity," *i.e.* of
shadowy transitoriness, is passed not only on the years in which he
is, in a measure, capable of enjoyment, and on the days of darkness,
but even on that which lies beyond them. The unknown future—the
undiscovered country—it was, from the point of view from which, for

9   Rejoice, O young man, in thy youth ; and let thy heart

the time, he looked at it, "vanity" to build too much even on that. Men speculated much and knew but little, and there was an unreality in sacrificing the present to that undefined future. What has been called "other-worldliness," involving the contempt at once of the duties and enjoyments of this world, was but a form of unwisdom. Asceticism, looking to that other world, needed to be balanced by the better form of Epicureanism.

9. *Rejoice, O young man, in thy youth*] Strictly speaking, as the beginning of the end, the opening of the *finale* of the book, these should be read in close connexion with chap. xii. The **Debater** turns with his closing counsel to the young. That counsel, like the rest of the book, has been very variously interpreted. (1) Men have seen in it the stern irony of the ascetic, killing the power of rejoicing in the very act of bidding men rejoice, holding before the young man the terrors of the Lord, the fires of Gehenna. Coarsely paraphrased, the counsel so given is practically this, "Follow your desires, take your fling, sow your wild oats, go forth on the voyage of life, 'youth at the prow and pleasure at the helm,' but know that all this, the 'primrose path of dalliance,' ends in Hell and its eternal fires." It is not without significance, from this point of view, that the counsel given is almost in direct contradiction to the words of the Law, brought, we may believe, into notice by the growing stress laid on the use of phylacteries, on which those words were written, which warned men that they should not " seek after their own heart and their own eyes" (Num. xv. 39). (2) Men have also seen in it the unchastened counsel of the lowest form of Epicureanism, "Let us eat and drink, for to-morrow we die. Leave no desire ungratified, seek the maximum of intense enjoyment, crowd the sensations of a life-time into a few short years." (3) Even the closing words have, by a strange ingenuity, been turned into a protest against asceticism. "God will judge you, if you slight His gifts. Self-denial is for Him no acceptable service. He rejoices in your joy, will punish the gloomy Pharisee or Essene who mortifies the flesh, by leaving him to his self-inflicted tortures." Once again men have looked at the shield on its gold or its silver side : and the Truth is found in seeing it on both. Once again we may recognise the method of one who spoke φωνήεντα συνέτοισιν ("full of meaning to those who have eyes to see"), and uttered his precepts with a double sense as a test of the character of those who heard or read them. The true purport of the words seems to be as follows. After the manner of chs. ii. 24, iii. 12, 22, v. 18, ix. 7, the **Debater** falls back on the fact that life is after all worth living, that it is wise to cultivate the faculty of enjoyment in the season when that faculty is, in most cases, as by a law of nature, strong and capable of being fashioned into a habit. So moralists in our own time, preachers of "sweetness and light," have contrasted the gloomy plodding Philistinism or Puritanism of the English as a people, "*qui s'amusent moult* (=*bien*) *tristement*" (Froissart), with the brightness and gaiety

cheer thee in the days of thy youth, and walk in the ways of
thine heart, and in the sight of thine eyes : but know thou,

of the French, and have urged us to learn wisdom from the comparison.
In good faith he tells the young man to "rejoice in his youth," to
study the bent of his character, what we should call his æsthetic tastes,
but all this is not to be the reckless indulgence of each sensuous
impulse, but to be subject to the thought "God will bring thee into
judgment." What the judgment may be the **Debater** does not define.
It may come in the physical suffering, the disease, or the poverty, or
the shame, that are the portion of the drunkard and the sensualist.
It may come in the pangs of self-reproach, and the memory of the
"*mala mentis gaudia.*"   "The gods are just, and of our pleasant vices
make whips to scourge us."   It is singularly significant to find an echo
of the precept so given in the teaching of the great Poet of the more
atheistic type of Epicureanism, obliged, as in spite of himself, to recognise the fact of a moral order in the world:

> " Inde metus maculat pœnarum præmia vitæ.
> Circumretit enim vis atque injuria quemque,
> Atque, unde exorta est, ad eum plerumque revertit;
> Nec facile est placidam ac pacatam degere vitam,
> Qui violat facteis communia fœdera pacis.
> Etsi fallit enim divom genus humanumque,
> Perpetuo tamen id fore clam diffidere debet."

> " Hence fear of vengeance life's best prizes mars;
> For violence and wrong take him who works them,
> As in a net, and to their source return.
> Nor is it easy found for him who breaks
> By deeds the common covenants of peace
> To lead a placid and a peaceful life.
> For grant he cheat the gods and all mankind,
> He cannot hope the evil done will be
> For ever secret."
>
> LUCR. *De Rer. Nat.* v. 1151.

Did the judgment of which the thinker speaks go beyond this? That
question also has been variously answered. The **Debater,** it is obvious,
does not draw the pictures of the Tartarus and Elysian Fields of the
Greek, or of the Gehenna and the Paradise of which his countrymen
were learning to speak, it may be, all too lightly. He will not map out
a country he has not seen.   But the facts on which he dwells, the life of
ignoble pleasure, or tyranny, or fraud carried on successfully to the last, the
unequal distribution of the pleasures and the pains of life, the obvious
retort on the part of the evil-doer that if this life were all, men could
take their fill of pleasure and evade the judgment of man, or the
misery of self-made reproach and failure, by suicide, all this leads to
the conclusion that the "judgment" which the young man is to
remember is "exceeding broad," stretching far into the unseen future

that for all these *things* God will bring thee into judgment.
10 Therefore remove sorrow from thy heart, and put away evil
from thy flesh : for childhood and youth *are* vanity.

12   Remember now thy Creator in the days of thy youth,
while the evil days come not, nor the years draw nigh, when

of the eternal years. Faith at last comes in where Reason fails, and
the man is bidden to remember, in all the flush of life and joy, that
"judgment" comes at last, if not in man's present stage of being, yet
in the great hereafter.

10. *Therefore remove sorrow from thy heart*] The two clauses
recognise the two conditions of happiness so far as happiness is attainable by man on earth. "Sorrow," better perhaps, **discontent** or
vexation, is by a deliberate effort to be put away from our "heart,"
i.e. from our mind. We are not to look on the dark side of things,
but to cultivate cheerfulness, to be "content" (αὐτάρκης) with whatever
life brings us (Phil. iv. 11). And the "flesh" too has its claims which
may legitimately be recognised. We need not vex it with the self-
inflicted tortures of the ascetic, but, in a sense as far as possible
different from "the rehabilitation of the flesh" which has been made
the plea for an unrivalled sensuality, consider and meet its capacities
for pure and innocent enjoyment.

childhood and youth are vanity] The Hebrew word for "youth" is
an unusual one and is not found elsewhere in the Old Testament. It has
been differently explained: (1) as the dawn or morning of life, the period
of its brightness; and (2) as the time when the hair is black as contrasted with the grey hair of age. Of these (1) seems preferable. The
prominent idea of "vanity" here is that of transitoriness. The morning
will not last. It is wise to use it while we can.

CHAPTER XII.

1. *Remember now thy Creator in the days of thy youth*] The word
for "Creator" is strictly the participle of the verb which is translated
"create" in Gen. i. 1, 21, 27, and as a Divine Name is exceptionally
rare, occurring only here and in Isai. xl. 23, xliv. 15. It is plural in
its form, as Elohim (the word for God) is plural, as the "Holy One"
is plural in Prov. ix. 10, xxx. 3; Hos. xii. 1, as expressing the majesty
of God. The explanations which have been given of the words as
meaning (1) "thy fountain" in the sense of Prov. v. 18, "thy well-
spring of sensuous joy," or (2) "thy existence," are scarcely tenable
philologically, and are altogether at variance with the context.

while the evil days come not] The description which follows forms
in some respects the most difficult of all the enigmas of the Book.
That it represents the decay of old age, or of disease anticipating age,
ending at last in death, lies beyond the shadow of a doubt; but the
figurative language in which that decay is represented abounds in
allusive references which were at the time full of meaning for those

thou shalt say, I have no pleasure in them; while the sun, 2
or the light, or the moon, or the stars, be not darkened, nor

that had ears to hear, but which now present riddles which it is not
easy to solve. Briefly, the two chief lines on which commentators have
travelled have been (1) that which starts as in the comment of Gregory
Thaumaturgus (see *Introduction*, ch. VII.) from the idea of the approach
of death as the on-coming of a storm; (2) that which assumes that
we have as it were a diagnosis of the physical phenomena of old age
and its infirmities, and loses itself in discussions as to what bodily
organ, heart, brain, liver, gall-duct, or the like, is specially in the
author's mind. It will be seen, as the imagery comes before us in
detail, how far either solution is satisfactory, how far they admit of
being combined, or what other, if any, presents itself with stronger
claims on our attention.

The "evil days" are those which are painted in the verses that follow,
not necessarily the special forms of evil that come as the punishment
of sensual sins, but the inevitable accompaniment of declining years or
of disease. There is the implied warning that unless a man has
remembered his Creator in his youth, it will not then be easy to
remember Him as for the first time in the "evil days" of age or infirmity.
In those days it will be emphatically true that there will be no pleasure
in them.

2. *while the sun, or the light*] The imagery falls in naturally with
the thought that the approach of death is represented by the gathering
of a tempest. It does not follow, however, that this excludes the
thought of a latent symbolism in detail as well as in the general idea.
The thought that man was as a microcosm, and that each element in
the universe had its analogue in his nature, was a familiar one to the
Greek and Oriental mind, and was susceptible of many applications. So,
to take an instance belonging to a different age or country, we find
an Eastern poet thus writing, *circ.* A.D. 1339,

> "Of all that finds its being in the world
> Man in himself the symbol true may find.
> *   *   *   *   *
> His body is as earth, and as the Heaven
> His head, with signs and wonders manifold,
> And the five senses shine therein as stars.
> The Spirit, like the sun, pours light on all.
> The limbs, that bear the body's burden up,
> Are as the hills that raise their height to heaven.
> Hair covers all his limbs, as grass the earth,
> And moisture flows, as flow the streams and brooks.
> So on the day when soul and body part,
> And from the body's load the soul is freed,
> Then canst thou see the body all a-tremble,
> As earth shall tremble at the last great day;
> The Spirit with its senses fall away,
> As stars extinguished fall on earth below;

₃ the clouds return after the rain : in the day when the keepers

> The last death-sigh with which the body dies
> Thrill through the bones, like tempest-blast and storm.
> As on that day the hills shall pass away,
> So does death's storm break up our mortal frame.
> A sea of death-damps flows from every pore :
> Thou plungest in, and art as drowned therein :
> So is thy dying like the great world's death;
> In life and death it is thy parallel."

From the *Gulschen Ras* of Mahmud, quoted in Tholuck's *Blüthen-Sammlung aus der morgenländischen Mystik,* p. 213.

It will be admitted that the parallelism is singularly striking and suggestive. With this clue to guide us we may admit all that has been urged by Umbreit, Ginsburg and others in favour of the "storm" interpretation and yet not reject the more detailed symbolic meaning of Jewish and other commentators. We may have the broad outline of the phenomena that precede a tempest, sun, moon and stars, hidden by the gathering blackness. A like imagery meets us as representing both personal and national calamity in Isai. xiii. 10; Jer. xv. 9; Amos viii. 9. The sun may be the Spirit, the Divine light of the body, the moon as the Reason that reflects that light, the stars as the senses that give but a dim light in the absence of sun and moon. The clouds that return after rain are the natural symbol of sorrows, cares, misfortunes, that obscure the shining of the inward light, perhaps of the showers of tears which they cause, but after which in the melancholy and gloom of age and weakness they too commonly "return." The mere anatomical interpretation which interprets the first four symbols as referring to the eyes, the brow, the nose, the cheeks, and finds in the "clouds after rain" the symptoms of the catarrh of old age, may be looked upon as a morbid outgrowth of prosaic fancy in men in whom the sense of true poetic imagination was extinct.

3. *in the day when the keepers of the house shall tremble*] Here, as before, there is a vivid picture which is also an allegory. The words represent (1) the effect of terror, such as that produced by tempest, or by earthquake, in the population of the city; and (2) the fact which corresponds to these in the breaking up of life. As in the previous verse the phenomena of the firmament answered to those of the higher region of man's nature, so these represent the changes that pass over the parts of his bodily structure. Here accordingly the mode of interpretation which was rejected before becomes admissible. The error of the allegorizers was that they had not the discernment to see that the decay of mental powers would naturally take precedence of that of the bodily organs and that they would as naturally be symbolized by sun, moon and stars. The "keepers" or "watchers" of the houses are in the picture those who stand at the gate as sentinels or go round about the house to see that there are none approaching with the intention to attack. In the allegory they represent the legs which support the frame at rest or give it the power of movement. The trembling is that of the

of the house shall tremble, and the strong men shall bow
themselves, and the grinders cease because they are few,

unsteady gait of age, perhaps even of paralysis. Not a few features
in the picture seem to indicate experience rather than observation, and
this fits in with the thought, suggested in the *Ideal Biography* (*Introduction*, ch. III.), of a form of creeping paralysis depriving one organ
after another of its functional activity yet leaving the brain free to note
the gradual decay of the whole organism.

and the strong men shall bow themselves] As the previous clause
painted the effect of terror on the slave sentinels of the house, so this
represents its action on the **men of might**, the wealthy and the noble.
They too cower in their panic before the advancing storm. Interpreting
the parable, they are the symbol of the arms as man's great instrument
of action. They too, once strong to wield sword, or axe, to drive
plough, or pen, become flaccid and feeble. The "hands that hang
down" (Job iv. 3, 4; Isai. xxxv. 3; Heb. xii. 12) become the proverbial type of weakness as well as the "feeble knees." It should be
added that the allegorizing commentators for the most part invert the
order of interpretation which has been here adopted, finding the arms
in the "keepers" and the legs in the "strong man." Something may,
of course, be said for this view, but the balance of probabilities turns in
favour of that here adopted.

and the grinders cease because they are few] Both this noun and
"they that look out" are in the feminine, and this determines their
position in the picture. As we found slaves and nobles in the first half of
the verse, so here we have women at the opposite extremes of social ranks.
To "grind at the mill" was the type of the humblest form of female
slave labour (Judg. xvi. 21; Isai. xlvii. 2; Exod. xi. 5; Job xxxi. 10;
Matt. xxiv. 41; Homer, *Od.* XX. 105—8). To "look out of the windows"
(*i.e.* the latticed openings, glazed windows being as yet unknown) was
as naturally the occupation of the wealthy and luxurious women of the
upper class. So the ladies of Sisera (Judg. v. 28), and Michal, Saul's
daughter (2 Sam. vi. 16), and the observing sage, or probably, Wisdom
personified (Prov. vii. 6), and Jezebel (2 Kings ix. 30), and the kingly
lover of the Shulamite (Song Sol. ii. 9) are all represented in this
attitude.

The interpretation of the parable is here not far to seek. The grinders
(as the very term "molar" suggests) can be none other than the teeth,
doing, as it were, their menial work of masticating food. They that
look out of the windows can be none other than the eyes with their
nobler function as organs of perception. So Cicero describes the eyes
as "*tanquam in arce collocati...tanquam speculatores altissimum locum
obtinent.*" "Placed as in a citadel, like watchmen, they hold the
highest places" (*de Nat. Deor.* II. 140). The symbolism which thus
draws, as it were, distinctions of dignity and honour between different
parts of the body will remind a thoughtful student of the analogy on
which St Paul lays stress in 1 Cor. xii. 12—26. Each member of

4 and those that look out of the windows be darkened, and
the doors shall be shut in the streets, when the sound of

that analogy may, of course, thus be used as a symbol of the other.
Here the gradations of society represent the organs of the body, and
the Apostle inverts the comparison.

4. *and the doors shall be shut in the streets*] The picture of the
city under the terror of the storm is continued. The gates of all
houses are closed. None leave their houses; the **noise of the mill
ceases. The bird** (probably the crane or the swallow) **rises** in the
air with sharp cries (literally, **for a cry**). Even the "daughters of
song" (the birds that sing most sweetly, the nightingale or thrush,
or possibly the "singing women" of ch. ii. 8, whose occupation
is gone in a time of terror and dismay) **crouch silently**, or perhaps,
chirp in a low tone. Few will dispute the vividness of the picture.
The interpretation of the symbols becomes, however, more difficult
than ever. The key is probably to be found in the thought that as we
had the decay of bodily *organs* in the previous verse, so here we have
that of bodily *functions.* The "doors" (the Hebrew is dual as representing what we call "folding doors") are the apertures by which the life
of processes of sensation and nutrition from its beginning to its end is
carried on, and the failure of those processes in extreme age, or in the
prostration of paralysis, is indicated by the "shutting" of the doors.
What we may call the dual organs of the body, lips, eyes, ears, alike
lose their old energies. The **mill** (a better rendering than "grinding")
is that which contains the "grinders" of verse 3, *i.e.* the mouth, by
which that process begins, can no longer do its work of vocal utterance
rightly. The words "he shall rise up at the voice of the bird" have
for the most part been taken as describing the sleeplessness of age, the
old man waking at a sparrow's chirp, but this interpretation is open to
the objections (1) that it abruptly introduces the old man as a personal
subject in the sentence, while up to this point all has been figurative;
and (2) that it makes the clause unmeaning in its relation to the picture
of the terror-stricken city, below which we see that of the decay of
man's physical framework. Adopting the construction given above, we
get that which answers to the "childish treble" of the old man's voice,
and find a distinct parallel to it in the elegy of Hezekiah "Like a crane
or a swallow, so did I chatter" (Isai. xxxviii. 14); the querulous moaning
which in his case was the accompaniment of disease becoming, with the
old or the paralysed, normal and continuous. The "daughters of song"
are, according to the common Hebrew idiom, those that sing, birds
or women, as the case may be. Here, their being "brought low,"
i.e. their withdrawal from the stage of life, may symbolise the failure
either of the power to sing, or of the power to enjoy the song of others.
The words of Barzillai in 2 Sam. xix. 35 paint the infirmities of age in
nearly the same form, though in less figurative language. "Can thy
servant taste what I eat or drink? Can I hear any more the voice of
singing men or singing women?" The interpretations which find in
the "daughters of song" either (1) the lips as employed in singing, or

the grinding is low, and he shall rise up at the voice of the bird, and all the daughters of musick shall be brought low ;

(2) the ears as drinking in the sounds of song, though each has found favour with many commentators, have less to commend them, and are open to the charge of introducing a needless and tame repetition of phenomena already described.

With the picture of old age thus far we may compare that, almost cynical in its unsparing minuteness, of Juvenal *Sat.* x. 200—239. A few of the more striking parallels may be selected as examples :

> "Frangendus misero gingiva panis inermi."

> "Bread must be broken for the toothless gums."

> "Non eadem vini, atque cibi, torpente palato,
> Gaudia."

> "For the dulled palate wine and food have lost
> Their former savours."

> "Adspice partis
> Nunc damnum alterius; nam quæ cantante voluptas,
> Sit licet eximius citharœdus, sitve Seleucus,
> Et quibus auratâ mos est fulgere lacernâ?
> Quid refert, magni sedeat quâ parte theatri,
> Qui vix cornicines exaudiet, atque tubarum
> Concentus."

> "Now mark the loss of yet another sense:
> What pleasure now is his at voice of song.
> How choice soe'er the minstrel, artist famed,
> Or those who love to walk in golden robes?
> What matters where he sits in all the space
> Of the wide theatre, who scarce can hear
> The crash of horns and trumpets?"

Or again

> "Ille humero, hic lumbis, hic coxâ debilis; ambos
> Perdidit ille oculos, et luscis invidet; hujus
> Pallida labra cibum accipiunt digitis alienis.
> Ipse ad conspectum cœnæ diducere rictum
> Suetus, hiat tantùm, ceu pullus hirundinis, ad quem
> Ore volat pleno mater jejuna."

> "Shoulders, loins, hip, each failing in its strength
> Now this man finds, now that, and one shall lose
> Both eyes, and envy those that boast but one....
> And he who used, at sight of supper spread,
> To grin with wide-oped jaw, now feebly gapes,
> Like a young swallow, whom its mother bird
> Feeds from her mouth filled, though she fast herself."

₅ also *when* they shall be afraid of *that which is* high, and fears *shall be* in the way, and the almond tree shall flourish,

5. *also when they shall be afraid of that which is high*] The description becomes more and more enigmatic, possibly, as some have thought, because the special forms of infirmity referred to called for a veil. The first clause, however, is fairly clear if we omit the interpolated "*when.*" **They** (the indefinite plural, with the force of the French *on*) **shall be afraid of a height**, or **hill.** The new form of the sentence, the opening words also, indicate that the picture of the storm has been completed, and that symbolism of another kind comes in. We see, as it were, another slide in the magic lantern of the exhibiter. To be "afraid of a hill" expresses not merely or chiefly the failure of strength of limbs to climb mountains, but the temper that, as we say, makes "mountains out of molehills," which, like the slothful man of Prov. xxii. 13, sees "a lion in the path." There are "fears in the way." Imaginary terrors haunt the aged. Here again we have a parallel in Latin poetry :

> "Multa senem circumveniunt incommoda; vel quòd
> Quærit et inventis miser abstinet, ac timet uti,
> Vel quòd res omnes timidè gelidèque ministrat."

> "Many the troubles that attend the old;
> For either still he sets his mind on gains
> And dares not touch, and fears to use his gains,
> Or deals with all things as with chill of fear."
> HORACE, *Ep. ad Pis.* 169—71.

So Aristotle among the characteristics of age notes that the old are δειλοὶ καὶ πάντα προφοβητικοί (timid and in all things forecasting fears) (*Rhet.* II. 23). The interpreters who carry the idea of a storm through the whole passage explain the passage : "They (the people of the city) shall be afraid of that which is coming from on high," *i.e.* of the gathering storm-clouds, but for the reasons above given, that interpretation seems untenable.

and the almond tree shall flourish] The true meaning is to be found, it is believed, in the significance of the Hebrew name for almond tree (*Sheked*=the early waking tree, comp. Jerem. i. 11), and the enigmatic phrase describes the *insomnia* which often attends old age. The tree that flourishes there is the tree of *Vigilantia* or Wakefulness. As might be expected, the discordant interpretations of commentators multiply, and we may record, but only in order to reject them, the more notable of these. (1) The almond blossoms represent the white hairs of age. Those blossoms are, however, pink and not white, and few persons would find a likeness in the two objects thus compared. (2) The verb rendered "shall flourish" has been derived from a root with the meaning "to loathe—scorn—reject," and the sentence has been explained either (2) he (the old man) loathes the almond, *i.e.* has no taste for dainties, or (3) turns away from the almond tree, *i.e.* has no welcome for the messenger of spring, or (4), with the same sense as (2), "the

and the grasshopper shall be a burden, and desire shall fail :

almond causes loathing." Anatomical expositors strain their fancies
to find in the almond that which answers to (5) the thigh bone, or (6)
the vertebral column, or some other part of the body which age affects
with weakness. Into the discussion what part best answers to the
almond we need not follow them.

and the grasshopper shall be a burden] The word translated "grasshopper" is one of the many terms used, as in 2 Chron. vii. 13, for insects
of the locust class, as in Lev. xi. 22; Num. xiii. 33; Isai. xl. 22, where the
A. V. has "grasshopper." It will be noted that in some of these passages
(Num. xiii. 33; Isai. xl. 22) it plays the part of the "mustard seed" of
the Gospel parable (Matt. xiii. 31) as the type of that which is the
extreme of diminutiveness. And this we can scarcely doubt is its meaning here. "That which is least weighty is a burden to the timidity of
age." Assuming the writer to have come in contact with the forms of
Greek life, the words may receive an illustration from its being the
common practice of the Athenians to wear a golden grasshopper in their
heads as the symbol of their being *autochthones*, "sprung from the soil."
Such an ornament is to the old man more than he cares to carry, and
becomes another symbol of his incapacity to support the least physical
or mental burden. As before we note a wide variety of other, but, it is
believed, less tenable, explanations. (1) The locust has been looked on
as, like the almond, another dainty article of food, which the terror of the
storm, or the loss of appetite in age, renders unattractive. Commonly
indeed they are said to have been eaten only by the poor, but Aristotle
(*Hist. Anim.* v. 30) names them as a delicacy, and the Arabs are said
to consider them as such now (Ginsburg). Entering once more on the
region of anatomical exposition we have the grasshopper taken (2) for
the bone of the *pelvis* which becomes sharp and prominent in age, (3) for
the stomach which swells with dropsy, (4) for the ankles swelling from
the same cause, and so on through various other members.

and desire shall fail] The word translated "desire" is not found
elsewhere in the Old Testament, and this rendering rests on a somewhat doubtful etymology. The LXX. version, which may be admitted
as shewing in what sense the word was taken at a very early date,
and with which the Rabbinic use of the word agrees, gives κάππαρις,
which the Vulgate reproduces in *capparis*, *i.e.* the caper or *Capparis
spinosa* of botanists. It is in favour of this rendering that it preserves
the enigmatic symbolism of the two previous clauses, while "desire"
simply gives an abstract unfigurative term, out of harmony with the
context. Possibly indeed the name was given to the plant as indicating
its qualities as a restorative and stimulant (Plutarch, *Sympos.*; Athenæus,
Deipnos, IX. p. 405). The pickled capers of modern cookery are the
buds of the shrub, but the berries and leaves are reputed to possess the
same virtues. Hence one of the Epicures in Athenæus (*Deipnos.* IX. p.
370) takes Νὴ τὸν κάππαριν (By the caper!) as a favourite oath, just as a
modern *gourmet* might swear by some favourite sauce. So understood
the meaning of the passage seems fairly clear. **The caper-berry shall**

because man goeth to his long home, and the mourners go
6 about the streets: or ever the silver cord be loosed, or the

fail, *i.e.* shall no longer rouse the flagging appetite of age. There shall
be a *longa oblivio* of what the man had most delighted in. It would
seem indeed from the account of the *capparis* given by Pliny (*Hist.
Nat.* xx. 59) that its medicinal virtues were of a very varied character.
It was a remedy for paralysis and diseases of the kidneys and the liver,
for tooth-ache and ear-ache, for scrofula and phagedænic ulcers. The
words describe accordingly the infirmity which no drugs, however
potent, can cure. It is as when Shakespeare says that "poppy and
mandragora" shall fail to minister the "sweet sleep" of yesterday, as
when we say of a man in the last stage of decrepitude that "no quinine
or phosphorus will help him now." See the *Ideal Biography* in the
Introduction, ch. III. So understood the **Debater** speaks with a scorn
like that of Euripides (*Suppl.* 1060) of the attempts of the old to revive
their flagging desires and avert the approach of death.

> μισῶ δ' ὅσοι χρῄζουσιν ἐκτείνειν βίον
> λουτροῖσι, καὶ στρωμναῖσι καὶ μαγεύμασιν.

"I hate them, those who seek to lengthen life
With baths, and pillows, and quack-doctor's drugs."

Substantially most commentators agree in this meaning. The anatomical school, however, identify it, as before, with this or that bodily
organ affected by old age, and one writer (Rosenmüller) thinks that the
point of comparison is found in the fact that the caper-berry as it
ripens, bends the stalk with its weight, and then splits open and lets the
seeds fall out.

because man goeth to his long home] Literally, **to the house of his
eternity**, *i.e.* **to his eternal home.** The description of the decay of age
is followed by that of death as the close of all, and for a time, perhaps
to link together the two symbolical descriptions, the language of figurative imagery is dropped. The "eternal home" is, of course, the grave
(the phrase is stated by Ginsburg to be in common use among modern
Jews), or more probably, *Sheol*, or Hades, the dwelling-place of the dead.
In Tobit iii. 6, "the everlasting place" seems used of the felicity of
Paradise, and it is, at least, obvious that the thought of immortality,
though not prominent, is not excluded here. The term *Domus æterna*
appears often on the tombs of Rome in Christian as well as non-Chris-
tian inscriptions, probably as equivalent to the "everlasting habitations"
of Luke xvi. 9, and in these cases it clearly connotes more than an
"eternal sleep." An interesting parallel is found in the Assyrian legend
of Ishtar, in which Hades is described as the "House of Eternity," the
"House men enter, but cannot depart from; the Road men go to, but
cannot return" (*Records of the Past*, I. 143).

the mourners go about the streets] Literally, in the singular, the
street or **market-place.** The words bring before us the most prominent
feature of Eastern funerals. The burial-place was always outside the

golden bowl be broken, or the pitcher be broken at the

city, and the body was borne on an open bier through the streets and open places of the city, and the hired mourners, men and women, followed with their wailing cries, praising the virtues, or lamenting the death, of the deceased (2 Sam. iii. 31; Jer. xxii. 10, 18; Mark v. 38). Sometimes these were short and simple, like the "Ah brother! Ah, sister! Ah, his glory!" of Jer. xxii. 18. Sometimes they developed into elegiac poems like the lamentations of David over Saul and Jonathan (2 Sam. i. 17—27), and Abner (2 Sam. iii. 32—34). So we have in the Talmud (quoted by Dukes, *Rabbin. Blumenlese*, pp. 256, 257) examples such as the following, "The palms wave their heads for the just man who was like a palm"—"If the fire falls upon the cedar what shall the hyssop on the wall do?" It is obvious that such elegies would often take the form of a figurative description of death, and that which follows in the next verse may well have been an echo from some such elegy.

6. *or ever the silver cord be loosed, or the golden bowl be broken*] The figurative character of the whole section reaches its highest point here. It is clear however that the figures, whatever they may be, are symbolic of nothing less than death. We have had the notes of decay in organs and in functions brought before us one by one. Now we come to the actual dissolution of soul and body. It will help us to a right understanding to begin with the golden bowl. The noun is the same as that used in Zech. iv. 3, 4, for the bowl of the golden seven-branched candlestick (better, **lamp**) of the Temple. It was the vessel, or reservoir, from which the oil flowed into the lamps. The lamp itself was, in the judgment of most students of the Mosaic ritual, the symbol of life—perhaps, even in its very form, of the Tree of life—in its highest manifestations. The symbolism of Greek thought harmonized with that of Hebrew, and "the lamp of life" was a familiar image. So when Pericles visited Anaxagoras, as he was dying of want and hunger, the sage said reproachfully "When we wish to keep the lamp burning, we take care to supply it with oil." (Plutarch, *Pericles.*) So Plato (*de Legg.* p. 776) and Lucretius (II. 78) describe the succession of many generations of mankind, with an allusive reference to the Lampadephoria, or torch races of Athens.

"Et quasi cursores vitai lampada tradunt."

"Like men who run a race, hand on the lamp of life."

So the "light of life" appears in Greek epitaphs,

Νὺξ μὲν ἐμὸν κατέχει ζωῆς φάος ὑπνοδοτείρη

"Sleep-giving night hath quenched my light of life."

Anthol. Graec. Ed. Jacobs, *App.* 265.

It can scarcely remain doubtful then that the "golden bowl" is life as manifested through the material fabric of man's body. And if so, the "silver cord" in the imagery of the parable can only be the chain

7 fountain, or the wheel broken at the cistern.   Then shall

by which, as in houses or temples, the lamp hangs, *i.e.* when we interpret the parable, that on which the continuance of life depends. Death, elsewhere represented as the cutting of the thread of life by the "abhorred shears" of the Destinies, is here brought before us as the snapping of the chain, the extinction of the principle of life. The anatomist commentators have, as before, shewn their lack of poetic feeling by going *in omnia alia* as to the interpretation of the symbols. The "golden bowl" has been identified with the skull or the stomach, and the "silver cord" with the tongue or the spinal marrow, and so on into a region of details into which it is not always pleasant to follow the interpreter.

or the pitcher be broken at the fountain, or the wheel broken at the cistern] Better, **or the pitcher be shattered.** As with the Hebrews so also with the Greeks, life was represented by yet another symbol almost as universal as that of the burning lamp. The "fountain of life" was with God (Ps. xxxvi. 9). It was identified in its higher aspects with "the law of the wise" (Prov. xiii. 14), with "the fear of the Lord" (Prov. xiv. 27). The "fountain of the water of life" was the highest symbol of eternal blessedness (Rev. xxi. 6, xxii. 17). Two aspects of this symbolism are brought before us. (1) There is the spring or fountain that flows out of the rock, as in Isai. xxxv. 7, xlix. 10. When men go to that spring with their pitcher (an "earthen vessel" as in Gen. xxiv. 17) there is an obvious type of the action of the body (we may, perhaps, go so far with the Anatomists as to think specially of the action of the lungs) in drawing in the breath which sustains life. The "cistern" represents primarily the deep well or tank from which men draw water with a windlass and a rope and bucket (1 Sam. xix. 22; Lev. xi. 36; Deut. vi. 11), a well like that of Sychar (John iv. 6). Here obviously we have another parable of the mechanism of life, pointing to an action lying more remote than that of the fountain and the pitcher, and, if we have been right in connecting that with the act of breathing, we may as naturally see in this the action of the heart. Death is accordingly represented under both these figures. There will come a day when the pitcher shall be taken to the fountain for the last time and be broken as in the very act of drawing water, when the wheel that guides the current of the blood "which is the life" shall turn for the last time on its axis. Into the more detailed anatomical explanations which find in the pitcher and the wheel, the liver and the gall-duct, or the right and left ventricle, we refrain, as before, from entering.

7. *Then shall the dust return to the earth as it was*] The reference to the history of man's creation in Gen. ii. 7 is unmistakeable, and finds an echo in the familiar words of our Burial Service, "Earth to earth, ashes to ashes, dust to dust." So Epicharmus, quoted by Plutarch, *Consol. ad Apoll.* p. 110, "Life was compound, and is broken up, and returns thither whence it came, earth to earth and the spirit on high." So the Epicurean poet sang,

the dust return to the earth as it was : and the spirit shall
return unto God who gave it.

> " Pulvis et umbra sumus."

> "Dust and shadows are we all."
>
> <div align="right">HOR. <i>Od.</i> IV. 7. 16—</div>

echoing the like utterance of Anacreon,

> ὀλίγη κόνις κεισόμεθα.

> "We shall lie down, a little dust, no more"—

echoed ín its turn by Shakespeare (*Cymbeline*, IV. 2),

> "Golden lads and lasses must,
>   Like chimney sweepers, turn to dust."

the spirit shall return unto God who gave it] We note, in the
contrast between this and the "Who knoweth...?" of ch. iii. 21, what
it is not too much to call, though the familiar words speak of a higher
triumph than is found here, the Victory of Faith. If the **Debater** had
rested in his scepticism, it would not have been difficult to find parallels
in the language of Greek and Roman writers who had abandoned the
hope of immortality. So Euripides had sung

> Ἐάσατ᾽ ἤδη γῇ καλυφθῆναι νεκρούς,
> Ὅθεν δ᾽ ἕκαστον ἐς τὸ φῶς ἀφίκετο,
> Ἐνταῦθ᾽ ἀπελθεῖν, πνεῦμα μὲν πρὸς αἰθέρα,
> Τὸ σῶμα δ᾽ ἐς γῆν.

> "Let then the dead be buried in the earth,
>   And whence each element first came to light
>   Thither return, the spirit to the air,
>   The body to the earth."
>
> <div align="right">EURIP. <i>Suppl.</i> 529—</div>

or as Lucretius at a later date,

> "Cedit item retro, de terra quod fuit ante,
>   In terras, et quod missum 'st ex ætheris oris,
>   Id rursum cœli rellatum templa receptant."

> " That also which from earth first came, to earth
>   Returns, and that which from the ether's coasts
>   Was sent, the vast wide regions of the sky
>   Receive again, returning to its home."
>
> *De Rer. Nat.* II. 998.

Or again,

> "Ergo dissolvi quoque convenit omnem animaï
>   Naturam, ceu fumus, in altas aëris auras."

> "So must it be that, like the circling smoke,
>   The being of the soul should be dissolved,
>   And mingle with the breezes of the air."
>
> <div align="right">LUCRET. <i>De Rer. Nat.</i> III. 455.</div>

8   Vanity of vanities, saith the Preacher; all *is* vanity.

Or Virgil, with a closer approximation to the teaching of the **Debater**,

> " Deum namque ire per omnes
> Terrasque tractusque maris, cœlumque profundum;
> Hinc pecudes, armenta, viros, genus omne ferarum,
> Quemque sibi tenues nascentem arcessere vitas;
> Scilicet huc reddi deinde, ac resoluta referri
> Omnia; nec morti esse locum; sed viva volare
> Sideris in numerum, atque alto succedere cœlo."

> "[They teach] that God pervades the world,
> The earth and ocean's tracts and loftiest heaven,
> That hence the flocks and herds, and creatures wild,
> Each, at their birth, draw in their fragile life;
> That thither also all things tend at last,
> And broken-up return, that place for death
> Is none, but all things, yet instinct with life,
> Soar to the stars and take their place on high."
>
> VIRG. Georg. IV. 220—227.

We cannot ignore the fact that to many interpreters (including Warburton) the words before us have seemed to convey no higher meaning than the extracts just quoted. They see in that return to God, nothing more than the absorption of the human spirit into the *Anima Mundi*, the great World-Soul, which the Pantheist identified with God. It is believed, however, that the thoughts in which the **Debater** at last found anchorage were other than these. The contrast between the sceptical "Who knoweth the spirit of man that it goeth upward?" (ch. iii. 21) and this return to God, "who gave it," shews that the latter meant more than the former. The faith of the Israelite, embodied in the *Shemà* or Creed which the writer must have learnt in childhood, was not extinguished. The "fear of God" is with him a real feeling of awe before One who lives and wills (ch. viii. 8, 12). The hand of God is a might that orders all things (ch. ix. 1). It is God that judges the righteous and the wicked (ch. iii.' 17). Rightly, from this point of view, has the Targum paraphrased the words "The Spirit will return to stand in judgment before god who gave it thee." The long wandering to and fro in many paths of thoughts ends not in the denial, but the affirmation, of a personal God and therefore a personal immortality.

8.   *Vanity of vanities, saith the preacher; all is vanity*] The recurrence at the close of the book, and after words which, taken as we have taken them, suggest a nobler view of life, of the same sad burden with which it opened, has a strange melancholy ring in it. To those who see in the preceding verse nothing more than the materialist's thoughts of death as echoed by Epicurean poets, it seems a confirmation of what they have read into it, or inferred from it. The **Debater** seems to them, looking on life from the closing scene of death, to fall back into a

And moreover, because the Preacher was wise, he still ₉

hopeless pessimism. It may be rightly answered however that the view
that all that belongs to the earthly life is "vanity of vanities" is one not
only compatible with the recognition of the higher life, with all its
infinite possibilities, which opens before man at death, but is the natural
outcome of that recognition as at the hour of death, or during the
process of decay which precedes and anticipates death. The "things
that are seen and are temporal" are dwarfed, as into an infinite
littleness, in the presence of those which are "not seen and are eternal"
(2 Cor. iv. 18). And there would be, we may add, even a singular im-
pressiveness in the utterance of the same judgment, at the close of the
great argument, and from the higher standpoint of faith which the
Debater had at last reached, as that with which he had started in his
despondent scepticism. It is, in this light, not without significance that
these very words form the opening sentence of the *De Imitatione Christi*
of à Kempis.

There remain, however, two previous questions to be discussed. (1)
Are the words before us the conclusion of the main body of the treatise,
or the beginning of what we may call its epilogue? and (2) is that
epilogue the work of the author of the book or an addition by some later
hand? The paragraph printing of the Authorised Version points in
the case of (1) to the latter of the two conclusions, and it may be noted
as confirming this view that the words occur in their full form at the
beginning of the whole book, and might therefore reasonably be expected
at the beginning of that which is, as it were, its summing-up and completion. In regard to the second question, the contents of the epilogue
tend, it is believed, to the conclusion that they occupy a position analogous to that of the close of St John's Gospel (John xxi. 24) and are,
as it were, of the nature of a commendatory attestation. It would
scarcely be natural for a writer to end with words of self-praise like
those of verses 9, 10. The directly didactic form of the Teacher ad-
dressing his reader as "my Son" after the fashion of the Book of
Proverbs (i. 8, ii. 1, iii. 1, 11, 21) has no parallel in the rest of the book.
The tone of verse 11 is rather that of one who takes a survey of the
book as one of the many forms of wisdom, each of which had its place
in the education of mankind, than of the thinker who speaks of what
he himself has contributed to that store. On the whole, then, there
seems sufficient reason for resting in the conclusion adopted by many
commentators that the book itself ended with verse 7, and that we have
in what follows, an epilogue addressed to the reader; justifying its admission into the Canon of Scripture and pointing out to him what, in the
midst of apparent perplexities and inconsistencies, was the true moral of
its preaching. The circumstances which were connected with that
admission (see *Introduction*, chs. II., III., IV.) may well have made such
a justification appear desirable.

9. *And moreover, because the Preacher was wise*] The opening words,
closely linked on, as they are, to the preceding, confirm the conclusion
just stated that verse 8 belongs to this postscript of attestation. The

taught the people knowledge ; yea, he gave good heed, and
10 sought out, *and* set in order many proverbs.   The Preacher
sought to find out acceptable words : and *that which was*

unknown writer of the attestation (probably the President of the Sanhedrin, or some other Master of the Wise, such as were Hillel and Gamaliel) begins by repeating the key-note of the opening of the book.   So
taken, the words are every way significant.   They do not name Solomon
as the author, but content themselves with recognising the enigmatic
name with which the unknown writer had veiled himself.   He, they
say, belonged to the company of the sages.   He "gave good heed"
(literally, **he hearkened** or **gave ear**), he "sought out" (we note
how exactly the word describes the tentative, investigating character of
the book, as in Judg. xviii. 2 ; 2 Sam. x. 3 ; Prov. xxviii. 11 ; Job v. 27,
xxviii. 27), he "set in order" (*i.e.* **composed**) "many proverbs."   The
word for "proverbs" is that which stands as the title of the Book of
Proverbs, but it expresses, more than the English term does, the para-
bolic, half-enigmatic character which is characteristic of most sayings of
this nature in the East, and as such is translated by "parables" in the
LXX. here, and in the A.V. in Ezek. xx. 49 ; Ps. xlix. 4 ; Num. xxiii.
7, 18, 24 and elsewhere.   The words have been pressed by some interpreters as a testimony to the Salomonic authorship, but it is obvious
that though they fit in with that hypothesis, they are equally applicable
to any one who followed in the same track and adopted the same method
of teaching.

   10.   *The Preacher sought to find out acceptable words*]   Literally,
words of delight, or **pleasure**, as in chs. v. 4, xii. 1.   The phrase reminds us of "the words of grace" (Luke iv. 22) which came from the
lips of Him, who, as the Incarnate Wisdom of God, was, in very
deed, greater than Solomon.   The fact is stated as by way of *apologia*
for the character of the book.   The object of the teacher was to
attract men by meeting, or seeming to meet, their inclinations, by
falling in with the results of their own experience.   We are reminded
so far of the words of Lucretius :

> "Nam veluti pueris absinthia tetra medentes,
>   Cum dare conantur, prius oras pocula circum
>   Contingunt mellis dulci, flavoque liquore,
>   Ut puerorum ætas improvida ludificetur
>   Labrorum tenus, interea perpotet amarum
>   Absinthî laticem, deceptaque non capiatur,
>   Sed potius tali pacto recreata valescat."

> "As those who heal the body, when they seek
>   To give to children wormwood's nauseous juice,
>   First smear the cup's rim with sweet golden honey,
>   That infant's thoughtless age may be beguiled
>   Just to the margin's edge, and so may drink
>   The wormwood's bitter draught, beguiled, not tricked,
>   But rather gain thereby in strength and health."

De Rer. Nat. IV. 11—17.

written *was* upright, *even* words of truth.   The words of the 11
wise *are* as goads, and as nails fastened *by* the masters of
assemblies, *which* are given from one shepherd.   And 12

and that which was written was upright]   The italics shew that
the sentence is somewhat elliptical, and it is better to take the two
sets of phrases in apposition with the "acceptable words" that precede
them, **even a writing of uprightness** (*i.e.* of subjective sincerity),
words of truth (in its objective sense).   The words are, thus understood, a full testimony to the character of the book thus commended
to the reader's attention.

11.   *The words of the wise are as goads*]   The general fact is, of
course, stated in special connexion with the book which furnishes the
writer's theme.   They assert that its words also, sweet as they seem,
are not without their sting, though, like the prick of the goad, it is
for good and not for evil, urging men on to strong and vigorous labour
in the fields of thought and action.   The comparison was a natural
one in any country, but we are reminded of what was said of the
words of Pericles that his eloquence "left a sting (κέντρον) in the
minds of his hearers (Eupolis, quoted by Liddell and Scott, *s.v.*
κέντρον), and in part also of the Greek proverb, consecrated for us
by a yet higher application (Acts ix. 5, xxvi. 14) that "it is hard to
kick against the pricks," as applicable to resisting wisdom as well
as to defying power (Æsch. *Agam.* 1633, Pindar, *Pyth.* II. 173).

as nails fastened by the masters of assemblies]   The word for "nails"
is found in this, or a cognate form, with that meaning in Isai. xli. 7;
Jer. x. 4; 1 Chron. xxii. 3; 2 Chron. iii. 9; and there is no adequate
reason for taking it here, as some have done (Ginsburg), in the sense
of the "stakes" of a tent.   The word "by" however is an interpolation, and the words taken as they stand would run **as nails fastened
are the masters of assemblies.**   The whole analogy of the Hebrew
is against our referring the last words to any but persons, and we
must therefore reject the interpretation that the "words of the wise
are as goads, as fastened nails which are put together in collections"
(Delitzsch).   The "masters of assemblies " (not, as it has been rendered
(Tyler) "editors of collections",) can be none else than the heads or
leaders of a body of learned men, like the Great Synagogue of the traditions of the time of Ezra and Nehemiah, or the Sanhedrin of a later date.
In "the fastened nail" we have a symbolism like that of Isai. xxii. 23;
Ezra ix. 8, and seen also in the Rabbinic proverb, "Well for the
man who has a nail to hang things on " (Dukes, *Rabbin. Blumenlese,*
p. 121).   In both these cases, it will be noted, the word refers
to persons.   It is the fitting emblem of fixity and permanence, and
forms the natural complement to that of the goads.   As it has been
well put (Ginsburg), the two words express the several aspects of Truth
as progressive and conservative.

which are given from one shepherd]   The noun is used often in the
O. T. both in its literal sense, and of kings and rulers as the shepherds

further, by these, my son, be admonished : of making many
books *there is* no end ; and much study *is* a weariness of
the flesh.

of their people (Jerem. ii. 8, iii. 15, xlix. 19, l. 44; Ezek. xxxiv.
passim), and of God as the great Shepherd of Israel (Ps. xxiii. 1,
lxxx. 1, and by implication, Ezek. xxxiv. 23). We have to choose
accordingly between the two latter meanings. The words either assert
that all the varied forms of the wisdom of the wise come from God,
or that all the opinions, however diversified, which are uttered by
"the masters of assemblies," are subject to the authority of the
President of the assembly. The first gives, it is believed, the most
satisfactory meaning, and so taken, the words express the truth declared, without symbolism, in 1 Cor. xii. 1—11. It was not, perhaps,
without some reference to this thought, though scarcely to this passage,
that our Lord claimed for Himself as the one true Guide and Teacher
of mankind the title of the "Good Shepherd," and condemned all
that had come before Him, assuming that character, as thieves and
robbers (John x. 8, 11), and that St Peter speaks of Him as the "chief
Shepherd" (1 Pet. v. 4) over all who exercise a pastoral office in the
Church of Christ.

12. *And further, by these, my son, be admonished*] Better, **And
for more than these** (*i.e.* for all that lies beyond), **be warned**. The ad-
dress "my son" is, as in Prov. i. 1, ii. 1, x. 15, that of the ideal teacher
to his disciple. It is significant, as noted above, that this appears here
for the first time in this book.

of making many books there is no end] The words, which would have
been singularly inappropriate as applied to the scanty literature of
the reign of the historical Solomon, manifestly point to a time when the
teachers of Israel had come in contact with the literature of other
countries, which overwhelmed them with its variety and copiousness, and
the scholar is warned against trusting to that literature as a guide to
wisdom. Of that copiousness, the Library at Alexandria with its countless
volumes would be the great example, and the inscription over the portals
of that at Thebes that it was the Hospital of the Soul (ἰατρεῖον ψυχῆς,
Diodor. Sic. I. 49) invited men to study them as the remedy for their
spiritual diseases. Conspicuous among these, as the most voluminous
of all, were the writings of Demetrius Phalereus (Diog. Laert. v. 5. 9),
and those of Epicurus, numbering three hundred volumes (Diog.
Laert. x. 1. 17), and of his disciple Apollodorus, numbering four
hundred (Diog. Laert. x. 1. 15), and these and other like writings,
likely to unsettle the faith of a young Israelite, were probably in the
Teacher's thought. The teaching of the Jewish Rabbis at the time
when Koheleth was written was chiefly oral, embodying itself in
maxims and traditions, and the scantiness of its records must have
presented a striking contrast to the abounding fulness of that of the
philosophy of Greece. It was not till a much later period that these
traditions of the elders were collected into the Mishna and the Gemara
that make up the Talmud. Scholars sat at the feet of their teacher,

Let us hear the conclusion of the whole matter: Fear 13
God, and keep his commandments: for this *is* the whole
duty of man.   For God shall bring every work into judg- 14

and drank in his words, and handed them on to their successors. The
words of the wise thus orally handed down are contrasted with the
"many books."

much study is a weariness of the flesh] The noun for "study" is
not found elsewhere in the O. T., but there is no doubt as to its
meaning. What men gain by the study of many books is, the writer
seems to say, nothing but a headache, no guidance for conduct, no
solution of the problems of the universe. They get, to use the phrase
which Pliny (*Epp.* VII. 9) has made proverbial, "*multa, non multum.*"
We are reminded of the saying of a higher Teacher that "one thing
is needful" (Luke x. 42). The words of Marcus Aurelius, the representative of Stoicism, when he bids men to "free themselves from
the thirst for books" (*Medit.* II. 3), present a striking parallel. So
again, "Art thou so unlettered that thou canst not read, yet canst
thou abstain from wantonness, and be master of pain and pleasure
(*Meditt.* VII. 8).

13. *Let us hear the conclusion of the whole matter*] The word for
"let us hear" has been taken by some scholars as a participle with a
gerundial force, " *The* **sum** *of the* whole matter must be heard,"
but it admits of being taken as in the English version, and this gives
a more satisfying meaning. The rendering "everything is heard,"
i.e. by God, has little to recommend it, and by anticipating the
teaching of the next verse introduces an improbable tautology. The
words admit of the rendering **the sum of the whole discourse**, which
is, perhaps, preferable.

Fear God, and keep his commandments] This is what the Teacher
who, as it were, edits the book, presents to his disciples as its sum
and substance, and he was not wrong in doing so. In this the **Debater**
himself had rested after his many wanderings of thought (ch. v. 7,
and, by implication, xi. 9). Whatever else might be "vanity and
feeding on wind," there was safety and peace in keeping the commandments of the Eternal, the laws "which are not of to-day or yesterday."

for this is the whole duty of man] The word "duty" is not in the
Hebrew, and we might supply "the whole **end**," or "the whole
work," or with another and better construction, **This is for every man**:
i.e. a law of universal obligation. What is meant is that this is the only
true answer to that quest of the chief good in which the thinker had
been engaged. This was, in Greek phrase, the ἔργον or "work" of
man, that to which he was called by the very fact of his existence.
All else was but a πάρεργον, or accessory.

14. *For God shall bring every work into judgment*] Once again
the Teacher brings into prominence what was indeed the outcome of
the book; though, as history shews, the careless reader, still more the
reader blinded by his passions, or prejudice, or frivolity, might easily

ment, with every secret *thing*, whether *it be* good, or whether *it be* evil.

overlook it. The object of the writer had not been to preach a self-indulgence of the lowest Epicurean type, or to deny the soul's immortality, though for a time he had hesitated to affirm it, but much rather to enforce the truth, which involved that belief, of a righteous judgment (ch. xi. 9), seen but imperfectly in this life, with its anomalous distribution of punishments and rewards, but certain to assert itself, if not before, when "the spirit shall return to God who gave it" (verse 7). From the standpoint of the writer of the epilogue it was shewn that the teaching of Ecclesiastes was not inconsistent with the faith of Israel, that it had a right to take its place among the Sacred Books of Israel. From our standpoint we may say that it was shewn not less convincingly that the book, like all true records of the search after Truth, led men through the labyrinthine windings of doubt to the goal of duty, through the waves and winds of conflicting opinions to the unshaken rock of the Eternal Commandment.

APPENDIX.

I.

I HAVE already in the "Ideal Biography" of the Author of Ecclesiastes (ch. III.), suggested a parallelism between the thoughts which have found expression in the writings of Shakespeare and Tennyson, and those that meet us in the Book with which this Volume deals. That parallelism is, I believe, deserving of more than a passing sentence, and I accordingly purpose to treat of it, as far as my limits permit, in the two following Essays.

I. SHAKESPEARE AND KOHELETH.

It lies almost in the nature of the case that the standpoint of a supreme dramatic artist involves the contemplation of the chances and changes of human life, of the shifting moods of human character, in something like the temper of a half-melancholy, half-genial irony. Poets, who, like Æschylus or Calderon, write in earnest to enforce what they look upon as a high and solemn truth, and to present to men the consequences of obeying or resisting it, who seek to present the working of a higher order, and characters of a loftier nobleness, than the world actually presents, have, in the nature of the case, little of that element. Those who write, as Sophocles did, impressed with the strange contrasts which human life presents in its ideal and its reality, its plans and their frustration, its aims and its results, who cannot bring themselves to think that it is the duty of the artist to present a false, even though it be a fairer, picture than what the world actually exhibits, manifest the irony of which we speak, as Bishop Thirlwall has shewn in his masterly Essay[1], in its graver forms, restrained, in part, it may be, by the dignity of their own character, in part by the conditions under which they work as artists, from dealing with its applications to the lighter follies of mankind. One who, like Shakespeare, worked with greater freedom, and, it may be, out of the resources of a wider experience, was free to present that irony in both its applications. That sense of the nothingness of life, which manifests itself in the melancholy refrain of "Vanity of vanities" in Koheleth, would be sure to shew itself in such a poet, in proportion, perhaps, as he had ceased to strive after a high·ideal, and learnt to look with an Epicurean tran-

[1] Cp. Thirlwall, "The Irony of Sophocles," *Philological Museum*, II. 483. *Remains*, III. I.

quillity on the passions of those who, though puppets in his mimic drama, had yet found their archetypes in the characters of the men and women with whom he had lived, and whose weaknesses he had noted. If the story of his own life had been that of one who had sought to find satisfaction in the impulses of sense, or in affections fixed on an unworthy object, we might expect to find the tendency to dwell on the various forms of the ironical, or the pessimist view of life, which is the natural outcome of the disappointment to which all such attempts are doomed. And this, it is believed, is what we find in Shakespeare, as the result of his personal experience, reproduced now in this aspect, now in that, according as each fitted in best with his purpose as an artist.

I have already shewn in the "Ideal Biography" of ch. III. that the Sonnets of Shakespeare present a striking parallelism to the personal experience that lay at the root of the pessimist tone of thought which the confessions of Koheleth present to us. There had been the element of a friendship which he thought to be ennobling, of a love which he felt to be debasing. But we may go further than this, and say that they manifest also, and not in that passage only, the tone and temper to which that experience naturally leads. Without discussing the many problems which those mysterious poems bring before us, this at least is clear, that they speak of a life which had not been free from the taint of sensuality, of a friendship which, beginning in an almost idolatrous admiration, ended in a terrible disappointment, and that the echoes of that disappointment are heard again and again in their plaintive and marvellous sweetness. The resemblance between their utterances and those of Ecclesiastes is all the more striking, because there is not a single trace that Shakespeare had studied the book that bears that title. He does not use its peculiar watchwords, or quote its maxims. Despite of all that has been written of Shakespeare's knowledge of the Bible by Archbishop Trench, Bishop Charles Wordsworth, and others, it does not seem to have been more than a man might gain, without study, by hearing lessons and sermons when he went to Church on Sundays, and as Ecclesiastes was not prominent in the calendar of Sunday lessons, and not a favourite book with the preachers of the sixteenth century, he probably knew but little of it. We have to deal, accordingly, with the phenomena of parallelism and not of derivation. But the parallelism is, it will be admitted, sufficiently suggestive. Does Koheleth teach that "there is nothing new under the sun," that "if there is anything whereof it may be said, See this is new; it hath been already of old time, which was before us" (Eccl. i. 10), Shakespeare writes

"No, Time, thou shalt not boast that I do change.
Thy pyramids built up with newer might,
They are but dressings of a former sight.
Our dates are brief, and, therefore we admire
What thou dost foist upon us that is old:
And rather make them born to our desire,
Than think that we before have heard them told.

Thy registers and thee I both defy,
Not wondering at the present and the past."

Sonn. 123.

Does Koheleth utter his belief that "the day of death is better than the day of one's birth" (Eccl. vii. 1), "that an untimely birth is better than the longest life" (Eccl. vi. 3), as growing out of the anomalies of a world in which "the race is not to the swift, nor the battle to the strong, neither yet bread to the wise...but time and chance happeneth alike to all" (Eccl. ix. 11); Shakespeare echoes the cry of that weariness of life:

"Tired with all these, for restful death I cry,
As, to behold desert a beggar born,
And needy nothing trimmed in jollity,
And purest faith unhappily foresworn,
And gilded honour shamefully misplaced,
And maiden virtue rudely strumpeted,
And right perfection wrongfully disgraced,
And strength by limping sway disabled,
And art made tongue-tied by authority,
And folly, doctor-like, controlling skill,
And simple truth miscalled simplicity:
Tired with all these, from these I would be gone,
Save that to die, I leave my love alone."

Sonn. 66.

The tendency which thus utters itself as in a personal subjective monologue took naturally another form, when, rising out of the feverish unrest which the Sonnets indicate, the writer passed into the true work of the poet-creator, contemplating man's nature as from without, and embodying the results of his boundless observation in the characters of his dramas, as if he had lived in each of them, identified at once with Coriolanus and with Falstaff, with Macbeth and with Malvolio. But the tendency, in such a case, remains. The man's experience determines the greater or less frequency of his choice of characters in which he can embody it. And what I seek to shew is that such a choice is traceable in the dramas of Shakespeare, and that no type of character appears so frequently, or is so conspicuously the reflection of what the poet himself had once been, as that of the contemplative half-sad, half-cynical temper which we find in Ecclesiastes. He has risen on the "stepping-stones of his dead self" to higher things, but he surveys that dead self with a certain loving complacency, and is not unwilling that for a time it should live again. He will shew that he understands the inner depths of the character that seems to many so inexplicable, and not seldom wins from them the reverence which of right is due only to that which is far worthier. Take, for example, the two types of character represented by the Duke and by Jaques, in "As You Like It." The former speaks in the nobler tones of Koheleth, the latter in the baser. The one has learnt that "sorrow is better than laughter," that "the heart of the wise is in the house of mourning" (Eccl. vii. 3).

> "Sweet are the uses of adversity,
> Which, like the toad, ugly and venomous,
> Wears yet a precious jewel in his head.
> And this our life, exempt from public haunt,
> Finds tongues in trees, books in the running brooks,
> Sermons in stones, and good in everything."
>
> *As You Like It*, II. 1.

Jaques, on the other hand, is emphatically "melancholy," but the temper is one which finds not "good" but evil in everything. For him, the sons of men are "as fishes taken in an evil net" (Eccl. ix. 12). His meditations on the sufferings of the wounded stag reveal but little of real humanity, but "he moralizes" the spectacle into "a thousand similes." All forms of life present to him the same picture of injustice and of wrong.

> "Thus most invectively he passeth through
> The body of the country, city, court,
> Yea, and of this our life."
>
> *As You Like It*, II. 1.

As the sight of brute suffering, so that of men, stirs him to no healthy sympathy. The Duke speaking as before, in the loftier moods of Koheleth, learns the lesson that

> "This wide and universal theatre
> Presents more woeful pageants than the scene
> Wherein we play in,"

but this is preceded by his kindly ministrations to the old and weary Adam, the very type of the "labouring man whose sleep is sweet to him" of Eccl. v. 12. Jaques joins in no such ministrations, but in the memorable speech of the Seven Ages, moralizes once more on the hollowness of human life, and paints, almost in the very colours of Eccles. xii. 3, 4, the decay and death in which it ends.

> "The sixth age glides
> Into the lean and slippered pantaloon,
> With spectacles on nose, and pouch on side,
> His youthful hose, well saved, a world too wide
> For his shrunk shank; and his big manly voice
> Turning again towards childish treble, pipes
> And whistles in his sound. Last scene of all,
> That ends this strange eventful history,
> Is second childishness, and mere oblivion,
> *Sans* teeth, *sans* eyes, *sans* taste, *sans* everything."
>
> *As You Like It*, II. 7.

And the secret of this evil cynicism is found in the previous life of this preacher of endless homilies on the "vanity of vanities." Of such homilies, the Duke tells him, no good can come. He will work

> "Most mischievous foul sin in chiding sin.
> For thou thyself hast been a libertine,

> As sensual as the brutish sting itself,
> And all the embossèd sores and headed evils,
> That thou with licence of free foot hast caught,
> Wouldst thou discharge into the general world."
>
> *As You Like It*, II. 7.

In "Timon of Athens" we have a variation on the same theme. He has sought happiness, as Koheleth did, in the life of wealth, magnificence, and culture. Poets and painters have ministered to his tastes and caprices. But among the thousand friends of his prosperity he finds but one faithful in adversity, and he loathes the very sight of the gold, with the absence or presence of which the friendship of the world wanes or waxes. He has used his wealth "unwisely, not ignobly," thinking that thus he will gather round him true and loving hearts, and finds that this also, as his wiser counsellor foretold, is "vanity of vanities."

> "Ah! when the means are gone that buy this praise,
> The breath is gone whereof this praise is made,
> Fast won, fast lost; one cloud of winter showers,
> These flies are couched."
>
> *Timon of Athens*, II. 2.

And so when he finds that the prediction is fulfilled, his love turns to gall and bitterness. The philanthropist becomes the misanthrope. As with Koheleth, men were hateful to him, and much more, women (Eccl. vii. 26—28).

> "Let no assembly of twenty be without a score of villains; if there sit twelve women at the table, let a dozen of them be as they are."
>
> *Timon of Athens*, III. 6.

Henceforward there is nothing for him but the moody curse of a solitary bitterness, and his faithful friends moralize on the transformation.

> "O, the fierce wretchedness that glory brings us!
> Who would not wish to be from wealth exempt,
> Since riches point to misery and contempt,
> Who would be so mocked with glory? or to live
> But in a dream of friendship?
> To have his pomp and all what state compounds,
> But only painted, like his varnished friends?
> Poor honest lord, brought low by his own heart,
> Undone by goodness."
>
> *Timon of Athens*, IV. 2.

Timon himself, however, cannot so moralize. The element of selfishness that had mingled with his seemingly limitless benevolence, seeking its reward in the praise and gratitude of men, turns to malignant scorn. He rails, as Shakespeare in his own person had railed, as in the Sonnet already quoted, at the disorders of society, in terms which again remind us of Ecclesiastes.

"Twinned brothers of one womb,
Whose procreation, residence, and birth,
Scarce is dividant: touch them with several fortunes,
The greater scorns the lesser: not nature,
To whom all sores lay siege, can bear great fortune
But by contempt of nature.
The senator shall bear contempt hereditary;
The beggar native honour.
It is the pasture lards the rother's[1] sides,
The want that makes him lean. Who dares, who dares,
In purity of manhood stand upright
And say, ' *This man's a flatterer?*' If one be,
So are they all; for every grise[2] of fortune
Is smoothed by that below: the learned pate
Ducks to the golden fool: all is oblique,
There's nothing level in our cursed nature
But direct villainy. Therefore be abhorred
All feasts, societies, and throngs of men!
His semblable, yea, himself, Timon disdains."

Timon of Athens, IV. 3.

Is not this almost as the very echo of the words which tell us how beggars had been seen riding on horseback, how the "poor man who had saved the city" was "no more remembered," how "time and chance happen alike to all" (Eccl. ix. 11—15), "how scarcely among a thousand men was one found faithful" (Eccl. vii. 28)? The one fact that kept him from utter despair was that he had such a friend.

"I do proclaim
One honest man—mistake me not—but one."

Timon of Athens, IV. 3.

In the account which Timon gives himself of this terrible transformation we trace the confession of an experience like that which Koheleth narrates in Eccles. ii. Apemantus, the cynic, who has not passed through that experience, whose moroseness is that of the man soured by the world's oppression and his own poverty rather than of one satiated with self-indulgence, taunts him with this extreme sensitiveness. He has a pessimism of his own, but it is that of apathy and scorn, and not of hatred.

"This in thee is a nature but infected,
A poor unmanly melancholy sprung
From change of fortune."

Timon allows that it is so, and makes that his *Apologia*. Apemantus does but

"Compound for sins he is inclined to,
By damning those he has no mind to."

---

[1] Apparently a Warwickshire name for ox.
[2] Grise=the "step" of fortune's ladder.

"Thou art a slave, whom Fortune's tender arm
With favour never clasp'd; but bred a dog.
Hadst thou, like us from our first swath, proceeded
The sweet degrees that this brief world affords
To such as may the passive drugs of it
Freely command, thou would'st have plunged thyself
In general riot; melted down thy youth
In different beds of lust, and never learned
The icy precepts of respect, but followed
The sugared game before thee. But myself,
Who had the world as my confectionary,
The mouths, the tongues, the eyes, the hearts of men,
At duty, more than I could frame employment;
That numberless upon me stuck as leaves
Do on the oak, have with one winter's brush
Fell from their boughs, and left me open, bare
For every storm that blows,—I, to bear this,
That never knew but better, is some burden;
Thy nature did commence in sufferance: time
Hath made thee hard in't."

Timon of Athens, IV. 3.

To one in such a mood, Nature did but minister, as it did to Koheleth, food for his absorbing passion. The ebb and flow of the ocean was the type of the changeable monotony of misery.

"Timon hath made his everlasting mansion[1]
Upon the beached verge of the salt flood;
Which once a day with his embossed froth
The turbulent surge shall cover; thither come,
And let my grave-stone be your oracle.
Lips, let sour words go by and language end,
What is amiss, plague and infection mend!
Graves only be men's works: and death their gain!
Sun, hide thy beams—Timon hath done his reign."

Timon of Athens, V. I.

And so, the end came, as it has to a thousand others plunged in the same wretchedness, with no outward sign of hope. Like Keats he wishes his name to be "writ in water." Like Koheleth he seeks to hide it from the memories of men. He writes his own epitaph, and it is this:

"Here lies a wretched corse, of wretched soul bereft;
Seek not my name: a plague consume you wretched caitiffs left!"

It was, perhaps, with a subtle touch of irony that Shakespeare, working, as experts think, on the rough materials supplied by an inferior writer, made the last couplet of the epitaph inconsistent with the first. In spite of his hatred of mankind the pessimist could not bear to

---

[1] We are reminded of the "long home," the "*domus æterna*" of Eccles. xii. 5.

be forgotten.   The one real mortification in Schopenhauer's life was
that men did not read his books.   The desire to be remembered is the
ineradicable ruling passion which yet remains in him whose fault was
that he had lived too entirely in the praise of men :

> "Here lie I, Timon; who, alive, all living men did hate,
> Pass by and curse thy fill; but pass, and stay not here thy gait."
>
> *Timon of Athens*, v. 4.

The life closed apparently in darkness, but the pity and sympathy of
the poet for a mood through which he had himself passed, and out of which
he had emerged, cannot leave it altogether without hope.   He can recognise and reverence the nobleness of spirit, which soured and thwarted,
was latent under this seeming blasphemy against humanity.   And so
he puts into the mouth of Alcibiades the judgement which we should
pass on such moods of perverted nature wherever they may meet us.

> "These well express in thee thy latter spirits:
> Though thou abhorr'dst in us our human griefs,
> Scorn'dst our brain-flow, and those our droplets which
> From niggard nature fall, yet rich conceit
> Taught thee to make vast Neptune weep for aye
> On thy low grave, on faults forgiven.   Dead
> Is noble Timon, of whose memory
> Hereafter more."
>
> *Timon of Athens*, v. 4.

The words are almost in the very note of David's lament over Saul
the outcast and the suicide, "The beauty of Israel is slain in thy high
places" (2 Sam. i. 19), of the *sie ist gerettet* ("she is saved") which the
angels utter over the Margaret of "Faust," of the lines in Hood's
"Bridge of Sighs" which describe the drowned outcast in the
Thames :

> "All that remains of her
> Now is pure womanly."

And so the preacher of hatred becomes in his death the benefactor
of his country which he had loved passionately, with a love that turned
to scorn, and Alcibiades "purified" by the "pity and terror" of
which Aristotle spoke (*Poet.* c. xiii.) as of the very essence of the work
of the tragic dramatist, offers peace to the Athenians on whom he had
come to wreak his vengeance.

I have dwelt at some length on Shakespeare's treatment of this
character, partly because, if I mistake not, the parallelism with some
aspects of Koheleth is a very striking one, partly because there are few
of his plays less generally read than that which supplies the parallelism.
I turn from this, the picture of one who has fallen in his conflict with
the pessimism that grows out of satiety and disappointment, and the
sense that "all is vanity," to that of one who, passing through a like
knowledge of good and evil gained by a like experience, has fought
and has prevailed.   Henry V. is obviously Shakespeare's pattern king,
such a monarch as he could picture himself to be, had an inherited

crown rested on his head. When he first appears on the scene he seems rapidly on the road to ruin, the grief of his father's heart, the companion of roysterers and debauchees. But the poet is careful to let us see that he has strength enough to pass through the ordeal. He is but "seeking in his heart," as Koheleth had done, "to give himself unto wine,...laying hold on folly...yet guiding his heart with wisdom" (Eccl. ii. 3), and he is confident that he shall not fail in the perilous experiment:

> "I know you all, and will awhile uphold
> The unyok'd humour of your idleness,
> Yet herein will I imitate the sun,
> Who doth permit the base, contagious clouds
> To smother up his beauty from the world;
> That when he please again to be himself,
> Being wanted, he may more be wondered at;
> By breaking through the foul and ugly mists
> Of vapours that did seem to strangle him."
>
> 1 *Henry IV.* I. 2.

The first step towards higher things is found in the call of duty. He is taught to see the evils of a country in which "the king is a child and the princes feast in the morning" (Eccl. x. 17). Such, as he himself then was, Richard II. had been.

> "The skipping king, he ambled up and down
> With shallow jesters and rash bavin[1] wits
> Soon kindled and soon burned: carded his state,
> Mingled his royalty with carping fools;
> Had his great name profaned with their scorns."
>
> 1 *Henry IV.* III. 2.

He is roused to the consciousness of the nobler possibilities of life by that mirror in which he sees his own likeness. As, to use a phrase of Kinglake's that floats in my memory, the "curled darlings of the Guards" were transformed into the "heroes of the Crimea," so here the boon companion of Pistol, Poins and Falstaff becomes the conqueror, first of Shrewsbury and then of Agincourt. In the care and trouble that haunt the sick-bed of his father "eating in darkness and having much sorrow and wrath in his sickness" (Eccl. v. 17) he learns how far more sweet is the sleep of the labouring man than that of "the rich man whose abundance will not suffer him to sleep" (Eccl. v. 12).

> "How many thousand of my poorest subjects
> Are at this hour asleep! O sleep, O gentle sleep,
> Nature's soft nurse, how have I frighted thee,
> That thou wilt no more weigh my eyelids down
> And steep my senses in forgetfulness?
> Why rather, Sleep, liest thou in smoky cribs,
> Upon uneasy pallets stretching thee,

[1] Bavin = brushwood.

And hushed with buzzing night-flies to thy slumber,
Than in the perfumed chambers of the great,
Under the panopies of costly state,
And lulled with sounds of sweetest melody?
O thou dull god! why liest thou with the vile
In loathsome beds, and leav'st the kingly couch
A watch-case or a common 'larum bell?
Wilt thou upon the high and giddy mast
Seal up the sea-boy's eyes, and rock his brains
In cradle of the rude tempestuous surge,
And in the visitation of the winds?
    *   *   *   *

Can'st thou, O partial sleep! give thy repose
To the wet sea-boy in an hour so rude,
And in the calmest and most stillest night
Deny it to a king? Then happy low, lie down!
Uneasy lies the head that wears a crown."

2 Henry IV. III. 1.

That father sees or thinks he sees the frustration of all his schemes
of ambition and mourns over them almost in the very terms of Koheleth, "There is a sore evil which I have seen under the sun, riches kept
for the owners thereof to their hurt...They perish by evil travail and he
begetteth a son and there is nothing in his hand...What profit hath he
that hath laboured for the wind?" (Eccles. v. 13—16).

"See, sons, what things you are!
How quickly nature falls into revolt
When gold becomes its object!
For this the foolish, over-anxious fathers
Have broke their sleep with thoughts, their brains with care,
Their bones with industry:
For this they have engrossed and piled up
The cankered heaps of strange-achieved gold;
For this they have been thoughtful to invest
Their sons with arts and martial exercises;
Where, like the bee, tolling from every flower
The virtuous sweets,
Our thighs packed with wax, our mouths with honey,
We bring it to the hive, and, like the bees,
Are murdered for our pains. This bitter taste
Yield his engrossments to the ending father."

2 Henry IV. IV. 5.

The lesson of that death-bed is not lost upon the nobler elements in
the nature of the son, and the change is perfected.

"The courses of his youth promised it not:
The breath no sooner left his father's body,
But that his wildness, mortified in him,
Seemed to die too: yea, at that very moment,

Consideration, like an angel, came
And whipped the offending Adam out of him,
Leaving his body as a paradise,
To envelope and contain celestial spirits."

Henry V. I. I.

He too has learnt the lesson of "vanity of vanities," but it leads him not to idle moralisings, like those of Jaques or the malignant misanthropy of Timon, but to "fear God and keep his commandments," to heroic deeds and high purpose, to a largeness of heart like that of the ideal Solomon. He hears his soldiers throw the burden of their suffering and death upon the king and feels that, if the majesty of the king rests only upon pomp and state, they are more than half-right:

"Upon the king! let us our lives, our souls,
Our debts, our careful wives, our children, and
Our sins lay on the king.
We must bear all.
O hard condition! twin-born with greatness,
Subject to the breath of every fool, whose sense
No more can feel, but his own wringing,
What infinite heart's ease must kings neglect
That private men enjoy?
And what have kings that privates have not too,
Save ceremony, save general ceremony?
And what art thou, thou idle ceremony?
What kind of God art thou, that suffer'st more
Of mortal griefs than do thy worshippers?
What are thy rents? what are thy comings in?
O ceremony, shew me but thy worth,
What is thy soul of adoration?
Art thou aught else but place, degree and form,
Creating awe and fear in other men?
Wherein thou art less happy, being feared,
Than they in fearing.
What drinkest thou oft, instead of homage sweet
But poisoned flattery? O, be sick, great greatness,
And bid thy ceremony give thee cure!
Think'st thou the fiery fever will go out,
With titles blown from adulation?
Will it give place to flexure and low bending?
Can'st thou, when thou command'st the beggar's knee
Command the health of it? No, thou proud dream,
That played so subtly with a king's repose,
I am a king that find thee, and I know
'Tis not the balm, the sceptre, and the ball,
The sword, the mace, the crown imperial,
The inter-tissued robe of gold and pearl,
The farcèd title running 'fore the king,
The throne he sits on, nor the tide of pomp
That beats upon the high shore of this world,

No, not all these, thrice-gorgeous ceremony,
Not all these, laid in bed majestical,
Can sleep so soundly as the wretched slave
Who, with a body fill'd and vacant mind,
Gets him to rest, crammed with distressful bread,
Never sees horrid night, the child of hell,
But, like a lackey, from the rise to set,
Sweats in the eye of Phœbus, and all night
Sleeps in Elysium; next day, after dawn,
Doth rise, and help Hyperion to his horse;
And follows so the everrunning year
With profitable labour to his grave:
And, but for ceremony, such a wretch,
Winding up days with toil, and nights with sleep,
Had the fore-hand and vantage of a king;
The slave, a member of the country's peace,
Enjoys it; but in gross brain little wots
What watch the king keeps to maintain the peace,
Whose hours the peasant best advantages."

Henry V. IV. I.

And in the strength of such thoughts he is able to preach to the murmurers the lesson which they need in the nearest approach to a Homily which the dramas of Shakespeare present to us and to tell them, as Koheleth tells his readers, of a righteous judge who "shall bring every secret thing to light whether it be good or whether it be evil."

"Every subject's duty is the king's, but every subject's soul is his own. Therefore should every soldier in the wars do as every sick man in his bed—wash every mote out of his conscience, and dying so, death is to him advantage ; or not dying, the time was blessedly lost wherein such preparation was gained : and in him that escapes, it were not sin to think, that making God so free an offer, he let him outlive that day to see His greatness, and to teach others how they should prepare."

Henry V., IV. I.

I take it that, though there may be many other passages in which we trace the hand of the Master Artist working with a more subtle power, Shakespeare reaches here, and in the prayer that follows, almost without a parallel in his other dramas, his highest ethical elevation. The heroic soul in whom he embodied what for the time at least was an ideal likeness of himself, has conquered the temptations of sense that deepen into malice, and has his faith fixed in the righteous judgment of God. And with this there is, as in a later scene of the play, a healthy capacity for the purer form of enjoyment such as Koheleth so often counsels. The reformed prodigal has found that after all there are some things that are not altogether vanity.

" A good leg will fall ; a straight back will stoop ; a black beard will turn white ; a fair face will wither ; a full eye will wax hollow ; but a good heart, Kate, is the sun and the moon, or rather the sun and not the moon; for it shines bright, and never changes, but keeps his course truly."

Henry V., v. 2.

On more familiar illustrations of the temper that thus moralises on the hollowness of things earthly I do not dwell. Wolsey's lamentations over his fallen greatness:

> "This is the state of man: to day he puts forth
> The tender leaves of hope: to-morrow blossoms,
> And bears his blushing honours thick upon him,
> The third day comes a frost, a killing frost;
> And when he thinks, good easy man, full surely
> His greatness is a-ripening, nips his root,
> And then he falls, as I do,"

Henry VIII., III. 1.

will occur to most readers. The thought that "as the crackling of thorns under a pot, so is the laughter of fools," finds its apt illustration alike in the imbecility of Shallow who found his "delights of the sons of men" in the merry nights of sin that he remembered in St. George's Fields (2 *Henry IV.* III. 3), and yet more in the death without honour of the supreme jester, "his nose as sharp as a pen and babbling of green fields" (*Henry V.* III. 3), his only nurse silencing the thought of God and of repentance, in the misery that taught Gloucester all too late that

> "The Gods are just, and of our pleasant vices
> Make instruments to scourge us."

King Lear, v. 3.

The temper that remains unmoved "fully set to do evil, because sentence against an evil work is not executed speedily" (Eccl. viii. 11) is brought before us in Gloucester's confession

> "Heavens, deal so still!
> Let the superfluous and lust-dieted man
> That slaves your ordinance, that will not see
> Because he doth not feel, feel your power quickly."

King Lear, IV. 1.

The supreme malignity of the mood that hates life because it has made life hateful is seen in Richard III.

> "O coward conscience, how dost thou afflict!
>   *   *   *   *   *   *
> My conscience hath a thousand several tongues
> And every tongue brings in a several tale.
>   *   *   *   *   *   *
>   There is no creature loves me;
> And if I die, no soul will pity me:
> Nay, wherefore should they? Since that I myself
> Find in myself no pity to myself."

Richard III. v. 3.

16—2

It would seem however, as if the myriad-minded poet felt that he had not exhausted the many aspects of what we have called the Koheleth mood of mind, that there yet remained to exhibit, in their highest manifestations, the results to which it leads when man is over-mastered by it, or in his turn, masters ·it, and the works of the poet's ripest and best years, and of the supreme culmination of his art, bring before us accordingly the characters of Hamlet and of Prospero. I accept, as in part adequate, the analysis of the former character which Goethe has given as that of a man upon whom is laid a burden which he is not strong enough to bear, and which therefore disturbs the balance of thought and will. From the stand-point of our present enquiry some fresh elements have to be added to that analysis. In Hamlet then, prior to the disclosure that haunts him afterwards night and day, we have the highest type of the Koheleth search after happiness in the path of culture. All perfections have met in him. He is nothing less than

> " The courtier's, soldier's, scholar's, eye, tongue, sword,
> The expectancy and rose of the fair state,
> The glass of fashion, and the mould of form,
> The observed of all observers."
>
> *Hamlet*, III. I.

He has studied man's life and nature less by the personal experience of their follies and their sins than in the drama which "holds, as 'twere, the mirror up to nature." He shrinks from the coarse revelry of the princes who "drink in the morning," keeping up a custom which is " more honoured in the breach than in the observance." He seeks for wisdom, and if for folly also, only that he may see "what is that good for the sons of men which they should do under heaven" (Eccl. ii. 3). He is beginning to feel the impulse of a new affection, in itself a pure and noble one, for Ophelia. Possibly there are memories lying behind of affections less pure which justified the warnings that Laertes gives his sister:

> " I am myself indifferent honest ; but yet I could accuse me of such things that it were better my mother had not borne me : I am very proud, revengeful, ambitious ; with more offences at my back than I have thoughts to put them in, imagination to give them shape, or time to act them in."
>
> *Hamlet*, III. I.

His discovery of the terrible disorder in the world that surrounds him has wakened conscience to a discernment, perhaps a morbid exaggeration, of a like disorder in himself, and this becomes, in its turn, an enfeebling element hindering him from bearing the burden that is laid upon him bravely like a man. He represents that aspect of the Koheleth temper which had its birth in the sight of iniquity where it looked for righteousness (Eccl. iii. 16), of power on the side of the oppressors while "the poor had no comforter " (Eccl. iv. 1). There is something significant in the contrast between the wider yet less balanced thoughts of one on whom rests the burden of the "world in the heart" (Eccl. iii. 11), the unfathomable mystery of the moral anomalies of the universe and the calmer, more worldly precepts of prudence which come from Polonius as one who has grown grey in courts and statecraft. Such precepts, it is surely the lesson which Shakespeare meant to teach, are of little value in ministering to a mind diseased. They may do for Laertes but not for Hamlet. There is a singular resemblance between those precepts and Bacon's Essay (xviii.) on 'Travel' which half suggests the thought that the poet, noting the weak points which such an eye as his could not fail to discern in the character of him who was the "greatest, wisest, meanest of mankind," and impatient of the pedantic moralisings that had nothing answering to them in the man's inner life, had that type of character in his mind when he drew the portrait of the "rash intruding fool" who schemes and plans, and utters his worldly maxims as if they were the oracles of God[1].

And what makes the burden more intolerable is that he is not allowed to bear it patiently and to refer it to the judgment of the Ruler who will bring "the secret things to light, whether they be good or evil." The "world is out of joint" and he, and none other, "is born to set it right." He must be the minister of vengeance, and in taking that office upon himself he does but make all things worse both for himself and others. And so the weariness of life, the "*satias videndi*" falls on him as it did on Koheleth. Below his simulated madness there is the real insanity of pessimism :

"It goes so heavily with my disposition that this goodly frame, the earth, seems to me a sterile promontory ; this most excellent canopy the air, look you,—this brave o'erhanging firmament, this majestical roof fretted with golden fire, why it appears no other thing to me than a foul and pestilent congregation of vapours. What a piece of work is a man ! How noble in reason ! how infinite in faculty ! in form, in moving, how like an angel ! in apprehension how like a God ! the beauty of the world, the paragon of animals ! and yet to me what is

---

[1] The suggestion may seem bold, almost to the verge of paradox, but is not made without a fairly close study of the original and the counterpart. The coincidences which I have pointed out between the counsel of Polonius and the Essay on Travel are, it will be admitted by any one who will take the trouble to compare them, striking enough. It may be said further that the whole phraseology of Polonius, shrewd yet slightly pedantic,

"full of wise saws and modern instances"

corresponds to that of Bacon as the collector of apophthegms and maxims and rules of prudence. May we not think that Shakespeare, through Hamlet, uttered his sense of the impotence of such counsels as applied to the deeper evils of the soul, when he makes the half-distracted prince declare

"Yea, from the table of my memory
I'll wipe away all trivial fond records,
All saws of books, all forms, all pressures past,
That youth and observation copied there."

Bacon's rise upon Raleigh's fall, about the time when Hamlet received the poet's last revision, and the part that he had taken in the proceedings against Essex were not likely to win the admiration of a man of letters who had known something of both his victims. To such a man he may well have seemed to embody the intriguing statecraft as well as the pedantry of Polonius.

this quintessence of dust? Man delights not me: no, nor woman
neither."

Hamlet, II. 2.

Has the theme of "Vanity of Vanities" ever been uttered in tones
of profounder sadness? Has the irony of the contrast between the
ideal and the actual in life ever been expressed more forcibly?

And with this there comes the thought on which Koheleth rings the
changes that death is better than life (Eccl. vi. 3, vii. 1), traversed in
its turn by the thought that life is better than death (Eccl. ix. 4, 9, 10),
the known than the unknown, the certainties of the present than the
uncertain chances of the future.

> "To be, or not to be, that is the question:—
> Whether 'tis nobler in the mind, to suffer
> The slings and arrows of outrageous fortune;
> Or to take arms against a sea of troubles,
> And by opposing, end them? To die,—to sleep,—
> No more; and, by a sleep, to say we end
> The heart-ache, and the thousand natural shocks
> That flesh is heir to,—'tis a consummation
> Devoutly to be wish'd. To die,—to sleep,—
> To sleep! perchance to dream;—ay, there's the rub,
> That makes calamity of so long life:
> For who would bear the whips and scorns of time,
> The oppressor's wrong, the proud man's contumely,
> The pangs of despis'd love, the law's delay,
> The insolence of office, and the spurns
> That patient merit of the unworthy takes
> When he himself might his quietus make
> With a bare bodkin? Who would fardels bear,
> To grunt and sweat under a weary life;
> But that the dread of something after death,—
> The undiscover'd country, from whose bourn
> No traveller returns,—puzzles the will,
> And makes us rather bear those ills we have
> Than fly to others that we know not of?
> Thus conscience does make cowards of us all;
> And thus the native hue of resolution
> Is sicklied o'er with the pale cast of thought;
> And enterprises of great pith and moment,
> With this regard their currents turn awry,
> And lose the name of action."

Hamlet, III. 1.

We feel that here, as in the case of Koheleth, the weariness of life
will not end in suicide. He talks too much of it for that, contemplates
it as a spectator from without, moralises on it, like Jaques, with a
thousand similies. Perhaps, we must add, as the thought of the undiscovered country has no purifying or controlling power, as conscience
leads only to cowardice and not to courage, suicide would have been

the lesser evil of the two. As it is, the cancer of pessimism is driven inward and eats into the inmost parts. We cannot doubt that Shakespeare had seen like phænomena in actual insanity, had felt the possibility of them in his own being. The moralising melancholy becomes a cynical and brutal bitterness. It is just after the soliloquy that he treats Ophelia with an almost savage ferocity. In the churchyard scene he speaks as one in whom the reverence for humanity is extinguished, moralises on the skulls of the lawyers, and of Alexander, and of Yorick, the well-loved friend of his boyhood, in tones that remind us at once of Jaques and of Timon. There are no "*lachrymae rerum,*" in that survey of mortality, hardly more than the *risus Sardonicus* which Tennyson has painted so vividly, as we shall see, in his Vision of Sin. The ruin is complete, or seems so. But the parallelism with Koheleth and with Shakespeare himself would not have been complete if, in this case also, there had not been in Horatio, the presence of the faithful friend, the "man who pleaseth God" (Eccl. vii. 26), to whom, as free from the passions that have plunged him in the abyss, he clings, as the drowning man to the hand that would fain have saved him. His last words are addressed to him:

> "Horatio, what a wounded name,
> Things standing thus unknown, shall live behind me!
> If thou didst ever hold me in thy heart,
> Absent thee from felicity awhile,
> And in this harsh world draw thy breath in pain
> To tell my story."
>
> *Hamlet,* V. 2.

And here, as in the case of Timon, the faithful friend sees a glimmer of hope even in the thick darkness. He will not despair even though the sufferer dies and make no sign. He loves him, will not God forgive?

> "Now cracks a noble heart. Good night, sweet prince,
> And flights of angels sing thee to thy rest."
>
> *Hamlet,* V. 2.

The last instance to which I call attention, that of Prospero, has the special interest of giving us the last, or all but the last, utterances of the great Master on the great mystery. As in *Hamlet* we have the history of a shipwrecked soul, so in the *Tempest,* almost as if its title and its opening scenes were meant to be a parable of the gist and drift of the whole book, we have that of one who has escaped from shipwreck and reached the desired haven of a supreme tranquillity. Prospero had sought wisdom at first in the "many books" of the making of which there is "no end" (Eccl. xii. 12). His "library" was "dukedom large enough." That study had left him exposed to treachery and baseness. He was shut out from the world, and knew its hollowness but he did not hate it or rail at it, as Timon and Hamlet did. He had found the well-spring of a new life and hope in the purest of all affections. He owns to Miranda all that she had been to him in the unconscious helplessness of her infancy,

"O! a cherubim
Thou wast that did preserve me! Thou didst smile,
Infused with a fortitude from heaven,
When I have decked the sea with drops full salt;
Under my burden groan'd; which raised in me
An undergoing stomach, to bear up
Against what should ensue."

Tempest, I. 2.

He has learnt,—Shakespeare himself, speaking through Prospero, has learnt,—that the sensuality that defiles the first stirrings of youthful love is the root of all bitterness, that then only can the man "live joyfully with the wife whom he loves" (Eccl. ix. 9), when passion has been controlled and purity preserved from stain, and

"Each to other gives the virgin heart."

And he too moralises on the chances and changes of life with the better form of Epicurean calmness. For him also

"All the world's a stage,
And all the men and women merely players,"

but the thought leads to no cynical revilings. It is not a Christian view of life and death. The ethics of Shakespeare are no more Christian, in any real sense of the word, than those of Sophocles or Goethe. But it is a view that commended itself not unnaturally to one who being himself the creator of the mimic drama that mirrored life, pictured to himself the great Workmaster as being altogether such an one as himself, the author of the great world-drama in which men and women were the puppets.

"These our actors,
As I foretold you, were all spirits, and
Are melted into air, into thin air;
And like the baseless fabric of this vision,
The cloud-capped towers, the gorgeous palaces,
The solemn temples; the great globe itself,
Yea, all which it inherit, shall dissolve,
And, like this unsubstantial pageant faded,
Leave not a rack behind. We are such stuff
As dreams are made of, and our little life
Is rounded with a sleep."

Tempest, IV. 1.

The pessimism which haunted Koheleth is absent from this calm contemplative acquiescence in the inevitable transitoriness of human life and of the world itself. It may be questioned perhaps whether the pessimism was not better than the calmness, testifying, even against its will, of higher possibilities, unable to satisfy itself with any belief that was, in its essence, though not formally, Pantheistic, and craving for the manifestation of a personal Will ruling the world in righteousness, and therefore "executing judgement against every evil work."

One more instance in which the final resting-place of Shakespeare's thoughts answers to that in which Koheleth rested for a time, and I have done. There is another drama, *Cymbeline* (A.D. 1605), which also belongs to the latest group of Shakespeare's writings. In that drama we have a funeral dirge sung over the supposed corpse of the disguised Imogen. It does not help to the development of any character in the play, but comes in, as it were, by way of parenthesis, and therefore may be legitimately considered as embodying the poet's own thoughts of what, if men could get rid of the Burial Service and other conventional decorums, would be the right utterance for such a time and place. And the dirge runs thus :

> "Fear no more the heat o' the sun,
> Nor the furious winter's rages;
> Thou thy worldly task hast done,
> Home art gone, and ta'en thy wages.
> Golden lads and girls all must,
> Like chimney sweepers, come to dust.
>
> Fear no more the frown of the great,
> Thou art past the tyrant's stroke;
> Care no more to clothe and eat ;
> To thee the reed is as the oak;
> The sceptre, learning, physic must
> All follow this and come to dust.
>
> Fear no more the lightning-flash,
> Nor th' all-dreaded thunder-storm,
> Fear not slander, censure rash,
> Thou hast finished joy and moan;
> All lovers young, all lovers must
> Consign to thee and come to dust."

Cymbeline, IV. 2.

So Koheleth had said of old "One generation passeth away, and another generation cometh" (Eccl. i. 4). "And how dieth the wise man? as the fool" (Eccl. ii. 16). "All go unto one place; all are of the dust, and all turn to dust again" (Eccl. iii. 20). "There is no work, nor desire, nor knowledge, nor wisdom, in the grave whither thou goest" (Eccl. ix. 10).

II. TENNYSON AND KOHELETH.

The conditions under which this paper is written forbid an analysis of life such as I have ventured to apply to the Sonnets and Dramas of Shakespeare in the Essay which precedes it. One may not, in the case of a living writer, remove the veil which shrouds the privacy of his home life, or draw conjectural inferences as to that life, however legitimate they may seem, from his writings. We must be content with what he has actually told us. And so, in the present instance, we must rest in the pictures which he himself has drawn of the Lincolnshire home, and the happy gatherings when

> "The Christmas bells from hill to hill
> Answer each other in the mist,"
> *In Memor.* XXVIII.

in what we know of the brothers, three of whom shared in different measures, the gifts and tastes of the poet's vocation; of the volume of early poems published by two of those brothers in their schooldays; of the Cambridge prize poem on Timbuctoo; of the new friendships and companionships which the life of Cambridge brought with it.

Of one of those friendships, however, the poet has himself taught us to think more freely, and to speak more fully. No one can read the *In Memoriam* without feeling that the world owes more than it knows to the man who will probably be scarcely remembered in the history of literature, except as having formed its subject. To that sacred influence, purifying and ennobling during life, yet more purifying and ennobling after death, we can trace in part at least, as well as to the early impressions of a happy home, that which forms one conspicuous element in the greatness of the poet's ripened genius, and places the name of Tennyson, along with those of Homer and of Virgil, of Dante, and Milton, and Wordsworth, in the list from which Byron and Burns, and even Shakespeare are excluded, of those who being in the first order of poets in their greatness are also first in their purity. The Sonnets of Shakespeare and the *In Memoriam* will occupy a prominent place in the history of English Literature at once as parallels and as antitheses. In both we have the outpouring of a fervent and deep affection, so profound and lasting, that we might almost apply to it the language in which David speaks of the friendship that bound to him the soul of Jonathan, "Thy love to me was wonderful, passing the love of woman." The thought of the parallelism seems to have come before the mind of the later poet when he wrote:

> "I loved thee, Spirit, and love, nor can
> The soul of Shakespeare love thee more."
> *In Memoriam,* LX.

But what a contrast between the luscious and sensuous sweetness of what his contemporaries called those "sugared sonnets" of the one poet, and the out-poured meditations, ever-rising to a clearer and calmer serenity, of the other. In this respect at least, and it is from this point of view alone that I am now contemplating the works of the two poets, the friendship which Tennyson has made immortal, comes nearer to the type of that to which we have been led to look as one element in Koheleth's recovery. Here also there was one who did in very deed "fear God" and "pleased Him" (Eccl. vii. 26). And it may be said freely, without going beyond the record, that the *In Memoriam* is itself also the history of a like recovery in the poet's inner life. He too had learnt to rise out of "the confusions of a wasted youth," had "held it truth"

> "That men may rise on stepping stones
> Of their dead selves to higher things."
>
> *In Memoriam*, I.

The earlier poems are in the tone of the *Mataiotes Mataiotêton*:

> "From out waste places comes a cry,
> And murmurs from the dying sun,
> And all the phantom, Nature, stands,
> With all the music in her tone,
> A hollow echo of my own,
> A hollow form with empty hands."
>
> *In Memoriam*, III.

His assured faith in the continued being and growth of the soul that has passed from earth is, as with Koheleth (Eccl. xii. 7), the triumph over a previous doubt:

> "My own dim life should teach me this,
> That life shall live for evermore,
> Else earth is darkness at the core,
> And dust and ashes all that is."
>
> *In Memoriam*, XXXIV.

He has communed with Nature, and her witness to him is as dreary and depressing as it was to Koheleth (Eccl. i. 2, 3, iii. 19, 20), or Hamlet:

> "Thou makest thine appeal to me;
> I bring to life, I bring to death;
> The spirit does but mean the breath;
> I know no more."
>
> *In Memoriam*, LV.

but he has learnt to look "behind the veil" and to "trust," however "faintly" the "larger hope."

It lies in the nature of the case, however, that the pessimist temper, so far as it had ever entered into the poet's consciousness at all, as more than what he felt was a possibility towards which he might drift as others had drifted, already lay behind him before he entered on the *In Memoriam* musings, as part of the "dead self" which had been made a "stepping-stone." We must turn to the earlier poems if we want to find parallels to that aspect of the Koheleth experience. And they are not hard to seek. In the Vision of Sin, in the Palace of Art, in the Two Voices, we may find, if I mistake-not, the most suggestive of all commentaries on Ecclesiastes.

The first of these poems deals with the baser, more sensuous form of the Koheleth experience of life (Eccl. ii. 8).

> "I had a vision when the night was late;
> A youth came riding towards a palace gate,
> He rode a horse with wings that would have flown,
> But that his heavy rider kept him down."

In the symbolism of those two last lines we may trace something like a reminiscence, though not a direct reproduction, of the marvellous *mythos* of the *Phædrus* of Plato (pp. 246, 254). The horse with wings that "would have flown" is the nature of man with its capacities and aspirations [1].

The "heavy rider" is the sensuous will that represses the aspirations and yields easily to temptation. And so :

> "From out the palace came a child of sin,
> And took him by the curls and led him in,
> Where sat a company with heated eyes,
> Expecting when a fountain should arise."

And then follows a picture of revel and riot, like that which Koheleth had known (Eccl. ii. 12). The fountain of sensual pleasure flows at last. The orgiastic ecstasy reached its highest point :

> "Twisted hard in fierce embraces,
> Like to Furies, like to Graces,
> Dashed together in blinding dew,
> Till, killed with some luxurious agony,
> The nerve-dissolving melody
> Fluttered headlong from the sky."

And then the vision changes, the mirth that has blazed so brightly, like the crackling of the thorns (Eccl. vii. 6) dies out, and the slow retribution comes :

> "I saw that every morning, far withdrawn
> Beyond the darkness and the cataract,
> God made himself an awful rose of dawn
> Unheeded: and detaching fold by fold
> From those still heights, and slowly drawing near,

---

[1] ἡ ψυχὴ πᾶσα παντὸς ἐπιμελεῖται τοῦ ἀψύχου...πάντα δὲ οὐρανὸν περιπολεῖ...τελέα μὲν οὖν οὖσα καὶ ἐπτερωμένη μετεωροπολεῖ τε καὶ ἅπαντα τὸν κόσμον διοικεῖ.

"The whole soul contemplates the whole that is without soul...It surveys the heavens...developed and with wings full grown it soars aloft and penetrates the Universe."

> A vapour heavy, hueless, formless, cold,
> Came floating on for many a month and year
> Unheeded."

That vapour is, as the sequel shews, the cynical pessimism which destroys all joy, and makes a man hate his life (Eccl. ii. 17) and find no beauty in nature, or comeliness in man or woman. The youthful reveller becomes

> "A gray and gap-toothed man as lean as death,
> Who slowly rode across a withered heath
> And lighted at a ruined inn."

And the monologue that follows can scarcely fail to remind us of much that we have met as we have traced the many wanderings of the soul of Koheleth. There is the same sense of the transitoriness of life, tempting men to drown it in oblivion (Eccl. ii. 22, vi. 12).

> "Fill the cup and fill the can:
> Have a rouse before the morn;
> Every minute dies a man,
> Every minute one is born."

There is the same contempt for the glory of living in the memories of men, after which so many strive without profit (Eccl. i. 11).

> "Name and fame! to fly sublime
> Thro' the courts, the camps, the schools,
> Is to be the ball of Time,
> Bandied in the hands of fools."

The anomalies of a world out of joint socially and politically do but stir in him the cynical "wonder not" (Eccl. v. 8) and he finds in these also, as Koheleth found, "vanity and *feeding upon wind*" (Eccl. viii. 10, i. 17).

> "He that wars for liberty
> Faster binds the tyrant's power,
> And the tyrant's cruel glee
> Forces on the freer hour.
> Fill the can and fill the cup;
> All the windy ways of men
> Are but dust that rises up,
> And is lightly laid again."

Here also time and chance happeneth alike to all (Eccl. ix. 11) and the days of darkness are many (Eccl. xi. 8).

> "Drink to Fortune, drink to chance,
> While we keep a little breath.
>   *   *   *   *
> Thou art mazed: the night is long,
> And the longer night is near"
>   *   *   *   *

and all that remains is but

"Dregs of life and lees of man."

The vision receives its interpretation from the voices that come from the mystic mountain range where the judgments of God hide themselves in clouds and darkness,

"Then some one said, 'Behold! it was a crime
Of sense avenged by sense that wore with time.'
Another said, 'The crime of sense became
The crime of malice and is equal blame.'
And one 'He had not wholly quenched his power,
A little grain of conscience made him sour.'"

The transformation presents a parallel, obviously, one would say, an unconscious parallel, to what we have seen in Shakespeare's *Timon*. And here too the wider thoughts of the seer lead him to look on that pessimism of the depraved and worn-out sensualist rather with pity and terror than with absolute despair. He dares not absolve, he dares not condemn;

"At last I heard a voice upon the slope
Cry to the summit 'Is there any hope?'
To which an answer pealed from that high land,
But in a tongue no man could understand,
And on the glittering summit far withdrawn
God made Himself an awful rose of dawn."

The "Palace of Art" presents the analysis of a far nobler experiment in life, answering to that of Koheleth when he sought to "guide his heart with wisdom" and surrounded himself with the "peculiar treasure of kings and of the provinces" and "whatsoever his eye desired, he kept not from them, and withheld not his heart from any joy and his heart rejoiced in his labour" (Eccl. ii. 8—10).

In this case the writer prologuizes and states in advance the moral of his poem. It will scarcely be questioned that it is identical with that which we have seen to be the moral of Ecclesiastes.

"I send you here a sort of allegory
(For you will understand it), of a soul,
A sinful soul possessed of many gifts,
A spacious garden full of flowering weeds,
A glorious devil large in heart and brain,
That did love Beauty only (Beauty seen
In all varieties of mould and mind)
And knowledge for its beauty; or if good
Good only for its beauty, seeing not
That Beauty, Good and Knowledge, are three sisters
That doat upon each other, friends to man,
Living together under the same roof,
And never can be sundered without tears.
And he that shuts Love out in turn shall be
Shut out from Love, and on her threshold lie

Howling in outer darkness. Not for this
Was common clay ta'en from the common earth,
Moulded by God and tempered with the tears
Of angels to the perfect shape of man."

And then the allegory begins. The man communes with his soul
after the manner of Koheleth (Eccl. ii. 1—3):

"I built my soul a lordly pleasure-house
Wherein at ease for aye to dwell,
I said, O Soul, make merry and carouse,
Dear Soul, for all is well."

That "pleasure-house" is filled with all that art can represent of the
varying aspects

"Of living Nature, fit for every mood
And change of my still soul."

It is filled also with all types and symbols of the religions of humanity,
regarded simply from the artist's stand-point as presenting, in greater
or less measure, the element of beauty, from St Cecilia, and the houris
of Islam, down to Europa and Ganymede.

"Nor these alone, but every legend fair
Which the supreme Caucasian mind
Carved out of Nature for itself, was there
Not less than life designed."

And poetry also in its highest forms ministered to the soul's delight;

" For there was Milton like a seraph strong,
Beside him Shakespeare bland and mild;
And there the world-worn Dante grasped his song,
And somewhat grimly smiled."

And with them were the typical representatives of divine philosophy,

"Plato the wise, and large-brow'd Verulam,
Masters of those who know."

The highest ideal of Epicurean culture in its supreme tranquillity
was at least for a time attained, and there was no contaminating element of the lower forms of baseness. The soul can say:

"All these are mine,
And, let the world have peace or war,
Tis one to me."

She found delight in tracing the evolution of organic, the development
of intellectual, life, and had placed beneath her feet, as Epicurus himself had done, the superstitions of the crowd, and, as Koheleth had
at one time done, had cast aside the memories of a national and
historical religion.

> "I take possession of men's mind and deed,
> I live in all things great and small;
> I sit apart, holding no form of creed,
> And contemplating all."

But the germ of retribution was already planted. As with Koheleth there was "the world set in the heart" (Eccl. iii. 11), the problems of the unfathomable universe:

> "Full oft the riddle of the painful earth
> Flashed thro' her as she sate alone,
> Yet not the less held she her solemn mirth
> And intellectual throne
>
> Of full-sphered contemplation."

And then, as with a stroke like that which fell on Herod, the penalty of her selfish search for happiness, her isolated eudæmonism, there fell on her as in a moment, the doom of "vanity of vanities" written on all her joys, and the mood of pessimism which was its first and bitterest fruit:

> "When she would think, where'er she turned her sight,
> The airy hands confusion wrought,
> Wrote 'mene, mene' and divided quite
> The kingdom of her thought.
>
> Deep dread and loathing of her solitude
> Fell on her, from which mood was born
> Scorn of herself: again from out that mood
> Laughter at her self-scorn."

Has the picture of one who is "*fessus satiate videndi*" been ever drawn by a more subtle master-hand? To such a mood, as seen in Koheleth, existence is a burden, and non-existence a terror (Eccl. ii. 17, vi. 3, ix. 5), the sleep of the grave, or the dreams that may haunt that sleep are equally appalling;

> "And death and life she hated equally,
> And nothing saw, for her despair,
> But dreadful time, dreadful eternity,
> No comfort anywhere."

It was a more terrible, if a less loathsome, form of retribution, than the cynical scorn of the "Vision of Sin," not without a certain element of greatness, and therefore that cry out of the depths was not uttered in vain:

> "What is it that will take away my sin,
> And save me lest I die?"

There is no other road to restoration than the old "king's highway" of penitence and prayer and self-renunciation. The deepest lesson of the poem is perhaps kept to the last. The joys of beauty, and culture, and art, and wisdom, are not lost utterly and for ever. The Palace of Art remains for the soul to dwell in, when it is purified from evil, no longer in selfish isolation, but in the blessedness of companionship. "Whatsoever things are noble, whatsoever things are pure, whatsoever things are lovely," are not forfeited by the discipline of repentance, but rather secured as for an everlasting habitation, withdrawn for a season, but only that they may abide with the soul for ever:

> "So when four years were wholly finished,
>   She threw her royal robes away.
> 'Make me a cottage in the vale,' she said,
>   'Where I may fast and pray.
>
> Yet pull not down my palace towers that are
>   So lightly, beautifully built;
> Perchance I may return with others there,
>   When I have purged my guilt.'"

In the "Two Voices" we have a fuller unveiling of what the poet pictured to himself as the working of the pessimist temper, to which life has become hateful, while yet it shrinks from death. Here also the unconscious echoes of the thoughts of Koheleth (Eccl. vi. 3) are distinctly heard:

> "A still small voice spake unto me,
>   'Thou art so full of misery,
> Were it not better not to be?'"

The soul makes answer to the tempter with feeble and faltering voice. It is in vain to urge the dignity of man's nature and his prerogative of thought. Nature cares for the race, not for the individual man. "One generation goeth and another generation cometh" (Eccl. i. 4).

> "It spake moreover in my mind
> 'Tho' thou wert scatter'd to the wind,
> Yet is there plenty of the kind.'"

In the language of the French cynic, "*Il n'y a pas d'homme nécessaire.*"

> "Good soul suppose I grant it thee
> Who'll weep for thy deficiency?
>
> Or will one beam be less intense,
> When thy peculiar difference
> Is cancelled in the world of sense?"

Hope that the future may be better than the past is repressed with a like sneer:

> "'Some turn this sickness yet might take,
>   Ev'n yet.' But he 'what drug can make
> A withered palsy cease to shake?'"

It is in vain to aim at the Epicurean tranquillity of culture or refined enjoyment (Eccl. ii. 24, v. 18).

> "Moreover but to seem to find,
> Asks what thou lackest, thought resigned,
> A healthy frame, a quiet mind."

ECCLESIASTES 17

As with Hamlet, this shrinking from the logical outcome of pessimism, lest it should tarnish his fair fame among his fellows, shews weakness and not strength. That desire to be remembered is also 'vanity,'

> "Such art thou, a divided will,
> Still heaping on the fear of ill
> The fear of men, a coward still.
>
> Do men love thee? Art thou so bound
> To men, that how thy name shall sound
> Shall vex thee, lying underground?"

The aspirations after the heroic life are shewn to be as hollow as the search for happiness. This also is vanity.

> "Then comes the check, the change, the fall;
> Pain rises up, old pleasures pall;
> There is one remedy for all."

The old question, who knows whether man is better than the brute creatures round him (Eccl. iii. 21) is asked and with the old answer:

> "If straight thy track, or if oblique,
> Thou know'st not, shadows thou dost strike,
> Embracing cloud, Ixion-like;
>
> And owning but a little more
> Than beasts, abidest tame and poor,
> Calling thyself a little lower
>
> Than angels. Cease to wail and brawl;
> Why inch by inch to darkness crawl?
> There is one remedy for all."

As with Hamlet, the voice that prompts to self-destruction is met in part by the fear of the unknown. We have no full assurance that death is the end of consciousness:

> "For I go, weak from suffering here;
> Naked I go, and void of cheer;
> What is it that I may not fear?"

The very weariness of life, which is the outcome of pessimism, testifies to the higher capacities, and therefore the higher possibilities, of the human spirit. The *Welt-schmerz*, the 'world set in the heart,' the thought of Infinity (Eccl. iii. 11), bears its unconscious witness,

> "Here sits he shaping wings to fly,
> His heart forebodes a mystery,
> He names the name Eternity."

Conscious as he is of the contradictions in his inner life, of the "dead flies" that taint the fair fame even of the best and wisest (Eccl. vii. 1).

> "He knows a baseness in his blood,
> At such strange war with something good,
> He may not do the thing he would."

Yet with him, as with Koheleth, faith at last prevails, and the goal of his many labyrinthine wanderings of thought is hope and not despair. And the faith comes to him, not through the careful balancing of the conflicting arguments of the Voice that whispered despair and of his own soul in reply, but partly through his inner consciousness of aspirations after a higher blessedness, partly through the contemplation of a form of life natural and simple enough, in which that blessedness is, in part at least, realised, in a fresh sympathy with humanity, in acts, or at least thoughts, of kindness (Eccl. xi. 1, 2).

> "Whatever crazy sorrow saith,
> No life that breathes with human breath,
> Hath ever truly longed for death.
>
> 'Tis life whereof our nerves are scant;
> Oh, life, not death, for which we pant,
> More life, and fuller, that I want.'

And what he sees is a village Churchyard, on "the Sabbath morn," and "the sweet Church bells begin to peal," and among those who are so "passing the place where each must rest" are three—husband, wife and child, bound together as by "a three-fold cord that is not easily broken" (Eccl. iv. 12).

> "These three made unity so sweet,
> My frozen heart began to beat,
> Remembering its ancient heat."

And so "the dull and bitter voice was gone" and a second voice was heard with its whisper,

> "A murmur 'Be of better cheer.'"

He looked back, as Koheleth looked back, on his previous mood of pessimism as a thing belonging to the past, and just as the last words of the one were those that said in tones, which though a sad tender irony might mingle with them, were far from being merely ironical, "Rejoice, O young man, in thy youth" (Eccl. xi. 9), so, in the new sense of life that dawned upon the thinker, this was the Voice that at last prevailed, as he looked on the blameless joys of the life of home, purified by the fear of God, and felt the calming influence of sky and stream and meadow-land and flowers,

> "So variously seem'd all things wrought,
> I marvelled how the mind was brought
> To anchor by one gloomy thought,
>
> And wherefore rather I made choice
> To commune with that barren voice
> Than him that said Rejoice, rejoice."

A later poem of Tennyson's, his "Lucretius," gives a new significance to these three earlier works, as shewing how deeply he had entered into that Epicurean teaching both in its higher and its lower aspects, of which we have seen so many traces in the words of Koheleth. With the profound insight which that study had given him he paints, on the one hand, the insane impurities which are the outcome of the soul's disease, and haunt the mind that has rested in sensuous pleasure as its goal, and of which the Poet's fourth Book presents but too full and terrible a picture; and, on the other, recognises the higher aim which makes the *De Rerum Natura* one of the loftiest and noblest poems of Latin, or indeed of any, literature. It had not been his aim, any more than it was that of Koheleth, to rest in mere negations.

> "My Master held
> That Gods there are, for all men so believe.
> I prest my footsteps into his, and meant
> Surely to lead my Memmius in a train
> Of flowery clauses onward to the thought
> That Gods there are, and deathless."

He too has known 'the two Voices' that tempt to self-slaughter and resist the temptation, as a man looks out at "all the evil that is done under the sun" (Eccl. iv. 1), of which he says:

> "And here he glances on an eye new born,
> And gets for greeting but a wail of pain;
> And here he stays upon a freezing orb
> That fain would gaze upon him to the last;
> And here upon a yellow eyelid fall'n,
> And closed by those who mourn a friend in vain,
> Not thankful that his troubles are no more.
> And me, altho' his fire is on my face,
> Blinding, he sees not, nor at all can tell
> Whether I mean this day to end myself,
> Or lend an ear to Plato, where he says,
> That men, like soldiers, may not quit the post
> Allotted by the Gods: but he that holds
> The Gods are careless, wherefore need he care
> Greatly for them, nor rather plunge at once,
> Being troubled, wholly out of sight, and sink
> Past earthquake—ay, and gout and stone, that break
> Body towards death, and palsy, death-in-life
> And wretched age...? "

The student will have noticed how singularly all this coincides with Koheleth's view of the 'vanity' of human life, one generation going and another coming (Eccl. i. 4), and with the picture of disease and decay in Eccl. xii. 3—6. Lucretius, like Koheleth, had aimed at the higher ideal of the life of the Garden of Epicurus. He turns to the Gods and says:

> "I thought I lived securely as yourselves—
> No lewdness, narrowing envy, monkey spite,
> No madness of ambition, avarice, none:
> No larger feast than under plane or pine

> With neighbours laid along the grass, to take
> Only such cups as left us friendly warm,
> Affirming each his own philosophy—
> Nothing to mar the sober majesties
> Of settled, sweet Epicurean life."

The agony which drove him to self-slaughter was that he had fallen from that ideal into the sensuous baseness with which he had made himself but too fatally familiar. He too had his "Vision of Sin," the "crime of sense avenged by sense," and found the haunting burden of it unendurable, and in words which again remind us of Koheleth (Eccl. i. 9, 11, iii. 20), utters his resolve,

> "And therefore now
> Let her that is the womb and tomb of all,
> Great Nature, take, and forcing far apart
> Those blind beginnings that have made me man,
> Dash them anew together at her will,
> Thro' all her cycles—into man once more,
> Or beast, or bird, or fish, or opulent flower:"

And doing this, he looks forward to the time

> "When momentary man
> Shall seem no more a something to himself,
> But he, his hopes and hates, his homes and fanes,
> And even his bones long laid within the grave,
> The very sides of the grave itself shall pass
> Vanishing, atom and void, atom and void,
> Into the unseen for ever."

With Tennyson, as with Shakespeare, there are few, if any, traces, that this striking parallelism with the Confessions of the Debater, is the result of any deliberate study of, or attempt to reproduce, them. The phrases of Ecclesiastes are not borrowed, admirably as they might have served to express his thoughts; there is no reference, however distant, to his experience. We have to do once more with parallelism pure and simple and not with derivation. What I have attempted to shew is that under every extremest variation in circumstances and culture the outcome of the pursuit of happiness, what we have learnt to call eudæmonism, after the Epicurean ideal, is sooner or later, that, in the absence of a clearer faith and loftier aim, the ideal breaks down and leaves the man struggling with the question 'Is life worth living?' perhaps finding the answer to that question in some form of a pessimist view of life and of the Universe. It will be admitted, I think, that, so far as I have proved this, I have added to the arguments which I have urged in favour of the view that I have maintained, both in the Notes and in the "Ideal Biography," as to the *genesis* and plan of Ecclesiastes.

III. A PERSIAN KOHELETH OF THE TWELFTH
CENTURY.

I have yet another instance of unconscious parallelism with the experience and the thought of Koheleth to bring before the student's notice. It comes from a far off land and from a more distant age than the two which I have already discussed. Omar Khayyam (=Omar, the Tent maker)[1] was born in the latter half of the eleventh century at Naishapur in Khorasan. He was in his youth the friend and fellow-student of Nizam ul Mulk, the Vizier of Alp Arslan, the son of Toghrul Bey. They read the Koran sitting at the feet of the Imam Mowaffek, the greatest teacher of his age and city. Another fellow-student became afterwards a name of terror as Hasan, the OLD MAN OF THE MOUN-TAINS, the head of the *Assassins* whose name and fame became a word of terror to the Crusaders. Omar, as acting on the Epicurean counsel, λάθε βίωσας (=live as hidden from view), asked his Vizier friend to "let him live in a corner under the shadow of his fortune," giving his life to the pursuit of wisdom. Like the Greek and Roman Epicureans, he devoted himself chiefly to astronomy and physical science. He was employed in reforming the Persian Calendar, and died, as the paragon of his age, in A.D. 1123. It was characteristic of the mood of thought, the workings of which we are about to trace, that his wish as to his grave was that it might be "where the North wind might scatter roses over him." Like the Koheleth of the "Ideal Biography," in his relation to the Jewish Rabbis of his time, he startled alike the orthodox Imams of Islam and the mystics of the Sufi sect, by the half-voluptuous, half-cynical strain which found utterance in his poems and his conversation. The writer of an article in the *Calcutta Review*, No. 59, draws an elaborate parallel between his poetry and that of Lucretius, but it does not seem to have occurred to him to carry the line of thought further and to note the many coincidences which the *Rubaiyat* (= *Tetrastichs*) presents to the thoughts and language of Ecclesiastes, as well as to those of the later Epicurean poet. To these the attention of the student is now invited.

The poem opens with the dawn of a New Year's day, and a voice calls as from a tavern where revellers are carousing, and summons to enjoyment

> "Come fill the Cup, and in the fire of Spring
> Your winter garment of Repentance fling,
> The Bird of Time has but a little way
> To flutter—and the Bird is on the wing."

---

[1] I owe my knowledge of the poet to the "Rubaiyat of Omar Khayyam," published by Quaritch, 1879. The name of the translator is not given.

Whether at Naishapur or Babylon,
Whether the Cup with sweet or bitter run,
   The Wine of Life keeps oozing drop by drop,
The Leaves of Life keep falling one by one.

Each morn a thousand Roses brings, you say,
Yes, but where leaves the Rose of yesterday?
   And this first summer-month that brings the Rose,
Shall take Jamshyd and Kaikobad away.

Well, let it take them."

The lesson drawn from that thought of the transitoriness of enjoyment is the old lesson of a calm and tranquil Epicureanism such as that of Eccl. ii. 24, v. 8, ix. 7.

"A Book of Verses underneath the Bough,
A Jug of Wine, a loaf of Bread—and thou
   Beside me singing in the Wilderness,
Oh, Wilderness were Paradise enow.

Some for the Glories of this World, and some
Sigh for the Prophet's Paradise to come;
   Ah, take the Cash, and let the Credit go,
Nor heed the rumble of a distant Drum!

Look to the blowing Rose about us;—'Lo!
'Laughing' she says 'into the world I blow,
   'At once the silken tassel of my Purse
Tear, and its Treasure on the Garden throw;'
    *   *   *   *   *

The Worldly Hope men set their Hearts upon
Turns ashes, or it prospers; and anon
   Like Snow upon the Desert's dusty face,
Lighting a little hour or two—was gone.

Think—in this battered Caravanserai
Whose portals are alternate Night and Day,
   How Sultan after Sultan with his Pomp
Abode his destin'd Hour, and went his way."

And this sense of the transitoriness of all things human (Eccl. i. 4—7, ii. 16) leads, as with the Epicureans of all times and countries, to the *Carpe diem* of Horace, the "let us eat and drink, for to-morrow we die" of 1 Cor. xv. 34, to the belief that there is "nothing better for a man than that he should thus eat, drink and be merry."

"Ah, my Beloved, fill the Cup that clears
To-Day of past Regret and future Fears.
    *   *   *   *   *

Ah, make the most of what we yet may spend,
Before we too into the Dust descend;
   Dust into Dust, and under Dust to lie,
Sans Wine, *sans* Song, *sans* Singer and *sans* End."

Man's aspirations after immortality are met with the scepticism of the "who knoweth?" of Pyrrho and of Koheleth (Eccl. iii. 21), or even with a more definite denial.

> "Alike for those who for To-Day prepare,
> And those that after some to-morrow stare,
> A Muezzin from the towers of darkness cries
> 'Fools, your reward is neither Here nor There.'"

The discussions of the Sages of his land, the making of many books without end, were for him but as the "feeding upon wind" (Eccl. xii. 2) and brought no satisfying answer.

> "Myself when young did eagerly frequent
> Doctor and Saint, and heard great argument,
> About it and about: but evermore
> Came out by the same door where in I went.
>
> With them the seed of Wisdom did I sow,
> And with mine own hand wrought to make it grow;
> And this was all the Harvest that I reaped :
> 'I came like Water and like Wind I go.'"

The problem of Life, the enigma of the Universe, found no solution. God had "set the world in the heart" of man to the intent that they might not "find out his work from the beginning to the end" (Eccl. iii. 11).

> "Up from Earth's Centre through the Seventh Gate
> I rose, and on the Throne of Saturn sate,
> And many a Knot unravell'd by the Road,
> But not the Master-knot of Human Fate.
>
> There was the Door to which I found no Key,
> There was the Veil through which I might not see:
> Some little talk awhile of ME and THEE,
> There was,—and then no more of THEE and ME.
>
> Earth could not answer: nor the Seas that mourn
> In flowing Purple, of their Lord forlorn ;
> Nor rolling Heaven, with all his Signs revealed,
> And hidden by the Sleeve of Night and Morn[1]."

Agnosticism has, perhaps, never spoken in the tones of a more terrible despondency than in the words that follow, though the language of Koheleth in Eccl. iii. 13, ix. 3, falls not far short of it.

> "Then of the THEE IN ME who works behind
> The Veil, I lifted up my hands to find
> A Lamp amid the Darkness; and I heard
> As from Without, 'The ME within THEE blind.'"

---

[1] We are reminded of the grand language of Job xxviii. 13, 14, but there the questioner, like Koheleth, was led to rest in a very different conclusion.

The sense of the infinite littleness of the individual life (Eccl. i. 4, 11), is expressed in words which remind us (once more a case of unconscious parallelism) of Tennyson's gloomier Voice,

> "When you and I behind the Veil are past,
> Oh, but the long, long while the World shall last,
>   Which of our Coming and Departure heeds,
> As the Sea's self should heed a pebble-cast.
>
> A Moment's Halt—a momentary taste
> Of Being from the Well amid the Waste—
>   And Lo! the phantom Caravan has reacht
> The NOTHING it set out from. Oh, make haste."

He takes refuge, like Koheleth (Eccl. ii. 3, ix. 7), from this despair, in the juice of the "fruitful Grape,"

> "The Sovereign Alchemist that in a trice
> Life's leaden metal into Gold transmutes."

He is not deterred from that sweet balm by the Prophet's prohibition, or fears of Hell, or hopes of Paradise,

> "One thing is certain, and the rest is lies,
> The Flower that once has blown, for ever dies."

None have come back from the bourne of that "undiscovered country" that lies behind the veil,

> "Strange, is it not? that of the myriads who
> Before us pass'd the doors of Darkness through,
>   Not one returns to tell us of the Road,
> Which to discover we must travel too."

Like Milton's Satan he has come to the conviction that,

> "The Soul is its own place and of itself
> Can make a Heaven of Hell, a Hell of Heaven,"

and gives utterance to the conviction:

> "I sent my Soul through the Invisible
> Some letter of that After life to spell,
>   And by and by my Soul return'd to me
> And answered, 'I myself am Heaven and Hell.'
>
> Heaven but the Vision of fulfilled Desire,
> And Hell the Shadow of a Soul on fire,
>   Cast on the darkness into which ourselves
> So late emerg'd from, shall so soon expire."

In words which remind us of Prospero's

> "We are such stuff
> As dreams are made of,"

or of Jaques'

> "All the world's a stage
> And all the men and women merely players,"

he writes his view of the world's great drama as seen from the half-pessimist, half-pantheistic, stand-point,

> "We are no other than a moving row
> Of Magic Shadow-shapes that come and go,
>   Round with the Sun-illumined Lantern held
> In Midnight by the Master of the Show;
>
> But helpless Pieces of the Game He plays
> Upon this Chequer-board of Nights and Days,
>   Hither and thither moves, and checks and stays,
> And one by one back in the Closet lays."

Koheleth's complaint that there is "no new thing under the sun" (Eccl. i. 9), that the course of Nature and of human life presents but a dreary monotony of iteration (Eccl. i. 5, 6, 14), oppresses him once more with a despair for which the wine-cup seems the only remedy: he knows not either the 'whence?' the 'whither?' or the 'why?' of life.

> "Yesterday, *this* Day's Madness did prepare;
> To-morrow's Silence, Triumph, or Despair:
>   Drink! for you know not whence you came, nor why:
> Drink! for you know not why you go, nor where."

In words which remind us of Heine, at once in their faint hope, and in the bold despair which equals almost the "*Tantâ stat proedita culpâ*" of Lucretius, he utters his last words to the Eternal, whom he can neither wholly deny nor yet trust in and adore,

> "What! out of senseless Nothing to provoke
> A conscious Something to resent the Yoke
>   Of unpermitted Pleasure, under pain
> Of Everlasting Penalties if broke!
>
> What! from his helpless Creature be repaid
> Pure Gold, for what He lent him dross-allay'd —
>   Sue for a debt he never did contract
> And cannot answer—Oh the sorry trade!
>
> Oh Thou, who didst with pitfall and with gin
> Beset the Road I was to wander in,
>   Thou wilt not with Predestin'd Evil round
> Enmesh, and then impute my Fall to sin!
>
> Oh Thou, who Man of baser Earth didst make
> And ev'n with Paradise devise the Snake:
>   For all the Sin wherewith the Face of Man
> Is blacken'd, — Man's forgiveness give—and take."

In this instance also, as in those of Koheleth, Jaques, Hamlet, Heine, Schopenhauer, and a thousand others, the pessimism, self-conscious and self-contemplative, finding free utterance in the play of imagination or of humour, did not lead to suicide, but to the effort, after the manner of Epicureans less noble than Lucretius, to narcotise the sense of wretchedness by the stimulation of the wine-cup. In words which half remind us of some of Heine's most cynical utterances and half of the epitaph said to have been placed on the tomb of Sophocles, he gives free vent to his thoughts as to the hard theory of destiny that had been pressed upon him under the form of the old parable of the Potter and the clay, and his refuge from those thoughts in the revelry which was rounded by the sleep of death,

> " 'Why,' said another, 'Some there are who tell
> Of One who threatens He will send to Hell
>   The luckless Pots He marred in making;—Pish !
> He's a Good Fellow, and 'twill all be well'[1].

> 'Well,' murmured one, 'Let whoso make or buy,
> My Clay with long Oblivion is gone dry:
>   But fill me with the old familiar juice;
> Methinks I might recover by and by.
>   *   *   *   *   *

> 'Ah, with the Grape my fading Life provide,
> Ah, wash the Body whence the Life has died,
>   And lay me, shrouded in the living Leaf,
> By some not-unfrequented Garden-side.

> That ev'n my buried Ashes such a snare
> Of Vintage shall fling up into the Air
>   As not a true believer passing by
> But shall be overtaken unaware."

Beyond this we need not go. The life of Omar Khayyam, so far as we know, did not end, as we have seen reason to believe that that of Koheleth, and even of Heine, did, in a return to truer thoughts of the great enigma. It will be admitted, however, that it is not without interest to trace, under so many varieties of form and culture, the identity of thought and feeling to which an undisciplined imagination, brooding over that enigma and seeking refuge, in sensual indulgence, from the thought that it is insoluble, sooner or later leads. The poets and thinkers of the world might, indeed, almost be classified according to the relation in which they stand, to that world-problem which Reason finds itself thus impotent to solve. Some there are, like Homer, and the unknown author of the *Nibelungen Lied*, who in their healthy objectivity seem never to have known its burden. Some, like Æschylus, Dante, Milton, Keble, have been protected against its perilous attacks by the faith which they had inherited and to which they clung without the shadow of a doubt. Some, like Epicurus him-

---

[1] Comp. Heine's words not long before his death "Dieu me pardonnera; c'est son metier."

self, and Montaigne, have rested in a supreme tranquillity. Some, like
Sophocles, Virgil, Shakespeare, Goethe, have passed through it, not
to the serenity of a clearer faith, but to the tranquillity of the Supreme
Artist, dealing with it as an element in their enlarged experience. Some,
like Lucretius, Omar Khayyam, Leopardi, and in part Heine, have
yielded to its fatal spell, and have "died and made no sign" after
nobler or ignobler fashion. Others, to whom the world owes more,
have fought and overcome, and have rested in the faith of a Divine
Order which will at last assert itself, of a Divine Education, of which
the existence of the enigma, as forming part of man's probation and
discipline, is itself a material element. Of this victory, the writer of
the Book of Job, and Tennyson, present the earliest and the latest
phases. An intermediate position may be claimed, not the less poetical
in essence because its outward form was not that of poetry, for the
writer of Ecclesiastes as in later times for the *Pensées* of Pascal.

INDEX.

Aberglaube, 47
abiit ad plures, 179
acceptable words, 226, 227
adder, deaf, 198
Æschylus quoted, 161, 181, 190
Alexandria, museum of, 49, 114
all is vanity, 110, 224
almond tree, 218
always white, 188
Anima mundi, 224
another generation cometh, 104
Antiochus Epiphanes, 120
Antiochus Sidetes, 191
apothecary, 195
Aristophanes, quoted, 106, 203
Aristotle, quoted, 17
ἀρχαιόπλουτοι, 195
Artaxerxes Mnemon, 155
assemblies, masters of, 227
Athanasius, 65

bedchamber, 203
Blaesilla, 95
breaketh a hedge, 196
Browning, quoted, 189
bulwarks, 191

caper-berry, 219
cast thy bread, 204
Catullus, quoted, 43, 200
charming of serpents, 198
Chasidim, 181
child, 200
"Christian Year," quoted, 128
Cicero, quoted, 132, 183, 200, 215
cistern, 222
cleaveth wood, 196
comforter, 138
consumes his own flesh, 140
crackling of thorns, 162
Croesus, 151
cranes of Ibycos, 203
commended mirth, 182
considered in my heart, 183
Creator, 212

dabar, 107
day of birth, 160
day of prosperity, 165
day of death, 177, 178
delirantium somnia, 185
dead lion, 186
dead flies, 192, 258
deaf adder, 198
days of darkness, 209
daughters of song, 216
doors, 216
desire, 219
dust, 222
duty of man, 229

eateth in darkness, 153
eat in the morning, 200
Ecclesiastes, meaning of word, 15; date
    and authorship of, 19—32; compared
    with Ecclesiasticus, 56—63; with the
    Wisdom of Solomon, 67—75; Jewish
    interpreters of, 75; parables in, 77,
    78; meanings of phrases in, 78; com-
    pared with Targum, 79 ff.; patristic
    interpreters of, 88; analysis of, 97 ff.;
    parallel between Shakespeare and,
    231 ff.; parallel between Tennyson
    and, 250 ff.; parallel between poem of
    Omar Khayyam and, 262 ff.
ἠθικὴ πίστις, 198
estate, 135
Euripides, quoted, 104, 134, 137, 160,
    173, 186, 208, 220, 223
Eternal Commandment, 230
evil days, 213

face to shine, 174
feedeth on wind, 110, 229, 253, 264
folding doors, 216
fountain of life, 222
full of words, 199

Gamaliel, 226
gardens and orchards, 115
gave good heed, 226

gave my heart, 109, 170
Gebini ben Charson, 77
Gehenna, fires of, 210
Gemara, the, 75, 228
Ginsburg, quoted, 90, 91
golden bowl, 221
good name, 159, 160
gracious words, 198
grasshopper, 219
great dignity, 195
Gregory of Nyssa, 91, 94
Gregory Thaumaturgus, 89, 92, 94
Gregory the Great, 99
Gulschen Ras, by Mahmud, quoted, 214
grinders, 215

Hades, 136
Haggadah, the, 75
Halachah, the, 75
have all one breath, 136
have no burial, 155
Herodotus, quoted, 135
higher, 149, 150
Hillel, 226
home, 220
Homer, quoted, 105, 118, 141, 193
Hood, quoted, 238
Horace, quoted, 112, 119, 124, 151, 152, 166 ,200, 201, 209, 218, 223
horses, keeping of, 195
house, keepers of, 214
house, of God, 145
Hospital of the soul, 228

Ibycos, cranes of, 203
In Memoriam, quoted, 250, 251
Irenaeus, 68

judgment, place of, 134, 212
Juvenal, quoted, 129, 151, 189, 191, 200, 217

Keble's "Christian Year," quoted, 128
keep thy feet, 145
keepers of the house, 214
king over Israel, 109
Koheleth, 16; biography of, 36; parallel between Shakespeare and, 231 ff.; parallel between Tennyson and, 250 ff. ; parallel between poem of Omar Khayyam and, 262 ff.

lamp of life, 221
Latin Fathers, the, 92
let thy words be few, 146
life, fountain of, 222
light is sweet, 208
little city, 191
little folly, 193
long home, 220
love or hatred, 184

Lucretius, quoted, 106, 107, 117, 123, 132, 136, 137, 146, 149, 154, 211, 223, 226

madness, 185
Mahmud, Gulschen Ras of, quoted, 214
mandragora, 220
Martial quoted, 42
masters of assemblies, 227
Mataiotes Mataiotêton, 251
matter, 229
Μηδὲν ἄγαν, 167
Metaphrasis, the, 89, 94
Midrashim, the, 75
Milton, quoted, 158, 265
Mishna, the, 75, 169, 228
moral suasion, 198
mourners, 221
Muratorian Fragments, 67
mischievous madness, 199
my son, 228

nails, 227
nard, 188
ne quid nimis, 119, 167
Nibelungen Lied, 267
Nirvana, 139
nobles, 200
no new thing, 108

oath of God, 175
ointment, 188
Omar Khayyam, biography of, 262; parallel between Ecclesiastes and, 262 ff.; poem of, quoted, 262 ff.
over much wicked, 167, 168
over the spirit, 177
Ovid, quoted, 131, 174

Paradise Lost, quoted, 158, 265
Pelagianism, 93
Pheraulas, 151
pitcher, 222
place of judgment, 134, 212
Plato, quoted, 17, 221, 252
Pliny, quoted, 203
Ptolemy, 64
Pyrrhonism, 137

ready to hear, 145
rebuke of the wise, 162
rejoice in thy youth, 210, 211
remembrance of the wise, 120
reward, 163
rich, 195
right hand, 193
right work, 139
righteous over much, 167, 168
Rufinus, 65

Sacian, 151
Sanhedrin, 226
satias videndi, 245

season, 201
see the sun, 164, 208
Seneca, quoted, 141
sentence, 180
serpents, charming of, 198
set in order, 226
Shakespeare, quoted, 40, 43, 122, 124,
  131, 187, 199, 223, 232, 233, 234, 235,
  236, 237, 238, 239, 240, 241, 242, 243,
  244, 245, 246, 247, 248, 249, 265, 266
Shechinah, 86
Sheked, 218
Sheol, 136, 189, 209
Shepherd, the Good, 228
silver cord, 221
sinister, 194
slaves, 115
slothfulness, 201
Solomon, Wisdom of, 67; compared with
  Ecclesiastes, 68, 69
Solon, 151
song, daughters of, 216
song of fools, 162
Sophocles, quoted, 128, 130, 139, 159,
  173, 176, 184, 187, 193
sorrow, 212
sow thy seed, 207
spirit of the ruler, 194
spirit shall return, 223
"sprung from the soil," 219
storm, 214
study, 229

suicide, 120
swallow up, 198

Targum, the, 75
Tennyson, parallel drawn between Koheleth and, 250 ff.; quoted, 250, 251,
  252, 253, 254, 255, 256, 257, 258, 259,
  260, 261, 265
threefold cord, 143, 144
thy hand findeth, 189
time and chance, 190
to do good, 133
"Two Voices," 126, 179, 252, 257, 260

unto one place, 136

vanity, 212, 229, 253
vanity of vanities, 102, 224, 225, 231, 234
vexation of spirit, 112, 122, 125
Virgil, quoted, 48, 105, 108, 123, 124,
  152, 161, 224
Voltaire, quoted, 205

Welt-schmerz, the, 258
wheel, 222
wisdom is good, 164
wise, remembrance of, 120: rebuke of,
  162
wonder not, 149
work of God, 183, 207

youth, 212

www.ingramcontent.com/pod-product-compliance
Ingram Content Group UK Ltd.
Pitfield, Milton Keynes, MK11 3LW, UK
UKHW010037140625
459647UK00012BA/1445